The Dynamics of Adoption

TREACHER + KATZ

The Dynamics of Adoption

Edited by
Amal Treacher and Ilan Katz

Jessica Kingsley Publishers
London and Philadelphia

First published in the United Kingdom in 2000 by
Jessica Kingsley Publishers Ltd,
116 Pentonville Road, London
N1 9JB, England
and
325 Chestnut Street,
Philadelphia, PA 19106, USA.

www.jkp.com

© Copyright 2000 Jessica Kingsley Publishers

Library of Congress Cataloging in Publication Data
A CIP catalog record for this book is available from the Library of Congress

British Library Cataloguing in Publication Data
A CIP catalogue record for this book is available from the British Library

ISBN 1 85302 782 0

Printed and Bound in Great Britain by
Athenaeum Press, Gateshead, Tyne and Wear

Contents

Acknowledgements

This book has arisen as part of the work of the Centre for Adoption and Identity Studies (CAIS, University of East London [UEL] and the Tavistock Clinic). We would like to thank the Department of Human Relations (at UEL) for its continued support for the Centre, and also those who attended the conferences that we have organized for their thinking and insights which have contributed to the book in important ways. Special thanks are due to Phil Cohen, who initiated the Centre, and also to Andrew Cooper and Barbara Prynn for their perseverance and input. We are also grateful to Amy Lankester-Owen and Janet Law for their editorial skills, and Linda Talbot whose knowledge of attachments eased the administrative path of this book considerably.

Amal would like to dedicate this book to Leila and Emmanuel (her birth grandparents) and to Alice and Tom (her adoptive grandparents). Ilan would like to dedicate it to Julia (his wife) and Daniel, Gideon and Talia (his birth children).

And so I am a Storyteller

And so I am a storyteller
I was born a storyteller
stories were my skin
I spun and was spun
self soothing stories
to wrap myself in
stories that were handed down
stories made and given
stories made for me to live in
stories withheld
stories whispered
stories never told
stories that crossed the lines
between fact and fantasy and fairy tale
and back again

Sometimes it seems to me
as if my life is living proof
of that poetic celtic truth
of the child within the crane bag
cast into the sea
the child that slips into the crack
between the worlds
to journey in the dark
of the oyster shell
the friction that creates the pearl
this journey is as long as it is hard
this journey is the making of a bard

So I have woven myself a story shawl
from these strands of a yarn

My Mother's House;
A story told in a dream.

For Rosemary;
How my mother came to take me in

What People Said;
Stories whispered around the baby's head

Wee Adopted Girl;
beginning to tell my story in the world

Knock Knock;
A story never to be told.

From 'The Making of Wee Bardy Bones';
The story whispered in the baby's cells,
the one the embryo might choose to tell

For Kathleen;
How my blood mother came to have me and to give me up

Roses in a Pewter Jar;
On hearing the death of my birth mother,
a story as told between strangers

My Mother's Songlines;
With thanks for the gift of my mother's stories.

I

Narrative and Fantasy in Adoption

Towards a Different Theoretical Understanding

Amal Treacher

Adoption is an emotive subject entangled in webs of confusion and fantasy. 'Mother', 'infant' and 'family' are not neutral systems of thought but terms loaded with emotions, beliefs and fantasies. An adoptive family has to be forged through the various discourses of family life and the social injunctions of what a family should be. Whether adopted or not, individual fantasies of family life are formed within these social and cultural demands. Elinor Rosenberg (1992) has pointed out that until recently (1970a) adoption was seen, unproblematically, as providing solutions for all those involved. This rather simplistic view of adoption led to a denial of its difficulties and complexities. The call for 'love' as if it will simply repair and make good the losses and absences of the human condition in general, and the adoption situation in particular, is no longer feasible or realistic.

One of the recurring themes of this collection is that fantasy is continually at play – creating demands for more love, and imaginings that life would have been better elsewhere and with different parents or child/ren. Such fantasies can centre on what could have been and can stir up feelings of pain, loss, fury, hope and love. It remains theoretically and emotionally challenging to struggle with understanding the shifts and overlaps between these feelings of loss, betrayal and abandonment experienced by those involved in adoption, and at the same time to bear in mind the inevitable losses and disappointments that occur through the sheer fact of being human.

For all of us, the tasks of maturation centre on placing oneself within and outside the family, to acknowledge the existence of others and to deal with frustration, loss and disappointment. For the adoptee and the adoptive family, these emotional processes occur alongside other psychic negotiations.

For example, the adoptee has to come to terms with having been given up by the birth mother and struggles to answer questions such as 'Why was I given up?', 'Does my mother remember me?' and 'Did my father know about me?' As Rose Golberg argues in Chapter 13, adoptions can be successful and reparative. She goes on, however, to warn that the importance of adoption should not be underestimated and to caution against making the fact of adoption a fetish around which all the difficulties of living hang. To estimate the impact of adoption requires careful thinking and distancing from reassuring fantasies and, as Alison Benton (Chapter 9) argues, the most dangerous of adoption fantasies are those that pretend that pre-adoption memories will fade and that the love of the adoptive family will conquer all.

The view that we (whatever our family history and experience) have to come to bear the complexity of being marks this book and the contributions. This collection is informed by psychoanalytic, social and cultural theory perspectives and is a contribution to a field in which social policy, welfare work and personal accounts are presented as if they have little connection with each other. It is intended to deepen theoretical debates about adoption. It is crucially not a handbook but aims to think through the emotionality and unconscious dynamics of adoption.

Contributions come from a range of backgrounds, and professional and personal involvement are not discrete experiences; for example my mother was adopted and I too was adopted as part of a family reconstitution when my mother remarried. Such personal experiences clearly have an impact throughout one's life. Some of these chapters are personal and others come from mainstream academia. Taken together and from their different vantage points, the contributors document, explore and understand the challenges that adoption presents. The book is structured so that the accounts of 'professionals' and of those personally involved are interwoven, presenting contrasting experiences and perspectives back to back. The poems of Margot Henderson, an adoptee, appear throughout the book and are intended to throw a different light on the experiences of growing up adopted. They serve as a documentation and a reminder of the emotions of the adopted daughter, adoptive mother and birth mother. Unfortunately, birth fathers are rarely present in this collection.

This introduction explores adoption conceptually and includes some theoretical background in order to frame the contributions within current social and psychoanalytic thinking. The conclusion by Ilan Katz (Chapter 14) explores the implications of current research and policy on practice. It is intended to highlight the dilemmas and pitfalls for professionals so that they can move towards more thoughtful practice. The challenge of this overall endeavour is to make a positive contribution to the adoption debate for everyone involved, whether personally or professionally.

John Triseliotis argues in Chapter 6 that adoption is bound by culture and its values and belief systems. He carries on to state that these 'are not static and neither is the adoption experience'. We are all bound by our historical and social context and this viewpoint is embedded in much contemporary theorization of subjectivity. Current thinking on identity from psychoanalysis to social and cultural theory centres on the ambiguity and contradictions embedded in inhabiting a human identity in contemporary western societies. The social and cultural spheres are now theorized as constituting identity itself; it is not that the social is stitched over a true self which then becomes distorted but rather that the social is the very stuff through which we become human. Within these accounts, conscious experience is fluid, contradictory and confusing. This is complicated even further if we take into account the unconscious and its systems of thought which are not amenable to conscious understandings. Meanings are multilayered and some may never be discovered; there is always another truth that cannot be known. The use of the word 'truth' is problematic. For those influenced by postmodern and Lacanian psychoanalytic thinking, the 'truth' does not exist; it is always socially constructed and to believe in 'truth' is both an illusion and part of the defensive structures of both the social and the individual. For those more reliant on modernist and object-relations psychoanalytic understandings, the truth is ambiguous and has to be struggled for. Further, through feeling and thinking, truth can be discerned; indeed, it is essential for psychic and social health. Further, to be human is always to be in processes and our meanings (personal and social) are forged and maintained within and through social and emotional relationships. Identity can never be taken for granted, assumed or conceptualized as in place. Currently, some commentators claim, all identities, whatever the family histories, are seen as 'adoptive'. Phil Cohen (1995) argues: 'lives and stories are enmeshed in a complex interweaving of disparate elements which can never be summed up as a totality but only ever grasped in partial and transitory ways' (Cohen 1995, p.3).

Or, as Margot Henderson writes:

> stories were my skin
> I spun and was spun
> self soothing stories
> to wrap myself in
>
> stories that crossed the lines

between fact and fantasy and fairy tale
and back again

Currently, in the social sciences there have been theoretical shifts which are increasingly orientated towards narrative and auto/biographical accounts as routes into theorizing subjectivity. Further, auto/biographical narratives are conceptualized as social and cultural, not as individual matters. From this viewpoint, common sense is overturned, for it is not that people reveal themselves through their life stories but rather that the self is constructed through the narrative, the confines of the social and linguistic conventions. Jerome Bruner (1987), in 'Life as narrative', argues persuasively that we '*become* the autobiographical narratives by which we "tell" about our lives' (Bruner 1987: 15). His argument is predicated on the viewpoint that linguistic and cultural conventions form and determine not only how we tell our narratives, and what is made present or absent, but more that these narratives form 'the essence' of who we are, what we experience and perceive. Bruner (1987) argues strongly that we become and are sustained through stories – our own and others.

John Simmonds (Chapter 2) explores the importance of storytelling in the construction of family history, and argues that the construction of a history involves facts, memory and emotion. Simmonds, as an adoptive parent and a social work lecturer and consultant, explores the dynamics of listening to and of telling narratives, and argues that it is important to be able to hear the different levels of the story and also the different emotional aspects that its various characters portray. One of the strengths of his exploration is his emphasis on the anxieties that can be and often are raised in the listener, be they professional or parent. Barbara Prynn (Chapter 5) approaches the anxieties experienced by social workers listening to birth and adoptive parents and adoptees. Prynn and Simmonds both raise the question of whether or not they and others can bear the feelings aroused by adoption.

Simmonds elaborates on the triangle of rescuer–victim–persecutor and argues that each aspect is beholden to the other and inextricably linked with it. Through exploring the issues of gratitude, Simmonds argues that this dynamic has shifted from the child having to be grateful to the adoptive parents, to the adoptive parents now having to be grateful to the child for rescuing them from what is currently seen as the tragic state of childlessness. The dynamics of gratitude exist within a particular cultural formation and contemporary culture currently is partly preoccupied with apology and making some reparation for past events. For example, the Child Migration Trust argues for the recognition of the damage done to children who were removed by involuntary migration to countries such as Australia and Canada. They plead for a public recognition that most of these migrant children have grown into adults with 'broken hearts and broken lives'. These dynamics of blame and responsibility – victim, persecutor and saviour – are taken into the self and form psychic dynamics. Crucially, the dynamics of blame and responsibility are not abstract and have a profound bearing on how professionals working within the area understand and intervene in the family, and on the personal responses of those involved.

The demands for compensation and recognition taking place currently in Australia for the 'stolen children' (children taken from their parents by Christian missionaries) are part of a movement to recover that which has been hidden from history, and to recover memories and address the damage done. Rebekka Göpfert's Chapter 3 on the 'Kindertransport' (the evacuation of Jewish children or 'kinder' to England during 1938–9) documents the experiences and histories of these Kinder. Göpfert's interviews gave some of the Kinder their first opportunity to tell their histories and to express their feelings. Interestingly, she points out that those Kinder who then moved to Israel and the USA, where there are cultural contexts for public memory, had easier access to their own recollections and found it easier to integrate their histories into their daily lives.

Narratives are also, as Paul Ricoeur (1984) argues, a means of placing oneself in time. For Ricoeur and Alisdair MacIntyre (1984), who are both from a philosophical background, concepts of unity of selfhood are understood as narratives which link birth to life and death. In this way, narratives are a poetic activity. As Michael Erbern (1997) puts it, narratives are not 'ungrounded in the world of facts but that the contour lines joining facts are a geometry belonging to the imaginative realm'. For some theorists, narratives and memories are the means by which we recognize the boundaries of self and other (MacIntyre 1984; Prager 1998; Ricoeur 1984). We need the words of others to keep memories buoyant; similarly, our memories and narratives are embodied and are the means by which attachments to others are experienced and expressed. Bollas (1995) explores stringently that health is based on two major capacities to move across temporal zones and to be able to disseminate experiences. Further, these capacities enhance movement from one thought to another, from a fantasy to a memory and from a feeling to a thought. A similar viewpoint is expressed in this book by both Simmonds and Göpfert, who argue that the ability to voice experiences and thoughts enables more healthy emotional development and psychic movement in adult life. Göpfert goes further and argues that silence and the denial of the 'right to grieve' caused the Kinder additional suffering, and became part of 'sequential traumatization'.

Narrative, memory and fantasy each partly constitute subjectivity, though these aspects must simultaneously be understood as both discrete and connected. Memory and fantasy are profoundly embroiled in the narrative structure and thereby influence what can be known or what has to be made absent. Memory and fantasy do not just work in the face of acceptable wishes and desires, for, when confronted with an unacceptable wish, desire or feeling, the ego works to repress it out of mind. Alongside the fantasy exist painful feelings of anxiety, shame, guilt or depression, which often have to be defended against, and cannot be allowed expression. Within a Kleinian framework, phantasy accompanies all thought and feeling.[1] As Robert Hinshelwood describes it: 'unconscious phantasies underlie every mental process, and accompany all mental activity' (Hinshelwood 1989: 32). He goes on to argue that the Kleinian tradition has centred on investigating the way in which 'internal unconscious phantasy penetrates and gives meaning to 'actual events' in the external world; and at the same time, the way the external world brings meaning in the form of unconscious phantasy' (Hinshelwood 1989: 37).

As has been argued above, however, all narratives are imbued with fantasy. Adoption is a central strand in the stories of Oedipus, Moses and many others. Freud (1909) wrote a short and provocative essay entitled 'Family Romance' in which he explores why so many children fantasize and believe that they have been adopted, kidnapped or abandoned due to extreme circumstances and through no fault of the 'original parents'. Crucially, one day these superior and original parents will return and restore the child to its rightful position. The fantasy has many nuances and variations but the basic scenario is this: young children are disappointed that their real parents do not live up to their exalted expectations of them, and their position in life, so they are replaced by a set of imaginary parents who are wonderful, understanding, powerful and extraordinary beings. Puzzled as to why this fantasy was so pervasive and why so many people were convinced that they had been adopted or kidnapped, Freud (1909) argues that this fantasy underpins much of the way children imagine their parents and their lives and that the narrative points to hoped-for status based on aristocracy.

1   Some schools of psychoanalysis spell fantasy with an 'f' to indicate both concious and unconcious processes. The Kleinian school spells phantasy with a 'ph' to indicate unconcious meanings. I have used both spellings in this chapter and the contributors have used whichever spelling they thought appropriate.

The Oedipus myth and the Family Romance narrative are common fantasies, in which there are differences between adopted and non-adopted children. While the Family Romance is charming on the surface, for all children there are involved a number of processes (as understood by psychoanalysis) such as omnipotence, anxiety, separation, control, inclusion/exclusion, revenge and fury. For the non-adopted child, however, the fantasy of adoption is the solution to various conflicts. For the adopted child, it is adoption itself that has produced psychic distress. The difference is crucial and Weider (1977) clarifies the difference thus: 'the adoptee's wish, in contrast to the blood kin child's, is to deny adoption, establish a fantasised blood tie to the adoptive parents, and thereby erase the humiliation adoption implies' (Weider 1977: 199).

Further, as Jean Linford (1994) points out, the poignant reality for adoptees is that they frequently have to live with feelings of abandonment, powerlessness, low self-esteem, shame, depression, lack of trust and feelings of unreality (Linford 1994: 10). Rosenberg (1992) and Linford (1994) argue that the adoptee cannot take for granted history, connection, bonds or a secure place within and outside the family. Adoptees speak of feeling alienated, strange, of looking in the wrong mirror, of not being able to place themselves and of their difficulty in finding a place of security when there is a whole 'retinue of ghosts' that litters the adoptive unconscious. Behind the ubiquitous and internal question 'Who am I?' lies a profound lack of knowledge of 'the mother who brought me into this mysterious world' (Linford 1994: 12). For the adoptee the question of 'Am I remembered?' cannot be taken for granted or approached with some security. The adopted child can be flooded with anxieties which centre on this question as well as (even if he is the most neglected figure in the adoption scenario) 'Does my father remember me?' or, perhaps more problematically, 'Did he know about me?'

The Family Romances of adopted children are based on partial bits of information and on fantasies of themselves and others. It is a potent mixture. The adoptive family receives snippets of information about the birth family from social services, but these are highly dependent on what is deemed 'appropriate' (and are open to the fantasies of those professionally involved). The adoptive parents themselves have their own fantasies and emotions, which they unconsciously relay to the child as they pass on the information. While all Family Romances are fantastical, the narratives and fantasies for the adopted child are mixed with layer upon layer of limited fact, fantasy and memory; currently most adoptions involve children, not newborn babies, and so they have experiences and memories of a life before adoption. The

Family Romance is a powerful narrative in which feelings of abandonment, rejection, rescue, loss, vulnerability, disappointment and insistent hope are experienced in their complex fashion. It is a fantasy in which life can be made tolerable and in which pain can be mitigated and triumphed over. It is one way of making a life, of telling the story of one's life, and of coming to terms with one's place and history.

We do not know, however, the fantasies and feelings of birth parents, who until recently were silenced. Treated moralistically and punitively, it is only recently that birth mothers (fathers still remain absent) have been granted the public space in which to express their experiences. Sallie Greenwood in Chapter 11 expresses her feelings and experiences about relinquishing her daughter. The pain persists, as do the fantasies. Greenwood concludes, but perhaps this is the starting point, with the recognition that her fantasy of reunion is with a baby not an adult woman. Time and fantasy are frozen in a space where once, briefly, there was a relationship. Greenwood's contribution explores the dynamics of being the one who relinquishes (into a closed adoption) and, as her daughter also relinquished her son (in an open adoption), the feelings of being a grandmother witnessing an adoption. Her personal experiences serve as a partial documentation of the changing experience of adoption. Their experiences are different and yet joined in terms of fantasy and feeling.

Birth mothers 'choose' (there is no other word available but it is clumsy in this context) to relinquish their child. In this respect, they are different from the adoptive parents and the adoptive child who have to be chosen. These central concerns about being chosen or not connect adoptive parents and adoptees. Yet, the issues for each of the participants are different. Prospective adoptive parents have to endure the bureaucratic processes of the state, at the end of which they may or may not be 'chosen'. This process may entail fantasies, such as what does it take to present my partner and myself, what can be divulged and what not? As Jackie Kay (1991) writes in the voice of her adoptive mother preparing for the assessment visit:

> I thought I'd hid everything
> that there wasnie wan
> giveaway sign left
>
> I put Marx Engels Lenin (no Trotsky)
> in the airing cupboard – she'll no be
> checking out the towels surely
>
> All the copies of the Daily Worker
> I shoved under the sofa

the dove of peace I took down from the loo
(Kay 1991: 14–15)[2]

The birth parent also has fantasies about the parents who have been chosen to nurture her child, and who, in turn, have chosen a child to nurture. The adoptive parents also have to present themselves to the birth parent and it is unknown what fantasies are in operation at these times. In presenting a fantasy of what may be wished for – calm, secure, presentable – they may give rise to the heartfelt plea expressed by Sallie Greenwood: surely there is more to them than this.

The contributions from Alison Benton (Chapter 9) and Damian McCann and Fiona Tasker (Chapter 10) both explore the question: what is good parenting? They prise apart the preconceived ideas of what is required to parent. For Benton it is the capacity to sustain nurture and containment no matter how impossible the circumstances. Crucially, she supported her daughter when she returned to her past in order to lead to her integration in the present. From this viewpoint, good parenting does not insist that there is only one central family.

For McCann and Tasker, different forms of the family are equally valid. Quoting from recent research, they point to the health and self-esteem of children who have been brought up by gay and lesbian couples. There is no difference, they argue. The fantasies persist, however, and their chapter outlines the uneven treatment given to prospective gay adopters and the various interventions made by social workers. For McCann and Tasker, how gay and lesbian couples are perceived and treated is frequently an individual matter, and the existence of equal opportunities is given a slight nod of recognition but is rarely fully accepted. There are two further dynamics at play: the influence of the media and the opinions of the birth parents. In a sense, an understanding of both adoption and sexual orientation share a common strand – how to think through their proper place without over/ underemphasizing so that the part stands in for the whole.

The place, motivations, functions and capacities of the professionals are crucial to the success of any placement. Various contributors discuss this: Luckock, McCann and Tasker, Prynn, and Richards all explore the motivations, anxieties, projections and fantasies of the professionals involved. Many social workers state that 'intuition' is their main strength, but, as Prynn points

2   The author gratefully acknowledges the kind permission by Bloodaxe: Newcastle-upon-Tyne for the use of this excerpt from *The Adoption Papers* by Jackie Kay, 1991 © Jackie Kay.

out, this can be unreliable. Professionals need confidence, which is frequently undermined, and a sense of security in their capacities while simultaneously they must be open to different ways of thinking. Barry Luckock (Chapter 12) documents a project undertaken in Sussex which revealed that while consultation was compulsory, professionals sought advice only at their own discretion. Usually they had a variety of informal sources that they turned to for advice. They took up formal advice and consultation only when they were insecure about how to proceed. So a useful resource was not used as, on the whole, social workers felt confident in their own professional judgement.

Social workers and allied professionals operate, however, with many preconceived notions, if not myths. These centre on: love is enough, children cannot remember their past, and a good family will repair the damage of the past. Perhaps the most powerful of all is the wish and pressure for a happy ending. Julian Lousada (Chapter 4) argues that much emphasis in adoption is placed on the future but this cannot be the reparative experience hoped for if the past and all that it entails is not faced fully. His primary concern is with denial, which can be, and frequently is, operative in adoption. For Lousada, the social and professional emphasis placed on a happy outcome paradoxically militates against more accepting possibilities and realistic outcomes. Benton similarly describes how, as an adoptive mother, she was told that she was 'making too much of things', that the past had little influence and was dismissed with the accusation that she was being fanciful and over-analytical. Several contributors to this book – Benton, Golberg, Lousada, Simmonds and Triseliotis – are concerned with knowledge; implicit in their chapters is the view that through the capacity to bear the pain of the adoptive history and the ability to know the fantasies involved – in short, to know and be known about – is the route to a healthier state. There are differences here and parents need to tread carefully about what they reveal and why; for, as Simmonds points out, it is at times difficult to know whether or not confronting the truth is helpful or punitive.

While it is a developmental task for all of us to locate ourselves both within and outside the parental couple, it is particularly difficult for adopted children who have often been the result of unwanted pregnancies. For the adoptee, there is the pain and difficulty of accepting passion – that of their adoptive parents, their birth parents or their own. Feelings can centre on shame, guilt and/or a lack of trust. Fantasies abound, and birth parents are imagined to be sexually promiscuous or as people with no boundaries. Alternatively, the birth mother is imagined to be an innocent being raped of her virginity. There is an endless variety of fantasies. However, most adoptees are taken in by infertile couples who also have feelings of loss, depression and shame, as well as anger and resentment of fertile couples who do not keep their child; but without them they would be childless and without their loved child. Feelings and fantasies surround each angle of the adoptive triangle – the child, the birth parents and the adoptive parents. This impacts on the child's fantasies and feelings about his or her own sexuality and body. Adoptive children can often feel shame and guilt about their developing bodies and passions, and despair that they will become like their 'wanton' birth parents. It may also be difficult for the adopted child, and I am speculating here, to feel the contempt that most non-adopted children have for parental intercourse. The child may wish to protect the adoptive parents who have suffered through childlessness from their feelings of derision. The adoptive child may also imagine that the adoptive parents do not indulge in sexual activity (this, after all, is a familiar fantasy) and so they are protected against knowledge that there is a parental couple from whom they are excluded.

Both Lousada and Golberg, writing as clinicians and from an explicitly psychoanalytic orientation, focus on the difficulty of truth and meaning, and also on how the truth can be processed and made bearable. Christopher Bollas in 'The functions of history' (1995) is preoccupied with how to transform the facts of a life – events that have happened that bear the marks of trauma – into meaningful thoughts and feelings. Bollas (1995) speaks of needing to turn away to find time and space in which to take in the meanings in the facts spoken. Explicit in the psychoanalytic stance is that events and facts do not in themselves carry meaning. The task is to discover the conscious and unconscious meanings of those involved. Turning to facts as if they will deliver meaning is a quest that cannot deliver. Facts are not enough for, as Bollas (1995) argues, 'fact' addicts strip events of meaning and interpretation, creating meaning where nothingness existed and paradoxically reducing the possibility of meaning and understanding (Bollas 1995: 113). Facts do not provide a container for the words and events to convey the meanings embedded. One of the emotional tasks within adoption centres on mourning: the adoptive couple mourning the child they could not have; the adoptive child mourning a birth family he or she may not know and a different life which can only be imagined; the birth parents mourning the child they gave up, for whatever reasons, and cannot know and nourish. For the professionals, mourning would require them to face their own fantasies about their personal lives alongside bearing witness to the pain and the endeavour to build something anew by those involved in adoption.

As stated above, identity is now theorized as based on ambiguity and contradiction and

> since adoptive identities are dependent on recognising the constitutive function of difference, might it not be better to make a virtue out of necessity and encourage adoptive parents and children to recognise that the different parts of their adoption story will never fit neatly together into a single shared plot around the classical unities of time, place and subject? (Cohen 1995: 3)

Cohen goes on to argue that it may become possible to negotiate those psychological defences – splitting, disavowal, denial – which are routinely mobilized when hearing the narrative or fantasy of another person. This would entail knowing and understanding what Cohen (1995: 3) terms 'the anxiety of influence', which is exerted by rival versions of a narrative. It may be easier said than done, to reject consoling fictions, or indeed fictions that fit neatly and do not allow differences of perception, fantasy and to have characters different from the one/s usually allowed for by the family script.

Barbara Prynn (Chapter 5) documents the current trend in adoption towards open adoptions and expresses her concerns about the unthinking way in which openness has been taken up and hailed as the new solution. For John Triseliotis (Chapter 6), however, adoptees need to have knowledge of their history and heritage as this, in his view, leads to a more solid identity. Currently, most adoptions are of children who have had disrupted family lives and have contact with their birth families so the issues of contact and open adoption are already part of contemporary practice. The effects are unclear and we do not yet know how contact and the attempt to be part of two families affects the adoptee. It is tempting to idealize this state as if it will mitigate fantasy and complexity but, as has been made clear in this introduction, fantasies are rife. It is an illusion to imagine that open adoption is a panacea and will militate against imaginings and longings for life to be different. It has to be understood that open adoption places demands on all involved. The professionals have to manage the situation and may be more challenged than they imagine. Sallie Greenwood (Chapter 11) describes her daughter's experiences in setting up an open adoption and tells how the professionals' anxieties, feelings and fantasies were uncontained and often acted upon. The professionals involved responded harshly and frequently in an unthinking way; this resulted in more distress for all concerned. Open adoption may also have pitfalls for the adoptee, who may be continually confronted with issues of belonging and loyalty. The adoptive parents may also fantasize that their child will prefer the other, 'real', family. There are also demands and expectations placed on the birth family. Lorraine Dusky (1996) expresses it poignantly: 'I was so filled with remorse that our visits would exhaust me emotionally. I couldn't give enough, do enough, be enough. I always came up wanting' (Dusky 1996: 5).

Greenwood (Chapter 11) argues that there is a powerful class bias in open adoption, in that it is particular forms of communication that are validated and valued. Class, which permeates so many social attitudes, is powerfully operant in adoption not only in terms of how open adoption is managed but also how adoptees perceive their new and usually more middle-class family. As part of Phil Cohen's poem expresses it:

> These strangers came from faraway
> and took me home with them.
>
> They were kind but old.
> I liked the flat and cats.
> I wanted a good cooker lady
> and a dad who's strong.
> I got a painter with a woolly hat
> and a man who lived for books and chat.
> They wanted a brainy head,
> they got a ragamuffin
> with street cred instead.

(Cohen 1999: 148)

Class is one of the silent dynamics of adoption, for currently much attention and emotion are devoted to transracial adoption. For many practitioners and academics it has become commonplace to argue that adoptees need to know their history, to have a full knowledge of their birth family backgrounds and the circumstances of their adoption. Triseliotis (Chapter 6) argues with commitment that full honesty and knowledge are necessary for the adoptee to be able to build and inhabit a strong identity. Tied in with this is knowledge of culture, history, language and traditions which are part of the adoptee's birth family but are not, necessarily, part of the adoptive family's heritage. For Ravinder Barn (Chapter 8), it is crucial for the black or mixed-race child to be placed in a black family. For Barn, the evidence is overwhelming that black children are psychologically damaged by adoption into a white family; to argue otherwise is to ignore political arguments and the psychological evidence available. Those for and against transracial adoption are united in the wish to pursue the importance of security and psychological well-being for the children involved, but the desirability or otherwise of transracial adoption remain contentious. For those against it, transracial adoption leads to identity confusion and conflict, while those for it believe that disorientation and damage are inflicted by life in an institution. For both it is the family and community that provide security and a safety net. However, those against transracial adoption believe that only a black family will provide the necessary armour against a racist and divided society; while those in favour believe that an adoptive family can love and nurture a child, helping him or her to mature into a person capable of sustaining solid relationships. The arguments centre on whether or not it is possible for anybody (whatever ethnicity or family background) to feel that they belong, to have a unified identity and to have a solid self-esteem. Many who are more cautious of transracial adoption draw upon postmodernist understandings of identity to argue their case. For example, both Phil Cohen (1995: 3) and Paul Gilroy (1994) identity is by necessity vexed and always precarious and it is not possible for anybody to be located in a homogenous culture with a unitary identity. Contradiction and conflict mark identity. For Barn (Chapter 8), however, this may be well and good, but what of the black adopted child who has suffered dislocation and distress, and who can only suffer more if not given the armour with which to face a society that so denigrates the other? Also, as Derek Kirton (1995) argues, there is no conflict between emphasizing the importance of 'race' and identity and seeing identity as relational and always in process. In short, it is to argue that such processes and relationships take place in a context shaped by 'race'. Barry Richards, however, identifies an added dimension in Chapter 7. He argues that beleaguered social workers, undermined by the media and society, are projecting their own anxieties and difficulties on to the black child adopted into a white family. Each side, however, accuses the other of not under-standing, of missing the point and of being so personally invested as not to be able to 'see the wood for the trees'. It is difficult at present to see how bridges can be built or a more imaginative way forward can be forged within this contentious aspect of adoption so that each side can allow the other's viewpoint to make a difference.

Various themes have run through this introduction and they are taken up and elaborated in the following chapters. One theme, and it verges on a moral imperative, is that all involved in adoption have to come to terms with difference. The adopting couple have to engage with and nurture a child who is not their flesh and blood; the adoptees have to allow themselves to be loved and sustained outside their birth families; the professionals need to face up to their fantasies of ties and kinship and what they consider to be a 'family'. To gain this knowledge is, perhaps, easier said than done and some of the contributions explore the difficulties of gaining knowledge. One of the common-sense injunctions embedded in adoption narratives is that it is better to forget. This book, however, is predicated on the view that it is both impossible to forget and that more damage is caused by a haunting of the past. John Steiner's (1985) article 'Turning a blind eye' explores the Oedipus myth to argue that the destruction caused was precisely due to turning away from knowledge. As I have tried to argue here, conscious and unconscious fantasies will always be in operation; they cannot be wished away through cognitive and emotional will. It is a delicate balance to understand the opportunities and difficulties that arise from being adopted and from adopting; and further to give these experiences their proper psychic space. Psychic and social health is dependent on the recognition that others have a separate existence from oneself, that the human condition is fraught with difficulties, that the past is never as one would wish, and that contained within the present are opportunities for new possibilities and negotiations. Adoption is a testimony to the fragile but precious human capacity for hope.

References

Bollas, C. (1993) 'Why Oedipus?'. In his *Being a Character: Psychoanalysis and Self-Experience*. London: Routledge.

Bollas, C. (1995) 'The functions of history'. In his *Cracking Up: The Work of Unconscious Experience*. London: Routledge.

Bruner, J. (1987) 'Life as narrative'. *Social Research 54*, 1, 11–32.

Cohen, P. (1995) *Frameworks for a Study of Adoptive Identities*, Working Paper no. 1. London: University of East London and Centre for Adoption and Identity Studies.

Cohen, P. (1999) 'Adoption story'. In A. Morris (ed) *The Adoption Experience*. London: Jessica Kingsley Publishers.

Dusky, L. (1996) 'Family reunions'. In S. Wadia-Ells (ed) *The Adoption Reader*. London: Women's Press.

Erbern, M. (1997) *Subjectivity Revisited*. Unpublished paper from seminar series: University of East London.

Freud, S. (1909) 'Family romance'. In *Standard Edition* vol. 9. London: Hogarth.

Gilroy, P. (1994) Foreword to *The Best Interests for the Child: Culture, Identity and Trans-racial Adoption*. London.

Hinshelwood, R. (1989) *A Dictionary of Kleinian Thought*. London: Free Association.

Kay, J. (1991) *The Adoption Papers*. Newcastle upon Tyne: Bloodaxe.

Kirton, D. (1995) *Race, Identity and the Politics of Adoption*. Working Paper no.2. London: University of East London and Centre for Adoption and Identity Studies.

Linford, J. (1994) *Journey of the Adopted Self: A Quest for Wholeness*. New York: Basic Books.

MacIntyre, A. (1984) *After Virtue*. Bloomington, IN: Indiana University Press.

Prager, J. (1998) *Presenting the Past: Psychoanalysis and the Sociology of Remembering*. Cambridge, MA: Harvard University Press.

Ricoeur, P. (1984) *Time and Narrative*. Chicago: University of Chicago Press.

Rosenberg, E. (1992) *The Adoption Life Cycle: The Children and their Families throughout the Years.* New York: Free Press.

Steiner, J. (1985) 'Turning a blind eye: the cover up for Oedipus'. *International Review of Psychoanalysis 12*, 28, 161–72.

Weider, H. (1977) 'The family romance fantasies of adoptees'. *Psychoanalytic Quarterly 46*, 185–200.

2

The Adoption Narrative

Stories that We Tell and Those that We Can't

John Simmonds

Adoption in context

Adoption policy and practice continue to remain controversial, complex and powerful areas of public debate. Their history reflects changing public and private perceptions of the status, purpose, needs and roles of children in relation to adults. Until the 1970s and 80s, the emphasis in adoption has been placed on the need of adults to become parents when, for one reason or another, they cannot have children of their own. It was a response to and recognition of the fact that, for some children, birth parents are unable to take up the parenting role. Embedded in this response is a powerful belief that children need parents. In attempting to control the process of adoption, society recognizes that parenting is a demanding, risky and difficult business. Through law, policy and procedure, society exercises its responsibility to regulate the process of who should become parents when adoption or fostering is the issue. Current debates about adoption include claims that sometimes the process is too slow (as was the case in the original permanency planning debates in the 1980s); or is too fast (when permanency planning policies time-limit attempts at rehabilitation); that it fails to be sensitive to issues of race and the development of identity (throughout the 1980s or 1990s); or that it creates insurmountable obstacles and makes harsh judgements about the suitability of who should adopt. Such debates will no doubt continue.

The intention of this chapter is to add another dimension to these debates by exploring adoption from a psychosocial perspective in which its meaning, rather than being defined by the regulatory process of law, policy and practice, is understood to be constructed in the course of the developmental history of the child and its family. I shall explore adoption by focusing on the importance of the adoption narrative as a vehicle that contains the family's joint and individual histories. In particular, I am concerned with those areas of the histories which are the painful, unacknowledged or unexpressed aspects of relationships that have developed over time.

Reflections: stories, adoption and family life

Over the past twenty years I have been involved in a number of personal as well as professional situations in which adoption has played a significant part. Some involved children who were being considered or prepared for adoption. Some involved families in which children had been placed but where real struggles had threatened the placement. Others involved adults who had been adopted as children and who were struggling with emotional issues in which adoption seemed to be a significant factor. Invariably these situations remind me of the enormous advantages and strengths involved in adoption as well as its risks and pain. I am also often left wondering about the relationship between some of these events and my experience as an adoptive father and those of my two adopted children. Can I allow myself to believe that things have actually gone rather better in my family than in some of the others that I have been in contact with? A recent experience at a friend's wedding has raised these issues once again. The bride's speech (as reported to me later – we had already left) included the revelation that the rivalry between herself and her sister was often heightened by the accusation 'You must have been adopted to be so awful'. I was left thinking that adoption seems to be one of those issues that can be acceptably used to put somebody down, to question their identity or their value or to reinforce their difference and the possibility of their rejection. What a lucky escape we had had, for our children had not heard this speech. How, I thought, could such a celebration include such insensitivity?

In thinking it over I became curious as to how I might have dealt with this if we had remained at the wedding. After all, my children are 18 and 12 and it would not have been the first time we had been through this kind of painful event requiring uncomfortable explanations and discussions. Would I have continued to reassure them about how much we loved them, or how we chose them and that made them very special, or how their birth mother was young and not ready to give them the love and care that small children need, or how people say cruel things sometimes without realizing? Or might I have just burst into tears at this unexpected reminder of something that is sometimes almost too difficult to think about? What story would I have told them? Who were the villains and who were the victims and who might come along to the rescue? Would it be a true story, the whole story, make believe or even a lie? Reflecting on this experience some time afterwards, I was struck by the importance of storytelling in the construction of our family history. Weaving together facts, memory and emotion to produce a tellable story for the audience I have in mind is an important part of my social competence.

The significance of stories in family life cannot be overestimated. They contain the many strands that link individuals, the group and its culture and history together in a meaningful way. Like all stories they contain good and bad characters, beginnings and endings, 'official' versions and secrets. As with all stories, there are identifiable narratives that organize the actors, the action and the script. The truth of these stories and their narratives is complex. As with my own struggle to find the right story to tell my children, or indeed myself when faced with an uncomfortable family event, the possible narratives I might have selected were constrained by a powerful requirement of all family stories, particularly those told to children: they emphasize the good and loving feelings that adults have towards children and the happy ending. For most children living with their birth parents, the birth narrative has a routine script because it is deeply embedded in a culture that makes it unproblematic. Conceived in and through love and born into love, what more is needed to have a happy ending? For individual parents though this narrative may be a gloss on the actual events of conception, pregnancy and birth. The beginning of 'Sleeping Beauty in the Wood' is a powerful example of this.

> There was once upon a time a King and a Queen, who were so sorry that they had no children, so sorry that it was beyond expression. They went to all the waters in the world, vows, pilgrimages, everything was tried and nothing came of it. (Opie and Opie 1974)[1]

The anxiety and sense of loss and tragedy felt by so many couples faced with problems in conceiving is eloquently expressed in the phrase, 'so sorry that it was beyond expression'. The search for a solution is poignantly described: 'They went to all the waters in the world, vows, pilgrimages, everything was tried and nothing came of it.' Then the joy and relief at the birth is simply expressed: 'At last however the Queen was with child and was brought to bed of a daughter.'

---

1   The author gratefully acknowledges the kind permission granted by Oxford University Press: London for the use of excerpts throughout this chapter from 'Sleeping Beauty in the Woods' In the Classic Fairy Tales by Opie, I. and Opie, P. (1974) © Opie, I. and Opie, P.

A story that begins with a profound struggle emerges into joy at the arrival of a baby who has 'all the perfections imaginable'. The pain of the story as it has emerged so far evaporates in the understandable idealization of the baby's qualities and the desire to secure these through the gifts of the seven fairies. The wish to mark this happy event with a grand and sumptuous christening seems both a celebration and an attempt, based on a powerful wish, to protect the baby from danger. Yet, in a way that reminds me of the 'wedding speech', the celebration is brought to a chilling halt by unanticipated events:

> But as they were all sitting down to dinner, they saw come into the hall an old Fairy, whom they had not invited, because it was now above 50 years since she had been seen out of the tower, and they thought her dead or enchanted. The King order'd her a cover, but could not give her a case of gold as the others, because they had seven only made for the seven Fairies... The old Fairy fancied that she was slighted, and mutter'd some threats between her teeth... Her turn coming next, with a head shaking more with spite than old age, she said that the Princess should have her hand pierced with a spindle and die of the wound. This terrible gift made the whole company tremble, and everybody fell a-crying. (Opie and Opie 1974)

This turn of events captures every parent's fear of a child becoming damaged by events — illness, heredity, poverty or ill-feeling. The only hope for modifying the curse comes from a young fairy, who says:

> Assure yourselves, O King and Queen, that your daughter shall not die of this disaster. It is true, I have not power to undo entirely what my ancient has done. The Princess shall indeed pierce her hand with a spindle: but instead of dying, she shall only fall into a profound sleep which shall last a hundred years, at the expiration of which a King's son shall come and awake her. (Opie and Opie 1974)

'Sleeping Beauty' encapsulates the fears of many parents. However, the demands of being a parent allow little time to dwell on these fears. Indeed, the routine story of 'happy endings' seems an important way of surviving the rigours, anxieties and fears that are part and parcel of the parenting task.

Adoption and curiosity

For the adopted child, this routine script does not represent the truth. His or her story is not culturally or historically located or sanctioned in any way that makes it unproblematic, so each child's birth story has to be constructed. Yet however it is constructed, it is a story that invites curiosity and this curiosity invariably leads to another story that is complex, painful and maybe unpalatable. It is a story in which rejection, abandonment and failure are realities and a happy ending cannot be routinely written into the script. While it is possible to be curious about 'normal' birth stories, their routine nature makes them largely unproblematic. Adoption, on the other hand, always invites curiosity, and the story will not routinely have a happy ending until the painful narratives of the birth parents, the adoptive parents and the child are woven together.

Adoption practice has struggled in various ways to deal with the problems of curiosity: letters from birth parents and the adoption social worker, life story books, advice and a formula for telling the birth/adoption story. Kornitzer (1976) advocates using the term adoption with small babies as a 'term of endearment … as a rhythm, as a sound, with loving overtones' (Kornitzer 1976: 121). Later in the child's development she advocates a story about 'mothers and fathers who wanted a baby and never had one, and how in the end they heard about some babies who had no fathers and mothers, and chose one of them to come home with them and to be their own for ever and ever' (Kornitzer 1976: 121). Very soon, Kornitzer says, 'the child will be told or will guess with great pleasure, that the story is really about him'. Wieder (1978), however, states:

> in the adoptees I have studied, their development and relationships to the adoptive mothers were clinically indistinguishable from blood kin children up to the time they were told of their adoption. After the disclosure, the children's behaviour, thought contents, and relationships showed dramatic changes…a toddler doesn't need to know he is adopted, he needs to know he belongs. (Weider 1978: 795, 799)

It appears that the longer the communication can be put off the better.

The most radical view is put by Ansfield (1971), who advocates that children should not be told because 'the knowledge will hurt them'. He suggests various ways of maintaining the secret including telling older siblings that 'the family is playing a game, and that no one is ever to know the secret, including the adopted child' (Ansfield 1971: 42). The debate has now moved firmly in the direction of children needing to be told the facts by their adoptive parents. All these ideas are aimed at providing both adults and children with access to a narrative which is in varying degrees psychologically and socially sound and is a satisfactory response to the problem of curiosity. Indeed, with the changing profile of children placed for adoption – older and with a more complex history – the debate has moved from the practice of 'secret' adoption (in order to maintain a firm psychological and social boundary around the 'new' family) to open adoption where both knowledge and contact introduce permeable and more flexible boundaries.

It is my contention that the capacity to be curious lies at the heart of an adopted child's ability to lay claim to his or her history and inheritance, to develop the capacity to sustain knowledge and to make sense of themselves and their world. Curiosity is the means by which individuals gain access to the narrative scripts that have for some reason become hidden, often because they contradict the kinds of narratives advocated by Kornitzer (1976) that have a more acceptable (i.e. anxiety-free or guilt-free) storyline. However, it is an understandable anxiety because of the real fears of what might be discovered if curiosity is allowed free rein. Sleeping Beauty's curiosity leads to disaster:

> About fifteen or sixteen years after, the King and Queen being gone to one of their houses of pleasure, the young Princess happen'd one day to divert herself in running up and down the palace, when going up from one apartment to another, she came into a little room on the top of the great tower, where a good woman was spinning with her spindle. This good woman had never heard of the King's proclamation against spindles. What are you doing there, said the princess? I am spinning, my pretty child, said the old woman, who did not know who she was. Ha! said the Princess, this is very pretty, how do you do it? Give it to me, that I may see if I can do so. She had no sooner taken it into her hand, than, whether being very hasty at it, somewhat unhandy, or that the decree of the Fairy had so ordained it, it ran into her hand, and she fell down in a swoon. (Opie and Opie 1974)

Absent parents, a powerful curiosity, something dangerous, a dark family secret, the sharp prick of sudden knowledge and the curse takes hold. Storytelling like this is a far cry from the requirements of adoption professionals. The notion of 'a story well told' is not acceptable in what should be a technical and rational process. Yet, our lives and our relationships are constructed through the stories we tell – the good bits, the bad bits, the exciting bits and the bits we cannot face. Our identities reflect these multilayered stories; consistent to some degree, ragged around the edges and always with an audience in mind.

Sophie, a woman in her mid-twenties and in therapy, illustrates the importance of storytelling in explaining why she feels so stuck in her life. She recounted that her adoptive parents, meeting her for the first time when she was a few months old, fell in love with her 'immediate smile'. Weaving this experience into their story of her adoption, Sophie becomes for them the eversmiling baby. 'But', she says with some anxiety, 'what if I hadn't smiled when my parents met me and what if I stopped smiling now?' A story told by her parents, with love and affection, had become a source of anxiety. Sophie wanted to be able to tell a different story about the unsmiling baby part of her who could grow up into an unsmiling child and adolescent not because she wanted to be unhappy but because she felt it was important to be allowed to show herself in this way if she needed to. She feared that her parents would not be able to accept this version of her, that it would reflect back to them a story that they could not bear to hear. She felt profoundly stuck – trapped by a story that gave only a very partial representation of her identity. If the rest of the story were to be told – and Sophie did feel a curiosity about this other story – then she felt that it would lead to her rejection by her parents.

While adoption is a fact in Sophie's story, the emotional meaning that adoption has in helping or hindering her development is critical. At the time she was recounting her story, as with Sleeping Beauty, Sophie's emotional development was hindered by what she experienced as the curse of the smiling baby. In her view, her parents could not face her pain or unhappiness and without their support or acceptance, she felt that she could not do so either. In order for Sophie to move on, I believe, it is necessary to understand the operation of some of the conscious and unconscious scripts that model her beliefs and values in relation to others.

The basis of this is rooted in attachment theory (Bowlby 1998, vols 1, 2 and 3; Ainsworth *et al.* 1978) and particularly its contribution towards developing our understanding of the concept of relatedness – the basis of engaging in meaningful interaction with the world. The capacity to find and construct meaning in experience is the basis upon which personal and social identities are constructed. The incorporation of the lived experience between the infant and its caretaker(s) into internal models of experience in relationships is a core, necessary and unavoidable part of the human developmental process.

Attachment scripts and narratives

Attachment is a system whose primary object is the achievement of physical proximity to an adult caretaker with the accompanying subjective experience of security. Bowlby (1988, vol. 1) describes its function in terms of the maintenance of a safe and nurturing environment. As a system, it becomes organized over the first six months of an infant's life. In the course of normal development, the attachment figure becomes internally represented in the child's mind so that the need for physical proximity is lessened. The child comes to develop trust and confidence in the responsiveness of the attachment figure if the carer has the capacity to hold the infant, and the effect of this is a deactivation of attachment behaviours such as monitoring the whereabouts of the attachment figure, signalling to the attachment figure to stay close and so on. A central feature of the internal modelling of the child's experience with its attachment figure is the coding of both the experience of being 'cared for' and the reciprocal experience of 'caring for'. The internalization of reciprocity in relationships is the key to the capacity to predict reasonably the emotional and behavioural responsiveness of others. It is also the key to escaping the activation and demands of attachment-driven behaviours.

The coding of reciprocity can be thought of in terms of scripts that tell a multilayered story involving different people or different parts of an individual's attachment history. An individual's attachment scripts are inevitably complex, being woven out of personal, intimate and extensive experience. However, embedded in the narratives of a secure attachment are scripts that encapsulate the reciprocity of the care-seeking/care-giving experience (Heard and Lake 1997). These narratives primarily emphasize a supportive and companionable quality of relating. Linked to key attachment qualities such as responsiveness, sensitivity and attentiveness, the supportive/companionable pattern provides a secure emotional base from which to explore the physical, emotional and social environment which can be full of possibility.

There are problems in describing attachment in this kind of way. Emotional responsiveness, sensitivity and physical proximity are the keys to meeting the child's attachment needs. The King and Queen's desire to protect their child in whatever way they could – to provide her with a safe space in which she could grow – is a reflection of this. Yet, as a description, it can sound idealized, as though there is an attainable and perfectible standard to which they need to aspire to match the perfections of their child. In reality a balance has to be achieved between the pleasures that come from having a close relationship with a small baby and developing child and the real demands and stresses of coping with a sometimes angry, demanding or messy baby. Winnicott's (1958) concept of 'good enough' is important here but, as every parent knows, it is not achieved without considerable emotional and physical cost.

When, for one reason or another, the needs of the attachment system are not met through an attachment figure, the individual child develops an insecure pattern of attachment. Attachment-related needs continue to exert a powerful influence on the child's behaviour but because of repeated earlier experiences where the attachment figure has been either emotionally unavailable or more actively rejecting, those needs are linked to a goal that is painful. The need to be close to the attachment figure and the expectation of unavailability or rejection produce unbearable conflict. In order to reduce this internal conflict, the child attempts defensively to exclude the attachment-related behaviours, resulting in patterns of behaviour such as compulsive self-sufficiency or compulsive care-giving.

In anxious attachment therefore a second, more problematic, pattern of reciprocity emerges in which the individual's relatedness is focused on being in either a dominating position in relation to the other or in a reciprocal position of submission. In either the dominant or submissive position, the individual attempts defensively to protect himself from the unbearable feelings of loss or anxiety that result from the emotional unavailability of the attachment figure.

The dominating/submissive pattern (Heard and Lake 1997), with its emphasis on control and avoidance, make for a form of relating where exploration and problem-solving can be highly problematic. The 'slight' felt by the older fairy in Sleeping Beauty, and her ensuing rage, seem to result from her feelings of being excluded from the baby's christening. However, rather than anticipating a supportive and welcoming response from the family and an attempt to make reparation for their oversight – 'The King order'd her a cover' – she anticipates further rejection. There seems to be no basis for exploration of her perception and fear of exclusion, or for a conversational: 'Where have you been, what have you been doing these past 50 years? Come and join us!' Rather, her mind is made up and her uncontained feelings turn to rage. She puts herself in the dominant position in order to avoid submitting herself to the unbearable risk of being excluded. What could be more powerful a defence against her vulnerability than to put a death curse on a small vulnerable baby in revenge? There is no doubt that in her arrival at the christening there was a problem to be solved; such oversights and misperceptions are part of everyday life. But they could be solved only by exploration and understanding between the King, Queen and the fairy – a joint curiosity. However, the deeply embedded code of reciprocity in the fairy's mind had already determined the outcome of this part of the story whatever intention the King and Queen might have had of changing it.

Karpman's (1968) 'drama triangle' provides a particularly helpful way of understanding the pattern of these defensive scripts and the narrative unfolding of stories through the different roles that individuals take up. At the centre of the triangle is the splitting and projection of feelings commonly associated with defences against emotional pain. They can also be thought of as defensive processes in relation to attachment conflicts. There are three basic scripts:

- When it is dangerous to feel anger, take the role of victim.
- Rather than feel vulnerable and in need of somebody, take the role of persecutor.
- When anger and vulnerability are the problem together, put

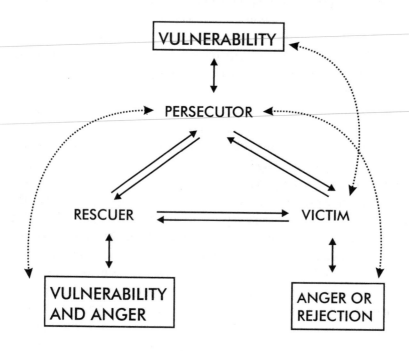

Figure 2.1 The dynamics of the drama triangle

yourself on the outside and care for and rescue the victim from the persecutor.

These scripts all describe a relatedness – persecutor–victim; victim–persecutor; rescuer–victim–persecutor. The persecutor needs the victim and the victim needs the persecutor; they also each need to be rescued from the other but the rescuer needs the persecutor to persecute the victim (Figure 2.1).

The framework in Figure 2.1 describes a psychological and social recipe for a stuck pattern of relatedness. The significance of understanding it as narrative is that it focuses our attention not on some static quality in the individual but on the fluid, unfolding quality of the roles that a person might find him or herself taking up in relation to other roles within the story. The characters in 'Sleeping Beauty', as the story is told here, have identifiable characteristics defining their roles – the persecuting older fairy, the rescuing younger fairy, the victim baby or parents. All of them are locked into these roles, leaving them little scope for individual emotional development. To take up other roles involves other emotions that are unbearable and is too great a challenge. We do not know, for instance, what the King and Queen did to the older fairy when she uttered her curse, but in the manner of these stories she was likely to have been killed. The King and Queen's hatred and desire for revenge then put them in the role of the persecutor. Similarly, what was the impact of the King's decree on spindle manufacturers or spindle operatives? Did they regard him as their persecutor as he deprived them of their livelihood when in the King's view he was attempting to rescue his daughter from the curse?

The 'drama triangle' therefore describes a system of interlocking defensive roles. As a system, it is rooted in anxious attachment where conflicted energy is focused on the physical whereabouts and emotional availability of an 'absent' attachment figure. The relationship scripts focus on the need to find people or situations that will act in complementary roles to the defensive position taken up. The impact that this can have on an individual's capacity for relatedness can be profound. In particular, these defences can make exploration of the physical, emotional and social world very difficult. Its impact might best be described in terms of what happens to curiosity.

Curiosity might be thought of as the key to the desire to learn. However, the human attachment system operates in antithesis to the exploratory system – when it is active and the individual is anxiously preoccupied with maintaining physical and emotional proximity to an attachment figure, then curiosity and exploratory behaviour become inhibited, conflicted or disappear. The supportive/companionable pattern of relatedness provides a secure basis for exploration because the attachment figure – internally or externally represented – does not have to be continually monitored for its whereabouts and emotional availability. Nor does there have to be undue concern if a difficult or worrying event occurs in the process of exploration; an explanatory and supportive response will provide, not necessarily painlessly, enough of a sense of safety for the individual to continue exploring.

In Sophie's story, her anxiety about the non-smiley part of her was intimately connected with the adoption story. In fact, she was so concerned about what this non-smiley part might reveal and what the consequences might be for her relationship to her adoptive parents that she suppressed it almost completely. When she might have appropriately signalled her distress or her anger to her parents, she feared that they would not be able to bear it. The only way she felt that she could maintain proximity to them was to smile in an undemanding and reassuring way. Without a sense that there was a securely delineated space for her needs inside their minds from which she could move on, she felt trapped. As a consequence her curiosity and need to explore had become seriously inhibited. Throughout her life, therefore, she often found herself in a passively anxious role, unable to understand things despite having the desire to do so. In relationships, she often found herself involved with men who turned out to be abusive, while she tried to placate them by smiling and looking the other way. Her curiosity needed to be stimulated to allow her to look more directly at these relationships and what they were doing to her; but the script that was associated with this always returned to her original adoption story – if I stop smiling, I will be abandoned for-ever. In order to control this powerful fear, Sophie had developed a script that kept people close but gave her very little and abused her a lot.

In thinking about Sophie's struggles in relation to adoption, it should be made clear that damage can be done by previous abusive experiences or disruption, especially when the child is adopted at an older age. This damage can be thought of as impacting on the development of a secure base narrative and the consequent continuation of attachment behaviours. However, although adoption may figure in the story, it is not the adoption *per se* that is the issue but the impact on the child's attachment history. Adoption is a cultural symbol that needs to be understood as part of a narrative which encapsulates important parts of an individual's story. The issue is what that story tells us about the nature of the individual's relatedness and whether he or she behaves in a supportive/companionable way or is accustomed to dominating and controlling. Whatever, the key to articulating these attachment narratives is curiosity.

The importance of a supportive/companionable relationship for exploring potentially difficult issues and the significance of curiosity are central to the following situation. I had been consulted about an assessment report that was being written about a girl of 8 who was fostered prior to being placed in a permanent family. The social worker writing the assessment report was qualified and experienced in social work but had not written this kind of report before. The conclusion to the report, which was detailed and gave a very positive picture of the girl, said that she was very suitable for a permanent placement and recommended that this should happen speedily. What seemed particularly gratifying was the fact that, despite just under twenty previous placements and numerous failed attempts at returning her to her mother, this girl appeared as 'normal' and well adjusted both in the foster home and at school. It seemed to be a clear example of the resilience of children in the face of adversity; a bad story with a potentially happy ending.

However, while discussing this with the social worker, I was struck by a comment in the assessment report that the child had a particular fascination with burglar alarms. She heard them go off even at some distance and would ask about it for days afterwards. The report also contained a paragraph describing a car journey where the girl had put considerable pressure on her foster father to turn around and look at what she was doing although he explained, as he was driving along, that he could not do this because it might cause an accident. Later, stopped at a red traffic light, he had turned around at which point the girl became very angry and said that she was going to complain and get him sacked because he was trying to kill her.

These fragments stood out in what was otherwise a reassuring and positive report. Did these events have some meaning? I struggled with my feelings of curiosity, fearing that something might spoil the happy ending. A happy family destroyed by the jealous and murderous attack of the slighted fairy. A planned happy placement brought to an end by the questions of a too-curious consultant.

The question that was forming itself in my mind was what could not be looked at for fear of what one might be forced to see. What feelings might be stirred up and what thoughts might one have as a result? Throwing caution to the wind, I asked whether the little girl's fascination with burglar alarms might tell us something that we had not yet realized. Was she ringing an alarm bell for us to hear? 'Well she's very happy with this family and I don't think there is much to be alarmed about,' said the social worker.

It seemed to me, however, that while focusing on her happiness was the safer option, it might be also be a defensive one. I wondered if this was what explained the danger in looking back during the car ride. I therefore asked the social worker,

> 'What might we or she see if we stopped looking steadfastly ahead to her new family and saw some of her experiences in past foster families?'

> 'Well, there were a lot of other families. And of course she was abused in a number of them.'

> 'What were you thinking of?'

> 'Well, in one family, the foster father put parcel tape over her eyes and mouth when she wouldn't get to sleep. In another, the foster father sexually assaulted her brother and maybe her too but nobody really knows. But she seems to have been able to put this behind her now.'

It is just as well then that we do not look back, I thought. There are two powerful and familiar social work scripts here. The first is driven by the hope that children surrounded by the love and warmth of responsive and mature parents can put the past behind them; children rescued from a persecuted past by a forward-looking love. This script is embodied in much policy and practice in social work with children. Yet, when it acts as a defensive script that prevents adults from thinking about the impact of these experiences on children, it may be unhelpful and sometimes dangerous.

The second script encapsulates the fear that looking at the past will create an impenetrable barrier to growth and development. In practical terms, the child might be thought to have the kind of history that no new parents could contemplate when choosing their desired child without being overwhelmed by rage, despair or fear. In Karpman's (1968) terms, the question seems to be, are children to be the victim of their past experiences by continually being reminded of them or can they be rescued from these experiences by the forward-looking love of a new family? Although there are crucial issues in both parts of this question, it is important to remember that both are based on a splitting off of unbearable feelings – a defence against the primary attachment need of a physically proximate relationship and an emotionally responsive adult.

In this example, then, the complex task for the social worker, the new family and, ultimately, for the little girl herself was how to tell a story that enabled her to make use of the opportunities of a new future without denying some of the real and horrifying experiences of her past. These experiences had important consequences for her identity, but they could not be allowed to dominate her relationship with the adult world or, indeed, adults' relationships with her. She needed to be able to signal her needs in a way that rang a bell for her adult carers so that their response could be supportive and companionable. It is important to understand the alarm she felt about needing something from adults when the response she received from the foster parent was tape over her eyes, but the message for her new family could not be clearer.

The assessment report was an important part of the regulatory framework for placement finding, adoption and, in the process, meeting the girl's needs. However, there were aspects of it where it might be understood to be playing a part in the story rather than being an observation or a commentary on it. The little girl herself was telling a story about the alarm bells that drew the attention of adults to the seriousness of her needs to be close to somebody who would keep her safe. Yet these seemed to provoke very powerful fears in the adults – myself included – of what happens if you try to relate to these fears. Do you try to rescue her from them, persecute her for stirring you up and making you anxious or become a victim to them by not thinking about them at all? These are all roles available in the narrative but, in bringing you closer to the little girl, they do so at the expense of other roles and their associated scripts, assigning them to other people to play. Unfortunately, the story then does not have a developmental but a defensive narrative that carries the risks that Sophie's experiences demonstrate.

The issue in the 'wedding speech' was therefore not my relief at having avoided it, or feeling outrage at it or protecting myself from it. It was important to hear the message in the story because it is one that reminds me that my role as an adult and parent includes hearing the painful and the anxious bits and not avoiding them. And that holds true for kings and queens as well!

References

Ainsworth, M.D.S., Blehar, M.C., Waters, E. and Wall, S. (1978) *Patterns of Attachment: A Psychological Study of the Strange Situation.* Hillsdale, NJ: Erlbaum.

Ansfield, J. (1971) *The Adopted Child.* Springfield, IL: Thomas.

Bowlby, J. (1998) *Attachment and Loss. Vol. 1: Attachment.* London: Hogarth and Institute of Psychoanalysis.

Bowlby, J. (1998) *Attachment and Loss. Vol. 2: Separation, Anxiety and Anger.* London: Hogarth and Institute of Psychoanalysis.

Bowlby, J. (1998) *Attachment and Loss. Vol. 3: Loss, Sadness and Depression.* London: Hogarth and Institute of Psychoanalysis.

Heard, D. and Lake, B. (1997) *The Challenge of Attachment for Caregiving.* London: Routledge.

Karpman, S. (1968) 'Fairy tales and script drama analysis'. *Transactional Analysis Bulletin 7,* 26, 39–44.

Kornitzer, M. (1976) *Adoption.* New York: Putnam.

Opie, I. and Opie, P. (1974) 'Sleeping Beauty in the wood'. In their *The Classic Fairy Tales.* London: Oxford University Press.

Wieder, H. (1978) 'On when and whether to disclose about adoption'. *Journal of the American Psychoanalytic Association 26,* 4, 793–811.

Winnicott, D. (1958) Collected papers: Through Paediatrics to Psychoanalysis. London: Tavistock.

My Mother's House

I am dreaming that I am
walking down an unfamiliar street
I am searching the windows
the doorways
for a woman
I do not know
but I know I am to meet

I am dreaming a door opens
a dark haired woman stands
within the frame
no words pass between us
she and I are strangers
yet somehow we are the same

I am dreaming
the woman beckons me
inside
she stands aside

My mother's house
has many rooms
she leads me up the stairway
through the layers of my self
finally she pauses
by a door
she stands aside

I know that I must pass
beyond this door
once I do so
nothing will be
as it has been before
I step inside
the secret room
as I look down
I see the floor
is made entirely of glass

Through this I see
many storeys
reaching back down to the earth
reaching back
beyond myself

Strangers gather
in these unfamiliar rooms
Who are they
Who am I
How can I step without falling

3

The Jewish Kindertransport from Germany to England, 1938–9

Rebekka Göpfert

In 1938–9, about ten thousand children aged between one and sixteen, mostly Jewish, from Germany, Austria, and some from Poland and Czechoslovakia, managed to escape to Britain, leaving their parents behind. At an age when stable and reliable surroundings and familiar people are necessary to create a safe atmosphere, these children were forced to emigrate, to leave their homes and their parents. In a foreign country the parents would have been the very people who could have helped the children to adapt to their new surroundings, but they were the ones who had to be left behind since, under this scheme, visas were granted only to children, not to adults.

This operation was, and is, known as 'Kindertransport'; the majority of the children were born between 1922 and 1938 and are today in their sixties to mid-seventies. Many of them still call themselves Kinder (German for children); whenever I talk about Kinder in this chapter, I am referring to children who escaped with the Kindertransport.

The year 1938 marked a turning point in German anti-Semitism. The Nuremberg Laws had already been introduced in 1935, but in 1938 open pressure against Jews reached its peak. In March of that year, Austria had been annexed to the German Reich, which meant that Austrian Jews had become victims of Nazi persecution practically overnight. Emigration became a more and more urgent last way out, but it was very hard to get a visa. Even if the whole family could not emigrate, every effort would be made to save the children.

News from Germany became worse and worse, and when Britain received reports of *Kristallnacht*, the pogrom night of 9–10 November when most German synagogues were burnt and Jewish shops were destroyed, the British government decided that something had to be done. On 21 November 1938, the British Parliament discussed the situation of Jews in Germany and passed a resolution that an unspecified number of Jewish children were to be admitted into Britain. Britain would issue as many visas as required, as long as the organizations involved could guarantee that the whole operation would be financed by private means and no money would be needed from official sources. The outbreak of the Second World War put a sudden end to the initiative. By then about ten thousand children had escaped to Britain.

In Germany and Austria, the local Jewish congregations, under general authorization from the German government, were responsible for the organization of the transports. They informed their members about the possibility of sending children to Britain, took registrations from the parents and handled the necessary paperwork. When there were more applications than available places on the trains, they had to select children.

The organization in Britain was mainly handled by the Central British Fund for German Jewry and the Jewish Refugees' Committee. In order to help organize the Kindertransport, the Refugee Children's Movement was founded. These three committees found places in families and hostels to house the children until they were old enough to live on their own; some of the children had relatives with whom they could stay. In various cases when difficulties between children and foster families arose, children were re-housed at least once, if not more often.

After the outbreak of war, some of the children who were then over the age of 16 were interned as enemy aliens; others were evacuated from the cities into the countryside in order to protect them from German air-raids. For the children this meant once again leaving the surroundings to which they had just adapted.

Today, the majority of the Kinder still live in England. After the war, some left for the USA, Canada, Australia or Israel. Very few went back to live in Germany. Probably more than two-thirds of them never saw their parents again; most now have a new family, with their own children and grand-children. Since the late 1980s they started to create a worldwide net of Kindertransport associations, organizing meetings and support groups. Members are thus provided with an opportunity to remember their history and are assisted in tracing information about the lives and deaths of their families. The various activities of contemporary Kindertransport organizations have proved to be very helpful for the process of remembering; through them many Kinder found out that there were others who had shared their experiences, they were able to contact people who came from the same city and who therefore were a valuable link to life before emigration.

Between 1993 and 1997 I interviewed twenty-seven Kinder. They talked about their lives, both before and after emigration, about their memories of their family and their friends, about their identities and about their relationship to Germany. They also talked about their lives today, about their professions, and about the traces and scars left by the experiences.

The interviews usually began with requests for biographical details and then moved on to the family background and family life, including the religious life at home and within the Jewish community. Initial experiences of discrimination, arrests of family members and open persecution were then spoken about. In most cases, the children could not remember or never knew when their parents first decided to put them on the transports and how the process of registration was handled. (Information on organizational details is evident in the written sources, though.) Also, recollections of saying goodbye were usually (with exceptions) vague, while the arrival in Britain was clear. One interviewee describes her feelings about it:

> And then everybody seemed to disappear and I can remember waiting, and an English lady ... came to fetch me and two other children. And I got in the car there, and all I can remember of the journey is continually asking the car to stop and getting out and being sick. And I must have been sick at least five or six times on that journey. Yes, I remember it very well. And I never knew who the two children in the car were till the 1988 [Kindertransport] Reunion when I put up a notice, and I was delighted that one of them was just sitting at the next table, and he read the notice, and that's Kurt Stern who met us in Jerusalem with his wife, and who I got to know since, and the other one, I thought was his sister, but in fact was his cousin who lives in America and who's also been to London and I've met since. And I was delighted to meet them and I was surprised how strongly I felt about them, what a strong emotion. I felt a tie with him and with his cousin Ruth, because somehow they'd been my last link with home, and I thought, I have very strong emotions for them, which was totally unexpected.

Interviewees then spoke extensively about their lives in the new surroundings and circumstances; very few Kinder had known beforehand the people they were going to stay with, and placements were usually unplanned. This resulted in many children being displaced more than once, since difficulties occurred quite often; the most frequent reason was that foster parents decided they no longer wished to keep the child. The Refugee Children's Movement, which was responsible for most of the children, had introduced a quite efficient scheme of regular but rare visits to every child's home. Unfortunately many cases of sexual abuse, exploitation as cheap home servants, and physical neglect were not seen or not investigated by the regular visitors; according to many interviewees, the inspectors spoke to the foster parents rather than to the children. Finally, even if it was a reasonable decision to move some children from their places, it usually meant an upsetting experience, being linked with issues of 'not being good enough' and of having to get used to new surroundings once again.

Other reasons for moves included evacuation and internment after the outbreak of war. To protect them from German air-raids, the Kinder were evacuated together with British children into safer, usually rural, areas. Here Kinder were often seen as German, of enemy origin. That they came from an enemy country was even more apparent when the children reached their sixteenth birthdays and were interned in camps as enemy aliens. They usually did not have to stay for very long, but it was once more made apparent that their presence in Britain was only tolerated, not wholly accepted.

Contact with the parents who had stayed behind was finally interrupted by the outbreak of war. This was usually remembered as painful since, in many cases, children thought that their parents were no longer interested in them or had even completely forgotten about them. Only when the children were old enough, or if somebody made an effort to explain the situation to them, were they able at least rationally to understand why they no longer heard from their parents.

Linked to this were the final biographical issues covered: life after the war; the search for parents and, in rare cases, reunion with them; professional lives; marriage and children; and in some cases emigration to the USA or Israel.

Reunion with the birth parents turned out to be quite difficult: one Kind remembers that having to leave the foster family she had grown very close to over the years meant a sort of repetition of her first separation from her birth parents many years earlier. Also, many parents had survived traumatic experiences themselves and were not prepared for how their children had grown up in the mean time. Severe conflicts were inevitable.

These are the main topics covered during the interviews. In addition, I asked all the Kinder whether they still spoke German, whether they spoke German to their own children, whether or not they had ever returned to their original towns and how they felt about Germany and Austria today. I wanted to know how they see themselves today, do they identify themselves as British, American, Israeli, German, Austrian or Jewish. This was the question to which answers varied the most.

In most cases people talked freely to me, even though the process of remembering was quite painful. For some of them, it was the first time that they had told their stories to anybody; others had talked about it with family or close friends. During almost every interview, the fact that I am a non-Jewish German researcher tended to come up, and I am well aware that this had a certain influence on how people talked to me and on what they told me.

So far, I have come to the conclusion that not only did the Kinder go through the common experience of violence and Nazi persecution in Germany, and the early separation from their parents, but also they were for a long time not allowed to grieve for what happened to them. If the Kinder were able to express their grief, it was in most cases very hard to find someone who would listen to them. This deprivation of the right to give voice to their suffering seems to me a further traumatization of the Kinder who, as children, were already the victims of violence.

Until very recently the Kinder were not acknowledged as 'real' Holocaust survivors (and might not even have seen themselves as such). In a sense they were never given the right to suffer or, more accurately, the right to express their suffering; most of them were constantly told to be grateful for being saved and not to complain, considering that millions had been killed and so few had survived the camps. During the interviews, all the Kinder said that they had been told that they had no right to be critical about their experiences since they had spent the war in a safe country, free from invasion and had not suffered hunger, cold or physical cruelty. The fact that their emotional needs were not met was completely neglected in these circumstances.

Interestingly enough, though, the same arguments are sometimes used today, when members of the second generation of the Kindertransport, that is, sons and daughters, complain of not being told of the experiences of their parents. Some Kinder claim that their own children have had a safe and wealthy home and a good education, therefore they should not complain about this lack of openness. Other Kinder wanted to spare their own children the hardships they had been through, and therefore kept silent when it came to their own childhood. In both cases, it is obvious that the unspoken is even more present in the families than the spoken.

The issue of guilt towards the non-survivors is closely linked to the forced gratitude towards the country which took the Kinder in, and to the people who looked after them. Gratitude was both demanded and taken for granted:

> Mrs Feirs always showed me off to all her friends as 'her little Czech refugee girl', and I was endlessly shown off with 'this is our little Czech refugee girl we are looking after', and I always felt like a false daughter. And I didn't like this, and all the conversations always went: 'Oh, you must be so grateful', and, 'Aren't you a lucky child that you've been

saved, and how grateful you must be to these good people.' Now, all that was right, but I didn't need to have it told to me by different sorts of people every single Sunday. So certainly, from having been quite a spoilt only child, suddenly to be opted a great charity wasn't something that I took very easily to, but on the other hand I was really – I was well treated.

Today, when the majority of concentration camp survivors are dead, the Kinder are among the last witnesses of the Holocaust and have finally stepped out of the shadow of the camp survivors. They have started telling their stories and have discovered that there is an audience for them. In this context it was interesting to see that children who re-emigrated to the USA or Israel (where a large percentage of the population are immigrants themselves and where the Holocaust plays a prominent role in the public memory) had much easier access to their autobiographies and found it easier to cope with their recollections, while those who stayed in Britain find it hard still to be seen as foreigners: they are British subjects, but not British. The Kinder in Britain are seen as refugees, while those who went on to another country after the war were seen as immigrants. Especially in the USA, being an immigrant is an experience shared with many others, up to this day. In Britain, however, it still seems to make a difference that the Kinder carry a not-English name, speak English with a foreign accent and cannot share the socialization of schooling and growing up with their British friends.

Marion Berghahn, herself a German, conducted an inquiry of Jewish immigrants of German origin who came to Britain both as children and as adults (Berghahn 1984). Her research, sociological rather than historical, considered the present lives of her interviewees, their integration into British society and their identity – German, British or both – and came to the conclusion that most of the German immigrants still felt a strong cultural attachment to the country they had to leave behind. This also makes it much harder to develop a feeling of belonging, especially when one takes into account that the country to which strong bonds still exist is the one from which they were expelled.

Consequences of the experiences of Kindertransport have still not been satisfactorily researched. Vernon Hamilton, a psychologist, carried out a study which included 388 Kinder currently living in the UK, North America, Israel and the European continent (Hamilton 1985). He claims that, in comparison with the general British population, no significantly higher degree of cases of mental illness could be found, while physical illnesses appeared much more frequently among Kinder. Hamilton (1985) points out, though, that women tend to be less satisfied with their adult and professional lives (one of the explanations might be that men had the chance to fight in the British army and thus were rewarded with a higher acceptance in British society). He also shows that the older the children were at the time of their arrival, the easier it was for them to cope with the separation from their families, while it was harder for them to become accustomed to the new language, society and school system. The group which were the most likely to settle down in their new surroundings were the Orthodox children. To a certain extent they had already been outsiders before emigration, so that their situation within society did not change drastically; of course, their family situations were as painful as those of non-Orthodox children.

The effects of Kindertransport may exist in a much more subtle form, however, and a Dutch researcher has found a way to describe these hidden scars. Hans Keilson's book is based on a follow-up study of the children whose parents were sent to a concentration camp and who were hidden by Dutch families (Keilson 1992). He writes about the effects of the early separation from their biological parents and about the difficulties in dealing with new families and the guilt of having survived, coming to the conclusion that the traumatization is repeated over and over again in later life. For this matter, he has created the term 'sequential traumatization', and I think that it describes very accurately the lives of the Kinder, too: recollections of persecution and humiliation by Nazis, early separation from parents, frequently changing surroundings, experiences of anti-Semitism also in Britain, loss of family members and survivors' guilt. All these are traumatic experiences existing up to the present and they make the Kinder much more vulnerable to further traumatizations.

References

Berghahn, M. (1984) *German-Jewish Refugees in England: The Ambiguities of Assimilation* New York: St Martin's Press.

Hamilton, V. (1985) 'A retrospective study of child refugees from Nazi Germany'. ESRC application, Department of Psychology, University of Reading.

Keilson, H. (1992) *Sequential Traumatization in Children: A Clinical and Statistical Follow-up Study on the Fate of the Jewish War Orphans in the Netherlands.* Jerusalem: Magnes Press.

Further Reading

Barnett, R. (1995) 'The other side of the abyss: a psychodynamic approach to working with groups of people who came to England as children on the Kindertransport'. *British Journal of Psychotherapy 15*, 2, 178–94.

Baumel, E.J. (1983) 'Twice a refugee: the Jewish refugee children in Great Britain during evacuation 1939–1943'. *Jewish Social Studies 45*, 2, 175–84.

Gillespie, V. (1994) 'Working with the Kindertransports'. In S. Oldfield (ed) *This Working-day World: Women's Lives and Culture(s) in Britain 1914–1945*. Bristol: Taylor and Francis.

Kushner, T. (1991) 'The impact of the Holocaust on British society and culture'. *Contemporary Record 5*, 2, 349–75.

For Rosemary

In the picture house
you began to lose
your life blood
and your child

Down the main street
and through the close[1]
straight forward and secret
you saw yourself home

In the living room
you bled discreetly
not wishing to offend
your sleeping father
in the sent in bed

In the early hours
home from the nightshift
my father found you
wrapped in bleeding sheets

The close women of the tenement
with whom you shared
the bluebell china
and the kitchen talk
they came and went

Then the Egyptian doctor
who both from heredity
and practice
was bound to be familiar
with such passing
in and out of life

He since confessed
his faith restored

1   Scottish word for small alley.

by your observance of last rites
and your refusal to commit
your unmade child to flame

Instead my father made
from his good watch box
a peg sized coffin
for your first misborn
and took you after
to the grave dug in the glen
long since the witness
of your early love

4

Infertility and the 'Bureaucratic' Child

Some Thoughts on the Treatment of Two Adopted Patients

Julian Lousada

The inescapable fact about adoption is that it is a bureaucratic process on the one hand, and a 'mission' of reparation on the other. The bureaucracy involves the prolonged experience of decision-making, vetting, waiting and placement. The mission of reparation is the wish to reduce the harm and pain that is associated with infertility. A powerful impetus when thinking about adoption is to think about the future, and pay too little attention to the intense experience of loss, bewilderment and failure that inevitably accompanies the experience of infertility. It is the basic premise of this chapter that it is not only the absent birth mother who has to be kept in the mind for the benefit of the adopted child, but also the experience of infertility for the adopting couple.

Although it is not centrally within the scope of this chapter, the impact of the experience of being 'vetted', passing or failing, and having one's child chosen by another must have an enormous impact upon both the marital relationship and the subsequent relationship with the adopted child. Additionally, the uncertainty of the process must reawaken very painful experiences of failure. I am reminded, for example, of an adoptive father who, having successfully adopted two children, spent a considerable amount of time writing a series of vitriolic letters and articles about his treatment at the hand of the 'vetting' agency, a retaliation it would seem not only about the intrusive, if necessary, process of vetting, but also an expression of the seemingly unprocessable hurt associated with not being able to have his own birth child.

Living happily ever after where the pain of the past is obliterated by the joy of the present is, I suspect, the wish in the minds of all couples without children who apply to adopt. From Moses on, the stories abound of the abandoned orphan who overcomes all manner of hardship only to be discovered and adopted into the land of plenty.

What the fairy stories do not describe is the hapless experience of all those princes before they meet their princesses. Prince Charming has one slipper, and the feet of an entire town to negotiate; Rapunzel's rescuer is blindly stumbling in a forest, perforce bumping into a whole manner of unseen obstacles; Sleeping Beauty's prince is hacking his way through a hundred years of growth of thick forests with no certainty of the outcome. What, I wonder, would have happened to their enthusiasm and their love, had they had to make public the most intimate details of their lives and negotiated a placement in order to gain the 'most beautiful' of children?

When I was doing my social work training many years ago, one of the first cases I was given was to prepare a vetting report for a couple being considered as adopters who, were they to be successful, intended taking their adopted child out of the country. I remember being told that this was a good initial training case as it would help me with my interviewing skills in a non-threatening situation. The couple had nearly completed the application process. I remember setting off eagerly and anticipated a good start to my training. An hour or so later I emerged feeling bullied, humiliated, quite unprepared and unable to think about the anger and pain that I had encountered. The combination of my inexperience and their largely un-explored feelings of failure and loss made a deadly cocktail.

My supervisor patiently listened to my account and commented that this couple had probably had quite enough of being 'investigated' and what I had to keep in mind on my next visit were the three general questions that the court would want to be satisfied upon:

- Would this couple be good parents?
- Would an adopted child 'fit' into their lives?
- Would the child grow up knowing of the adoption?

Much emphasis was laid upon this last point. It was precisely this question that had provoked the hostility in the first interview. It is the intensity of these three questions, which in one way or another dominate the vetting, and I suspect it is the shared knowledge that they cannot be answered with any degree of accuracy, that provided the terrain for the conflict that I so unwittingly stumbled upon.

My supervisor added that I must remember that I was helping an unfortunate couple come together with an unlucky child and there are not many happy endings in our line of work!

I start with this anecdote, which has probably become caricatured with the passing of time, because I think it highlights some important issues. First, the enormous pressure to have a happy ending; second, how invasive the experience of application can be; and third, the wish to make a very complex process straightforward. These injunctions are all predicated upon denial, which, I suspect, is one of the primary dynamics in the process of application for, and lived experience of, adoption.

I want to say at the outset that I am not an expert in adoption; indeed, in my career as a social worker I had only limited experience of this area of work. This chapter is based principally on my experience of treating a number of adopted patients over quite a few years. The experience of treating these patients has posed questions in my mind and it is these questions and thoughts that I want to discuss in this chapter. I should emphasize that I am not suggesting that what I shall describe is true for all adoptions. It is also worth pointing out that adoptions at birth are not nearly as common as they once were; I imagine different issues will arise in the case of later adoptions. I have organized my thoughts loosely under three headings:

- The infertile couple and the 'bureaucratic child'
- Telling
- Sexual boundaries and the internal couple.

The infertile couple and the 'bureaucratic child'

The patient (to protect confidentiality I have changed any identifying details) to whom I will refer most is in her late twenties. She is attractive and intelligent, but at the same time a very troubled and unhappy person who seemed unable to hold on to her capacities in such a way as to enable her to secure lasting relationships, or to develop her undoubted academic talents in such a way as to give her the satisfaction of an experience of maturation. Her internal objects had an exaggerated quality; there was, I suppose, little evidence of sustained 'depressive position' functioning. She seemed to find it difficult to discover the capacity for a reciprocal relationship in which she could, as it were, explore the potential for a creative intercourse. Habitually, she was either in supplication towards her objects, or convinced of a threatening and mendacious other. It was not, I think, surprising that she was a member of a far left organization which demanded loyalty of thought and prescribed 'correct' behaviour. She was promiscuous in an adolescent sort of way, and troubled by persistent, perverse sexual fantasies. However, on the other hand, she provoked in me unusually strong feelings of compassion and rescue, that are, I think, readily associated with the orphan. The beginning of her treatment was characterized by an almost instantaneous 'attachment' to me in which I became the idealized parent/man and therapist, but as in all idealized object relations the underpinning persecutory anxiety remained hard to confront. I had the experience of being captured by something that I knew was prejudicial to the therapy but about which I could not, for some considerable time, become clear.

In retrospect the intensity of the early months of treatment drew attention to some crucial issues concerning beginnings. In announcing her uncertainty that I was the right therapist for her, she demonstrated a process that was being undertaken prematurely. I have constantly been struck by the repetition of this aspect of her behaviour as if nothing could be completed in its 'own' time, but in some way had to be forced. I think this was also a defence against discovering how things come together, especially in the context where there is, or appears to be, an element of choice as is the case in adoption, and repeated in the patient's/therapist's 'choice' of each other. The confusion that characterized our beginning seemed to be informed by two projects, mine that was concerned with a beginning and hers that was concerned to avoid one, or more accurately her wish seemed to be to develop the fantasy that we were in some way 'meant for each other', known to each other, and therefore the experience of uncertainty, choice and conflict could be avoided. What I felt she wished to experience was in effect a 'natural conception', or to put it the other way, the 'arranged' nature of our relationship was experienced as very hurtful and fragile. In the one instance the maternal relationship could be taken for granted, in the other it had to be learnt.

For the birth child there is the experience of what Winnicott (1956) describes as the 'primary maternal preoccupation'. However, for my patient this primary experience was greatly complicated by the absent birth mother, her substitution by what is in effect a stranger, whose preoccupation was at least in part elsewhere. The fact that this young woman was my first 'training patient' drew to my attention the importance she had for my future. In these circumstances I became aware of two complementary, but initially separate, projects. First, one which had as its objective the realization of my ambition, and second, the hoped-for good experience of a treatment for my patient. I do not mean to imply that these two projects are for ever separate, but just to point out that they start from different positions, and that this needs to be recognized. It is my view that it is the complexity of the primary maternal preoccupation for the adoptive mother, bringing together as it does the mother and infant, that is one of the most powerful dynamics of adoption. I was very concerned with the questions as to what I was doing, and why, as a psychotherapist. Time and again I found myself unclear and lacking confidence in not only my ambition but also my competence. It was hard to admit that our project had been not in the celebration of a completed pregnancy, but in failure: those 'failures' in me which prompted me to seek therapy and subsequently training, and the 'failure' of the original mother to keep and nourish her baby. It is, I am sure, the residue of this shared knowledge that has such an influence on the experience of adoption and treatment alike. Put very bluntly, adoption has to overcome two things: first, the experience of the failure of creativity (i.e. the parental infertility) and second, the failure of the infant's capacity to create the idea of the wanted child in the birth mother.

For adopting parents the preoccupation is with their own failure and also the need to integrate the idea of the adopted baby that has to develop without, before it is able to develop within. There is in the mind of the adoptive parent an internal representation of a baby, but it is not, it seems to me, principally the baby they hope to adopt, but rather the baby they longed for, tried and failed over a long period to create. The loss of this baby is excruciating. I am not just drawing attention to the immense historical pain of infertility, but also drawing attention to the fact that the adoptive baby in the mind exists in the company of, and is unconsciously compared with, the wanted birth-child.

A mother of two teenage adopted children once said in conversation with me:

> I love my two children very much, but I have an inner fantasy I would never admit to other adoptive parents. They'd think I was disloyal. I would like to see the face and body of the biological child I couldn't have. We have gorgeous people in our family, bright people with brilliant minds. I'm sure it would have been a wonderful child.

There are two major dichotomous dangers that confront the thinking about adoption: one is to assume the fact of adoption to be the source of anxiety which must be kept in mind constantly as a potential difficulty, and the other to assume that the fact of adoption is of no importance. This dichotomy has in one way or another been a continuous preoccupation. There would be times when it would be possible to consider both these possibilities, but others when I would be accused of completely missing the point, and the constant accusation was that I was 'in another world'. When I could bear to consider this accusation I realized guiltily that it was quite probably right and that the world I was in was one in which babies were born, not bureaucratically arranged, intuitively known as being of oneself, as opposed to learnt about. I suppose I came to think that it was not only my patient who was concerned with what she knew or did not know, but that I realized as I struggled to understand which of the parental objects was being referred to, that 'not knowing' felt intolerable. I felt under tremendous pressure therefore to arrive at premature formulations, to put things in their 'proper place' long before I was in any position so to do. It seemed as if the anxiety caused for my patient of not knowing her place was extremely persecutory.

My thoughts initially were concerned with the anxiety associated with what was not known, and how available this gap was for a whole range of projections. What I found hard to come to terms with was not a gap that was empty and had to be filled, but a gap, a space, that had content. My patient had been 'put up' for adoption between 10 and 12 weeks of age.

> Even in the most favourable circumstances, there had been an experience of moving from one mode of being mothered to another. This may be felt at quite a primitive level – smells and shape of mother's body are different, the way of being held, fed, put to bed, will all be a little different … Even for a small baby, this transition in primary care is deeply registered, even though it is not understood. (Rustin 1991)

The residue of this largely unconscious 'knowledge', and the loss and pain associated with it, constantly vied with the actual experience of being parented. There is, however, another way of considering what can be thought about, and that is the question of who it is that is being thought about. It seems to me that some of the pain informed by the 'gap or space' might be associated with the realization that parent and child may not be primarily thinking about each other.

The patient I have described has a powerful wish that she will meet someone who will know all about her, and will be rescued and loved free of any doubt. Being known about is not, I think, concerned only with the discovery of the birth parent, powerful as this wish inevitably is, but the wish to know and feel secure about what is in the mind of the parent, in effect to be reassured that it is she who is there and not an 'other'.

Let me return briefly to how we might think about infertility. It is not just a narcissistic blow, but also inhibits the maturational experience of making the transition from being a child to becoming a parent. I suspect that this has considerable implications for the marital relationship. For those couples who want a child and discover they cannot have one, there is an enormous problem to overcome, namely their mutual failure of creativity. It seems to me that this failure in creativity dominates the experience of adoption for parent and child alike.

The secret that adoption can seek to hide is not just the illegitimacy of the child, but the failure of the couple to reproduce. I suspect the psychological future of the child largely depends upon the parents' capacity to come to terms with their experience of infertility and the loss of their biological child.

Joan Raphael-Leff (1993) writes movingly about the relentless quality of this experience:

> While trying to conceive, each month becomes a cycle of elation and deflation, each fertile outsider a potential reminder of their 'failure'. When a couple find they are unable to produce a baby of their own making the impact of this incapacity pervades their present relationship and invades past and future. Genetic immortality is curtailed. Love-making becomes baby-making. Persecutory guilt, mutual recriminations and sorrow and the non-materialisation of their joint-procreative project are coupled with an irrational sense of personal inferiority. In the case of assisted conception, invasion of their sexual privacy by technology and experts reawakens heightened feelings of childish incapacity and shame alongside renewed hope, deep gratitude, rage and bitter-sweet dependency. With preparation for adoption fears about taking in a stranger, anxieties about the selection process, being examined and found wanting, vie with every parent-to-be's doubts about their own capacity to be a good enough parent and to get/deserve a good baby. (Raphael-Leff 1993)

Telling

Referring once again to my original training, there was the slogan that adopted children 'should grow up knowing' of their adopted status, and should be protected from accidental 'discovery' so commonly reported by adoptees. Leaving aside the obvious question as to the nature of this accident, there is the equally obvious harm that late telling, especially during adolescence, can have. We are left with the thorny question as to when/how it is best to tell.

My patients report being 'told' from the age of about two and a half to three years. They described how their mothers constructed stories that emphasized how 'special' they were, how they had been 'chosen', and represented the birth mother in a rather idealized way as a loving, forlorn teenager forced by circumstances to give up her child.

I think one can only be sympathetic to the immense difficulty, and pain, that adoptive parents are faced with. In effect they are heard to be saying, 'I love you but you are not mine and I am not yours'. The dilemma seems to be that at precisely the time the adoptive parents have discovered a security and intimacy with the child, they feel under the obligation to introduce the child to the idea of the 'real birth mother' and the adoption. There is a real integrity in this process, but I think it inevitably makes the child aware of his or her parents' sense of failure and loss. It seems to me that 'telling' must in essence provoke feelings of catastrophic and inexplicable abandonment. The idealization of the story of their adoption, that my patients described, inhibited the necessity for a period of mourning and anger. My patient described experiences of disintegration, for example describing a memory of originally living in an idyllic country cottage, complete with pony and stream, which became replaced by ever more mundane housing. Another patient described being told at the age of just over three and responding by cutting open the breasts of her mother's dressmaking dummy as if to discover their contents, for which she received her first slap, leaving her feeling 'dirty and extremely guilty'. The cutting not only referred to a wish to find out, but also drew attention to her wish to attack and damage the absent mother. Freud (1917) in 'Mourning and melancholia' suggests that for an object to be given up it must first be taken in and valued; only then can the depression be tolerated. However, for the adopted child at this early age it is the idea of the birth mother that has to be given up, an idea with little substance in reality.

> Where a child has no contact with the biological parents outside the very earliest infancy – there is no organised experience, no memory to be drawn upon to construct the parent… so how can a child construct such a representation … observation seems to show a wish … but without enough bricks to build as it were. (Hodges 1984)

There is, it seems to me, a further complication associated with early telling and this concerns its repetition. Being told that I am not yours and you are not mine when the infant is already trying to establish what is me, what is you, and what is in my control is at best confusing, but the repeated information can also be experienced as very punishing.

Peller (1963) suggests that early and repeated telling is both confusing and destructive. She suggests that it is impossible to tell the young child the story of her adoption without implying at the same time the cruelty of desertion and rejection, or at least providing all the key elements for such a fantasy: 'out of this the child creates a longing for the original parent … as if something crucial was missing to the detriment of establishing the self in the real world' (Peller 1963).

The dilemma is this: can early telling be incorporated without it being experienced as a sadistic attack, at a time when the need for a reliable container is at its strongest? I vividly remember my daughter's repeated questioning about where she came from and how she came to be in her mother's tummy, and the visible pleasure and reassurance she obtained from our answers. I can equally imagine how devastating it would have been had she not obtained the answer she so confidently expected.

Sexual boundaries and the internal couple

I have frequently wondered how the experience of adoption alters the oedipal experience. Certainly, for my patients, its negotiation has been fraught with difficulties. Most notable has been the capacity to establish in their minds a parental couple capable of intercourse on the one hand, and the capacity to manage ambivalence without recourse to splitting. The creation of what Ronald Britton (1989) refers to as the 'Third Position' which

> provides the infant with a prototype for an object relationship of a third kind in which he is a witness and not a participant ... a capacity for seeing ourselves in interaction with others and entertaining another point of view whilst retaining our own, for reflecting on ourselves, whilst being ourselves. (Britton 1989)

I shall return to this in a moment. What Britton draws our attention to is a resolution that involves looking. The capacity to look, as with my daughter, is informed by the knowledge of a capacity to process what was found – difficult as it necessarily is. Furthermore, this capacity reflected the reliance in her mind of the parental couple. While not wanting to romanticize my daughter's experience, it did seem to contrast with the anxiety provoked in my patients. Looking for them required not only some rudimentary knowledge of their abandonment by the birth mother and their adoptive mother's infertility, but also, and I am being rather speculative here, the necessity to establish who is who and who does what.

In the transference my penis seemed to be a substitute for the nipple and much of my patient's confusion, distress and subsequent acting out was associated with her discovery of its true character. I think this reflected how her father was in the early days – both father and mother – which made the process of establishing whether she was the daughter or lover extremely difficult. I want to draw attention to what Winnicott (1962) describes: 'An altered sense of obligation in these families where the incestuous wishes are not, owing to the absence of a blood relationship, subject to the usual controls' (Winnicott 1962).

Although I feel rather cautious about being so emphatic, I was none the less made aware in the transference of a very concrete preoccupation with seduction, and the unreliability of sexual boundaries. There was a repeated dream of a very decrepit couple sitting in a bath on the kitchen floor, and outside the window a white foal was jumping playfully around; this dream seemed to draw attention to her sexuality and expected fertility, but also something was decaying, and deadly. Instead, parental objects were associated with hateful and confusing thoughts, and I think an uncertainty as to what distinguished one parent from another. The confusion in her boundaries was vividly described when she told how her father had not only described but also demonstrated the use of her first tampon. It seemed as if she was unable to resolve her longing for, her expectation of, seduction, and her fear of it. The therapy bore an uncanny resemblance to the solutions she acquired at home. The sessions were either flooded with, or starved of, material. There was an oscillation between a sensuous intimacy, and a sadistic and highly eroticized attack upon the therapy; both were forms of defence against a 'loving intercourse'. There are many ways we might usefully consider this splitting that I do not have space to pursue here. One aspect does, however, seem worth ending upon.

Some two years into therapy, I took the decision to move my consulting room from my home. I argued to myself that it would be better all round. For my family I thought there would be a liberation from the need to keep my patients in mind, and for my patients I felt that the intrusion of young children was not what they should have expected. With the passing of time I suspect that both these arguments are deeply flawed. I had anticipated how the move might provoke associations with the parental disruption that my patient had experienced. To my surprise the move was greeted with a rather shallow protest, principally criticizing the dreadful room that I now occupied, which I did not much like either. By contrast, in the counter-transference I was very concerned with 'being in a strange place' as if therapy that took place in my home was somehow inherently superior to that in my rented room.

For some time I was preoccupied with these thoughts, and indeed worried as to whether I had done the right thing. In passing, I remember thinking that I was given too little guidance by those who should know better, which I suspect is the constant experience of child and adoptive parents alike who long for certainty, and believe that it exists, but who for some reason have the experience of it being denied to them. It seemed as if I was left holding all the anxiety about the move. I was struck by the absence of reference to my family being elsewhere, no ready evidence of feelings of victory or loss. There was something both chilling and distressing about my patient's capacity to forget their existence, as if she could do without them. It was as if any triangular relationship posed irreconcilable conflicts, and the 'capacity for seeing oneself in interaction with others' was impossible for her to achieve.

I think the move inadvertently reproduced precisely the solution she found in her own family, namely that in effect the mother ceased to exist. I think the fantasy was that she now had me entirely to herself, what Britton (1989) refers to as an Oedipal Illusion, 'a phantasy relationship in which the child denies the relationship in order to recruit one parent into an exclusive relationship. In that phantasy different facets of the parent's personality as well as the relationship to the other parent is denied'. Britton writes:

> Internally she had one self in loving union with an idealised mother (i.e. birth mother) and another self in alliance with a father (adoptive father) seen as epitomising anti-mother love. The link between these two selves was missing, as was the link between the internal parents. (Britton 1989)

What I had failed to realize was how very important being in my home was; the proximity of my wife and child, even when she complained bitterly, was immensely reassuring (i.e. they survived). It was this that was shattered by the move, repeating as it so accurately did the experience with her parents when she became her father's princess, her mother's triumphant rival, and the parents as a couple ceased to exist.

Finally, it seems to me that the adopted child has one other major obstacle to contend with and that is the impossibility of fantasizing about being adopted. The fantasy solution of the biological child's conflict – adoption (I am thinking here of Freud's writing on the 'Family romance', 1909) is the fait accompli underlying the adoptee's distress. Jill Hodges (1983) puts it well:

> All adolescents have the task of freeing themselves from the emotional ties to the idealised infantile object. This means achieving some integration of phantasy and reality to the parents … But perhaps the inner conflict over the parents cannot, for the adopted child, be on firm ground. It cannot be fought in one arena, because it has occupied two psychological spaces throughout the child's development. (Hodges 1983)

Much of this chapter has in one way or another been concerned with what can be remembered and how it can be processed. In this connection, I came across the following, which seemed a hopeful way to end. Edgar Reitz (1993), interviewed in the Observer about his film Heimat, says:

> Remembering is a creative act. Our past is a pile of broken pieces. When we remember, we take these little mosaic pieces and build a new life with them. When we write down memories or make a film about them, we rescue a bit of life away from death and put it on a level where it can exist longer. In that there is a kind of love. (Reitz 1993)

Acknowledgements

This chapter was first published by the British Association of Psychotherapists in a monograph entitled *Family Secrets* (1996 no. 6). We are grateful to them for their permission to reproduce it in this volume.

References

Britton, R. (1989) *The Oedipus Complex Today*. London: Karnac.

Freud, S. (1909) 'Family romance'. In *Standard Edition* vol. 9. London: Hogarth.

Freud, S. (1917) 'Mourning and melancholia'. In *Standard Edition* vol. 14. London: Hogarth.

Hodges, J. (1983) 'Oedipus was adopted'. *Bulletin of the Hampstead Clinic 6*, 171–4.

Hodges, J. (1984) 'Two crucial questions: adopted children in psychoanalytic treatment'. *Journal of Child Psychotherapy 10*, 47–57.

Peller, L. (1963) 'Psychoanalytic theory as it applies to adoption'. *Bulletin of the Philadelphia Association of Psychoanalysis 13*, 10–14.

Raphael-Leff, J. (1993) 'Transition to parenthood-infertility'. Unpublished paper.

Reitz, E. (1993) Interview (about film Heimat). *Observer*.

Rustin, M. (1991) 'The meaning of home and family for the adopted child'. Unpublished paper.

Winnicott, D.W. (1956) 'Primary maternal preoccupation'. In his *Through Pediatrics to Psychoanalysis*. London: Hogarth.

Winnicott, D.W. (1962) 'Providing for the child in health and crisis'. In his *Maturational Processes and the Facilitating Environment*. London: Hogarth.

5

The Adoption Experience from a Social Worker's Point of View

Barbara Prynn

I came into adoption work almost by accident. I was looking for an interesting part-time job near my home. It was my belief at the time that why people became social workers was partly out of curiosity about other people and other families. It would be true to say that I was wholly ignorant of both legislation and practice in the area of adoption. This chapter reflects my experience in the field since that time.

Adoption is one of those issues about which everyone has an opinion. While many people's lives have been touched by adoption, only relatively recently has it been discussed openly. One reason for such secrecy is that adoption represents something wholly unacceptable: the giving or taking away of children and placing them with strangers. This practice is unheard of in some cultures, where it is shocking that, on the one hand, parents might damage or give away a child and, on the other, that no one in the extended family would take the child in.

This deep-rooted abhorrence of the very existence of adoption is one reason why, in a sense, it is continually being reinvented. Because the whole enterprise is deemed unacceptable, there is always a hope that a new trend or approach will (literally) legitimize it. This is also why the names given to the participants and the process are often changed. 'Natural parents' became 'first parents' became 'birth parents'. Adoption social workers became placement or family placement workers. The change of name also represents a change of function or a changed attitude to the function. The child, the adopters and the birth parents used to be positioned at the angles of the 'adoption triangle'. This has become a 'circle', presumably to demonstrate movement between the parties rather than fixed positions.

It has been said that 'adoption is the management of hope' (J. Hutten 1984, personal communication). I take this to mean that it is the hope of adopters that they will be given a child who will fulfil their wishes and desires for parenthood; it is the hope of the birth parent that the child is really going to have a better life; it is the hope of the child mature enough to be aware of what is happening that the tensions and difficulties of the past will be over; and it is the hope of the social worker that everything will work out well for all concerned.

What are social workers looking for in adopters? This too has changed over time. When I was new to the field I was told that my colleagues and I were looking for 'stickability'. How could we tell if the applicants had the necessary qualities? We were looking for people whose commitment to the child was unshakeable. It may be that this was based on a fear of our own failure, but it was an important feature nevertheless. The active involvement of the adopters' extended family and religious or other beliefs were positive traits. The extended family and the social group together provided a community who could support the family system as a whole as well as its individual members. A willingness to allow the child to behave bizarrely or inappropriately in regard to chronological age, while simultaneously holding in mind the target of 'normality', was helpful. Being available and consistent and thinking about the child – in other words setting aside space and time which were not eroded by other personal or family concerns – was essential. It was also helpful if the potential adopters had kept in touch with people from earlier phases of their lives, because this provided them with continuity and was an example to the children that relationships might endure over time.

Adopters hope that things will work out for them as a family. Almost by definition they are believers in environment rather than heredity, but at the same time they are in an invidious position with regard to birth parents. While it is difficult for childless adopters to think about their baby's birth parents without a degree of envy, it is also hard to think compassionately of someone who they know has harmed a child. When the child behaves particularly badly, making them feel incompetent, it is all too easy to imagine that the roots of such behaviour lie in inherited characteristics.

I see the constant search for and acceptance of changing policy and practice as a method of defence against the pain, guilt and responsibility involved in the task, for when things work out badly, all participants suffer. Social workers have to protect themselves, and their defences are analogous to those employed by nurses (see Menzies Lyth 1970). Grasping enthusiastically at the latest idea is a way of suggesting that somehow the mistakes of the past will not be repeated, but in this almost manic embrace of the new, good practice employed in the past is in danger of being lost. Before casework became counselling – and something which social workers ask other people to do – there was among adoption workers an awareness of the needs of babies and small children that seems to have been lost. It is moving to read in a file from the late 1950s how the childcare officer agonized about whether or not to leave a 19-month-old baby in a placement which was supposed to move forward to adoption. She had concerns about the new father's attitude to the little boy and knew that to move the child at his age could be very damaging. (The little boy in question had a successful adoption and is now happily married with two children.)

Now babies and young children are kept in 'short-term' foster homes until such time as their legal situation has been sorted out and an adoptive family found. When they are moved on, regardless of the length of time they have been in their foster home or of their vulnerability, their capacity for attachment may have been irreparably damaged. But in the present context, when notes are kept recording actions taken with an awareness of possible complaints in the future, the above dilemma would not have been articulated let alone written out in the file.

For an adopted person probably the easiest story to come to terms with is of the very young unsupported mother who cannot tell her parents what has happened to her or who is made by them to give up her child. In the past, girls in this situation were 'punished' by being sent to harsh institutions during their pregnancies. At the same time, other young women in almost identical situations were struggling to keep their babies with them.

When I was very young and newly qualified, a wise child psychiatrist said to me that I should be careful – this was in the context of work in a child guidance clinic – not to always identify with the child and to try to think of and understand the parents. I have not forgotten this advice and it is as apposite in adoption as in other work with parents and children. As an adoption social worker it is possible to identify with the pain of contemplating giving up a child and the apparent impossibility of seeing a way out of the problems arising from an unhelpful family and a difficult economic situation. At the same time identification with the child raises the question of whether being given up for adoption is ever the right solution.

In the past adoption social workers might have been responsible both for work with the birth mother/family and the adopters. Now they are responsible only for the adopters. Another worker will try to manage the tensions inherent in working with children and their birth parents. It is the adoption worker who holds the balance and must hold in mind the needs of all three parties. This is impossible because their needs are in conflict. Identification with an abusive birth parent is difficult, although someone with mental health problems who has had a rough deal may elicit considerable sympathy. In this case, contemplating placing the children in another family may be very hard for both social workers to think about. Where a child has been removed from the birth family the social worker will tend to identify with the child's hurt, and may reject the child's residual attachment to the birth parent. It is the social worker's task to enable the child to retain a balanced perspective about the birth family, especially as (see p.75) there may be continued contact between them. The carrying out of this task is problematic, because it seems that the way in which the social worker manages the pain and conflict of working with the child is by 'splitting' – that is, that the child becomes 'all good' and the birth parent 'all bad'. It is only in this way that the underlying conflict in working with children separated from their birth families, and therefore in adoption, can be managed. To see the birth family as 'all bad' enables social workers to idealize adopters and to defend themselves against these conflicts by pinning their hopes on finding the 'right' adoptive family.

Adopters may be more like, and more congenial to the social worker and they may even share interests. Even so, the relationship between adopters and social worker is a difficult one. They are neither clients nor colleagues, friends nor acquaintances but a mixture of these. It is therefore easy for the social worker to ignore the power dynamic when things are going well. The social worker (backed by the team and the adoption panel) can promote adopters or terminate their approval but during most contacts between the two this fact is not acknowledged (at least by the social worker).

Children who are placed for adoption now have very complex histories and finding families for them has become more and more difficult. It has been one of the revelations of recent decades that children who were placed for adoption as babies may also demonstrate difficulties in attachment in their adoptive families. These two factors have engendered a kind of desperation among adoption workers. Somehow the tried and tested characteristics that were looked for in adoptive families have become less significant and the qualities which adopters must demonstrate are today very much in the eyes of the beholder.

People who remind one of positive aspects of one's own parents, or of oneself, may be seen as more acceptable than those who do not. Thus one worker may be in favour of taking on a family while another is against it. These identifications may not be conscious and they tend to be very powerful. It is important to remember that one is not placing oneself or one's own children. A social worker should not need to like people to see them as possible adopters. If it is comfortable to visit the home of adoptive applicants, it is easy to imagine the child placed there and to anticipate further pleasant visits. In such a situation the worker may avoid raising difficult issues in regard to child-rearing or other potential problems and become protective and proprietary about the family. Indeed, it is common for social workers to refer to 'My Family X'.

An example of the idealization and fantasy involved in searching for adopters is to be found in the descriptions of families sought in photo-listings (examined by Ryburn 1992) where social workers' fantasies are clearly set out. The prescription 'must be the only or the youngest child in the family' says something about a social worker's perception of psychological space, ignoring potential adopters' capacity to manage the needs of a group of children.

There is a paradox in current adoption practice which can function defensively. As finding adoptive placements becomes more and more difficult – looked-after children's backgrounds involve more moves, more abuse, more potential attachment difficulties and potential adopters know this – so the criteria for family choice are reduced. Further changes reflect the priorities of cash-strapped adoption agencies; decisions may be made on the basis of low-cost adoption being cheaper than fostering in the long run, and much cheaper than a therapeutic children's facility.

'Matching' in adoption dates from the time when most adopted children were babies. The physical characteristics, social and educational position of adopters and birth parents would be matched. Since adoption has become a search for families for older children, adopters have been expected to take on any child instead of seeking children who resemble them, as if this was somehow wrong. This is a denial that physical resemblance is important. Of course, photo-listing is all about the conscious or unconscious choice of children who resemble the adopters, though somehow this fact has been neglected in discussions of how no significance should be attached to matching.

For the adopted child it may be comforting to look like the parents, and it avoids the necessity of explaining why the child does not look like them. It seems that this is a possible argument against transracial placement, which is the only context in which physical matching is now thought of as important.

By the early to mid–1980s a growing proportion of social workers came from ethnic minorities. Those in the adoption field were alarmed and angered by the number of black children being placed in white families. They saw this as the loss of those children to their communities. The Association of Black

Social Workers and Allied Professions was instrumental in promulgating the same-race placement argument (Barn 1993). Research at the time (Gill and Jackson 1983) confirmed that black children adopted into white families might not have a strong connection or identification with the communities from which they came.

White adopters who had in good faith and with good will adopted black children were made to feel that they could not by definition be good enough parents. Any difficulty experienced by the family over the years was attributed to the transracial nature of the placement regardless of the complexities inherent in all adoptions. White parents were said to be unable to help their black children to combat racism and to promote their children's identity.

'Blackness' was defined in a political sense. In practice this meant that a child with either or both parents from the Caribbean, Africa or Asia could be placed with a family who were not racially or culturally from the same background. But it is necessary to be aware of cultural as well as racial differences. It is no more or less appropriate to place a child from West Africa with African Caribbean adopters than it is to place them with a white family.

It was assumed that because of their own experience of combating racism the new family would be able to help the child. This view has not been supported by research (Tizard and Phoenix 1993) which shows that being black might be neither sufficient nor necessary to teach one's children how to deal with life in a racist society. The same assumption also collapsed identity issues into one essential point and neglected other aspects of identity which adopted people must grapple with over a lifetime.

White social workers were made to feel inadequate when working with black families. It became impossible for groups of social workers to discuss the merits or demerits of same-race or transracial placement. While many, in the pejorative language of the time, were called 'colour blind' and were capable of presenting arguments for transracial placement, they were unable to for fear of being labelled racist themselves.

The prescription in the Children Act 1989 to take note of a child's race, culture and religion, although not a new idea in childcare legislation, has promoted a difference in matching. While much more attention is now paid to cultural (including religious) background, there is still a difficulty when considering cultural diversity in a field of work which continues to be Eurocentric. The earlier overarching political definition of 'blackness' has given way to a diversity of definitions which confuse culture, race, ethnicity and nationality.

It is inappropriate that adoption social workers should seek to remedy society's ills by their placement decisions and by using looked-after children and adopters in an almost experimental way. This limited perspective ignores the fast growing though still small area of inter-country adoption. Past and present governments have been determined to regulate adoption from abroad and to make it easier (Department of Health 1992). A large proportion of children who are adopted from abroad are 'black' in the political sense. Defining the actions of inter-country adopters as wrong because they wish to adopt transracially is to deny them and their children help and support. This tactic makes it impossible for adopters to ask for help from statutory authorities because they are aware of the prevailing attitude towards them.

It is in this area of adoption work in particular that the defence of oversimplifying the issues may be seen. Maintaining a 'politically correct' attitude to both kinds of transracial adoption allows social workers to feel satisfied that their practice is anti-discriminatory. It is because of this stance that adoption social workers have been criticized in the press and elsewhere. One of the arguments against same-race placement is that children are kept waiting too long for adoption because of the social workers' need to match appropriately according to their idiosyncratic policies. While this argument disregards the fact that an increasing number of white children are also spending much longer being looked after before permanent families are found for them, it cannot be dismissed.

At the same time as it has become acceptable to place children with single men or women or with gay or lesbian couples, adoption seems still to be wedded to modern western European family forms. It may be argued that a damaged or disturbed child may be best placed with a single person or that a lesbian couple are the best family for a sexually abused child. It can also be argued that the complexities which looked-after children bring may be best handled in a joint family where adult children are as involved in childcare as their parents. There is resistance among social workers to consider such settings, perhaps because they seem less like the family they have in their minds. Such resistance highlights the need for social workers to examine their approach to 'difference' in all its forms. One could argue that the child needing permanent family placement at the end of the millennium comes with so many diverse problems that it may be necessary to have a village to raise that child – or, if not a village, more than one or two people in parental roles. Yet the lessons to be learned from other cultures – extended family care, joint family living – have not been grasped enthusiastically. There is concern among social workers that since one task of adoption is to repair damage which has resulted from insecure attachment to previous parent figures, there must be one specific person in the adoptive family who will become the child's new attachment figure. This perspective ignores the fact that children will choose from among all available adults the one to whom they wish to be closest; and that in non-western societies the extended family group is responsible for the children. These kinds of relationships we expect to have with our own children are not universal.

As has been said, one aspect of the social worker's defence against the pain of the work as a whole is to project all negative feeling into the bad and abusive birth parents and all the positives into the adopters. Having chosen a family – the choice is not made by adoption workers alone, though the burden of failure (as well as success) easily becomes personalized – social workers' pride and confidence in their own abilities are badly shaken when there is a disruption. Social workers' feelings of guilt and remorse must go somewhere. So the adopters are now seen as 'all bad' instead of 'all good' and social workers are protected from feeling responsible for what has occurred. Because the relationship with the child must continue and the social worker must retain hope for the child's future, the adopters may be left on their own to manage their feelings of failure, pain, anger and loss. They may indeed not wish for further contact with the social worker or the child, but it is the social worker's job to help them to deal with their complex feelings. Often this does not happen.

In a situation where good, supportive and analytical supervision is provided, these defence mechanisms may be redundant. In a climate where supervision is more about watching one's back and making sure that procedures are followed than about encouraging and supporting the development of insightful modes of work, it is less likely. Social workers are forced to manage themselves and the feelings which arise from their work. It is perhaps inevitable that their negative feelings will be projected on to the only parties to a disruption who, because of it, have become expendable.

How may the risk of disruption be minimized? When people apply to adopt they do so because they want to begin or increase their family. By taking on children beyond babyhood, all adult parties to the negotiation are aware that there is a degree of altruism in their action. If the adopters' desire is firm they will be prepared to leap through whatever hoops are presented to them by the adoption agency. Nevertheless, they are unlikely to anticipate the stress they may feel when they are asked to consider their own childhoods in detail, especially if this is the first time they have done so, by someone who is effectively sitting in judgement upon them.

There are many reasons why adopters find such probing uncomfortable and it is the social worker's task to make it as easy as possible. It is not so long – in the early 1980s – since it was a routine requirement that adopters should be asked about their sex lives; now this is regarded as an intrusion. Yet for many applicants – especially for people in whose cultures intimate matters are never discussed with strangers – questions about family relationships and behaviour may prove to be unwelcome and difficult, even though they know that their answers will determine whether or not they are approved as adopters. This difficulty has never been resolved and it may be one reason for the shortfall in ethnic minority families coming forward to adopt.

How might it be done differently? Behind and underpinning the adopters' role are their own experiences of loss and change. Were there disruptions in their own childhood? Potential black adopters are sometimes people who were left with grandparents in the Caribbean when their parents came to Britain and who joined them in later childhood. Examining their own memories and responses to their childhood experiences can be helpful in allowing adopters to imagine the feelings of children to be placed with them.

'Openness' in adoption means two things. The first is the opening of files and, through them, life histories and possible access to birth family members of adult adoptees. It seems that this goes hand-in-hand with other aspects of openness, which are now judged to be a good thing, such as more public discussion about sex or income or family secrets, of which adoption may have been one. As with these other aspects of social life, openness in the adoption context can sometimes go too far and advocates of openness may be overstepping the mark when they suggest that adult adoptees who seem not to be interested in their backgrounds are in some way remiss (Lifton 1994).

The fact that adoptees do 'search' for their past is one stated motive for encouraging continued contact between adopted children and their birth families; it is hoped to avoid the possible trauma that can result both from the lack of information and from the searching for it. Thus the second form of openness implies the transformation of the previously described adoption triangle, whose points were the adopters, the adopted child and the birth family, into the adoption circle. Here the three elements are seen as continuing to react upon one another either by means of letter exchanges or meetings.

The idea of openness came from Australasia (Ryburn 1996) and in spite of concerns about how contact could be managed, especially where children have been abused, adoption with contact has been seized upon in the UK as a good idea. While in Australasia it is not uncommon for adopted children to have staying contact with their birth families this is not a variant which has yet arrived in the UK. On the other hand, face-to-face contact with a variety of birth family members or 'letter box' contact (in which adopters and maybe their children communicate indirectly with birth families through the mediation of the adoption agency) is now expected in almost all adoptions.

To a degree, openness and contact are uncontentious. It is probably valuable for a child whose feelings about the birth parents are ambivalent, fearful or murderous to know that they are still alive and to begin to consider them as whole people. However, the avidity with which contact has been grasped upon by social workers seems to me to expose a fundamental problem: adoption is considered as second-best. The constant refrain about 'real' and 'natural' parents in the press and elsewhere is a continual reminder to adopters and their children that they are by definition 'unreal' or 'unnatural'. By continuing contact or by making it an indispensable part of the adoption scene, guilt about social work intervention in removing the child is assuaged.

Outcomes in Australasia have been mixed, though a firm commitment to the idea of contact remains (O'Neill 1994). As Triseliotis (1996) has said, contact following adoption is dependent upon the maturity of birth parents and their acknowledgement that the children have two sets of parents. Where this condition is not met it is doubtful whether contact of any kind will be in the best interests of the child.

One of the tasks of adopters is always to bear in mind that their child has two sets of parents and to help the child to come to terms with this (with contact, it is not easy to forget it). Adopters have to accept that the child may need to experiment with some to-ing and fro-ing between the two sets of parents and that this is an important constituent of the child's own journey to make new and different relationships with both.

Questions about degrees and kinds of contact are considered by the social work participants, and there are often as many answers as there are social workers involved. If there are several children in a family and each social worker is identifying with one of them, the ensuing sibling rivalry makes decision-making very complicated. It is the case that discussions (or arguments) about contact between workers are based more on the principle – whether there should be contact – rather than on the needs of an individual child. It is hard enough to see the child clearly in the present; it is much more difficult to try to predict how contact may need to change as the child grows and the adoptive family as a whole takes a view. It is anxiety about, and a desire to control, an eventual positive outcome that makes social workers try to determine what will happen when their involvement has ended. One underlying concern is whether the plan for the child with the adopters, to which the social worker has been a party, will ultimately be shown to be successful. Another is to do with the difficulty of letting go, of not knowing what will happen next.

There are, however, positive moves afoot. Concern among adoption agencies about the current difficulty of finding families for children and about avoiding the risk of disruption has led to questions being asked about practice, and to a search for new solutions. In November 1998 the Department of Health produced the Quality Protects Initiative, a blueprint for the reform of children's services listing eleven objectives for social services departments. It is interesting to note that the first one reads: 'To ensure that children are securely attached to carers capable of providing safe and effective care for the duration of childhood'; and that sub-objective 1.2 is 'To maximise the contribution adoption can make to providing permanent families for children in appropriate cases' (Department of Health 1998). The intention here is to ensure that adoption is considered as soon as it becomes clear that there is no realistic prospect of the birth family providing the basis for safe and adequately effective parenting and to avoid children staying unnecessarily long in the care system. Sub-objective 1.3 asks local authorities 'to reduce the period children remain looked after before they are placed for adoption, or placed in long-term foster care'.

I believe that this is the first time that 'attachment' has figured in a government circular. It is heartening to see it. One may hope that it heralds a return to considering the multiplicity of needs of children who are placed for adoption, and that the profile of potential adopters will no longer be reduced to a few obvious attributes. It will be interesting to follow the necessary changes in adoption which will follow these directives.

References

Barn, R. (1993) *Black Children and the Public Care System.* London: Batsford.

Department of Health (1992) *Review of Adoption Law.* London: Her Majesty's Stationery Office.

Department of Health (1998) *Quality Protects: Transforming Children's Services.* London: Her Majesty's Stationery Office.

Gill, O. and Jackson, B. (1983) *Adoption and Race.* London: Batsford and BAAF.

Holmes, J. (1993) *John Bowlby and Attachment Theory.* London: Routledge.

Lifton, B.J. (1994) *Journey of the Adopted Self.* New York: Basic Books.

Menzies Lyth, I. (1970) 'A case study in the functioning of social systems as a defence against anxiety'. *Human Relations 13,* 95–121.

O'Neill, C. (1994) 'To attach or not?' *Children Australia 18,* 2, 13–17.

Ryburn, M. (1992) 'Advertising for permanent placements'. *Adoption and Fostering 16,* 2, 8–16.

Ryburn, M. (1996) 'A study of post-adoption contact in compulsory adoptions'. *British Journal of Social Work 26*, 5, 627–46.

Tizard, B. and Phoenix, A. (1993) *Black, White, or Mixed Race? Race and Racism in the Lives of Young People of Mixed Parentage.* London: Routledge.

Triseliotis, J. (1996) 'Maintaining the links in adoption'. Paper given at Family Rights Group conference on open adoption; based on J. Triseliotis, J. Shireman and M. Hundleby (1997) *Adoption: Theory, Policy and Practice.* London: Cassell.

What People Said

You never know what you're getting
she might be bad blood

You can't blame a wean
for what her mother did
my mother said

She'll give you a sore heart

Sure your own can give you that

The doctor said
you must on no account
adopt a baby
you are not well enough

My mother bowed her head

Consider an older child
the doctor said

The canon of the parish said
So you want a baby sure you do
and I will guarantee you this
she will never lose you a night's sleep

Nor did you
my mother always said

My granny said
when she took me
the first time
and wrapped me in her shawl

She's all there that one
and I will tell you this
she will be there for you
when your own are far away

The nuns said
It's never too early
so tell her right away
and by the way
if you hold her this way
she'll never dirty a nappy

Children said
your mummy and daddy
aren't your real mummy and daddy

6

Identity Formation and the Adopted Person Revisited

John Triseliotis

The initial studies concentrating on the disclosure of adoption and linking identity with genealogy and background information have highlighted, among other things, the meaning of adoption to the adopted person and its relationship to aspects of identity formation. Though much more still remains to be learnt, these studies have possibly yielded the most decisive insights on the construction of the experience of adoption (Haimes and Timms 1985; McWhinnie 1967; Sachdev 1989; Triseliotis 1973; Triseliotis and Russell 1984). The purpose of this chapter is to review briefly the available knowledge on identity formation in relation to the adopted person and raise a number of questions still requiring answers.

Adoption is bound by culture, values, traditions, social, religious and other beliefs. These are not static and neither is the adoption experience. For example, some of the circumstances that motivated adopted people in the 1950s and 1960s to search for their roots continue to be the same, but others have changed because the social context has also changed. Within a climate of secrecy it was a very determined person who set out on a quest then. Now the pressure is on those who do not search to do so.

In spite of the generally very favourable overall outcomes achieved through adoption, especially for children placed when very young, there is also evidence that at certain points in their development some children display a somewhat higher rate of emotional and behavioural difficulties (Bohman and Sigvardsson 1990; Brodzinsky and Schechter 1990; Lambert and Streather 1980; Seglow, Pringle and Wedge 1972). This may not be surprising because adopted children, unlike others, have additional hurdles to overcome connected with their adoption and the construction of their identities. The extra tasks can act as a stress factor at certain points during childhood, for example, when the children are becoming more aware of the meaning of adoption, or in adolescence when they strive to achieve their separateness and find answers to questions of who they are. The same studies equally suggest that many of the problems displayed earlier and in adolescence disappear by the late teens and with time. In the end, these studies found that those adopted do not differ significantly from the rest of the population. Studying adopted children at a specific point in their childhood does not often tell us how they will develop in adult life.

The additional tasks

The studies in origins referred to earlier suggest that the satisfactory resolution of the adoption experience largely relies on the way the adopted child achieves a number of additional tasks not faced by others. For children adopted transracially or inter-country, these tasks increase even further in number and complexity. Having to accomplish extra, mainly psychosocial, tasks imposes added strains and stresses on the adopted child striving to develop relationships and achieve a sense of self. These extra hurdles could be summarized as:

1. Re-attachment to new parent(s).

2. Integrating in the developing self the knowledge of being adopted, which in turn involves:

   (a) awareness of being adopted and the gradual understanding of its meaning and implications

   (b) awareness of one's ancestry and, where relevant, of one's ethnic heritage

   (c) having access to genealogical, ethnic and other related information, including, where desired, face-to-face contact

   (d) the acknowledgement of the difference between psychosocial and biological parenting and, where relevant, the acknowledgement of one's ethnic and/or racial heritage and difference

   (e) dealing with the sense of loss and rejection that adoption inevitably conveys.

3. The formation of an identity that is based on a positive resolution of the above attributes.

Re-attachment to new parent(s)

The research literature on the subject of attachment suggests that, for satisfactory development, infants and very young children need to attach themselves to one or more people who can provide a warm, caring, secure and stable environment. It is further asserted that the nature of the initial bond made in childhood, whether it is a secure or anxious one, will have consequences for the future functioning, well-being and mental health of the individual.

As a concept, attachment and bonding between children and their primary carers seems particularly crucial in the early years of life when children are totally dependent on others. The construction of self seems to be largely dependent on the quality of these early experiences. Orbach (1997: 32) refers to attachment as being 'at the core of an enlivened human existence'. For the older child the task is mainly one of integration rather than attachment (see Howe 1997). Depending on their previous experiences, children who make the transition from one set of carers to another, such as in the case of adoption, have the task of emotionally attaching or re-attaching themselves to their new carers. A failure to attach may be attributable to the quality of parenting, the child or both.

The whole concept of attachment and re-attachment is a complex and controversial one. Though more has recently been learnt on how it operates, much more work is still needed concerning its aetiology, how to recognize it and how to measure its strength (World Health Organisation (WHO) 1992). A research project which studied attachment behaviours in young children adopted in Britain from Romania concluded that attachment disorder behaviours were positively associated with duration of severe deprivation. However, a substantial number of children exposed to it did not develop it, suggesting different levels of resilience on the part of children with possibly genetic factors being at play (O'Connor, Bredenkamp and Rutter 1999). Where optimum conditions prevail, children, when adopted young, seem to have little difficulty in attaching themselves to their new carers.

Knowledge and understanding about being adopted

Unlike the past, the issue now, as Brodzinsky, Schechter and Henig (1992) also point out, is not whether or not to disclose adoption but when and how. Furthermore, with the great majority of adoptions by non-kin in Britain now involving older children, the emphasis has shifted from disclosure to managing openness and contact. The disclosure of adoption introduces young children to the idea of something different, though they do not yet understand its full meaning. The concept of two families, of a biological and a psychosocial one, and in the case of inter-country adoption of two ethnic heritages, becomes central to the explanations, while also stressing the permanency of the arrangement and the commitment.

Revealing adoption, assisted reproduction or the reality of the status of other separated children, including those of divorce, should not have been a scientific but a moral issue. Nevertheless, the studies referred to here have empirically shown that being truthful and honest with children about their status, circumstances, roots, genealogy and general background is central to their identity formation and their mental health. Evasiveness, secrecy and avoidance have been found to generate mistrust (Triseliotis 1973). Telling the truth is also embodied in the legal codes of all countries, even though its adherence may be variable. Sharing such information with children is not, therefore, a matter of choice, but an obligation on parents and substitute carers. The research findings lend support to the UN Convention (1989) on the Rights of the Child, article 21, which states: 'Parties should undertake to respect the right of the child to preserve his her identity (nationality, name, family relations as recognised by law) without unlawful interference.'

Through the studies cited earlier we have also learnt that disclosure has to be part of a process, rather than a once and for all occasion. Neither should parents wait for the child to ask. The responsibility lies with them to take the initiative in explaining, discussing and sharing information. The reluctance of some parents to take the initiative is summarized in the following comment, which was one of many: 'Maybe my parents waited for me to ask and I waited for them to take the initiative and eventually we never talked about it' (Triseliotis 1973: 44).

Though for a minority of parents telling continues to be surrounded by strong emotional blocks (Tizard 1977), more recent studies suggest that almost all parents now seek opportunities to talk to the children about their adoption (Craig 1991). Parents, as we have found, have to strike a balance between avoiding oppressing the child with their insistence and frequency of telling, and using appropriate opportunities to return to the subject. We know that some children, and even adults, refuse to listen until they feel ready, and some may never come to feel like that. Many adopted children and adults also prefer to choose with whom to share this important aspect of their lives. Choice seems to give them more control, even though there is no protection for those who are also visibly different and exposed to possible negative attitudes.

The difference between knowing and understanding

Adopted children have not only to know that they are adopted, but also to understand and integrate this knowledge and its meaning into their developing selves. For children adopted when very young it is not apparently until around the ages of 5–7 that they cognitively begin to grasp the meaning and some of the implication of adoption (Brodzinsky 1984). Even if understanding comes later, disclosure has to start earlier so that children can feel that they 'always knew'. There is no agreement about when telling should start, but most researchers suggest that the earlier the better. It is this increasing understanding and awareness that may also bring to the surface some strong feelings and emotions about adoption. This awareness, if not the level of the reaction to it, is unavoidable and possibly painful, but it also seems to be the route towards a fuller genealogical and eventually personal identity.

Access to genealogical and other related background information

The knowledge and gradual understanding of the meaning of adoption also bring to the surface a number of related questions that have to be truthfully and honestly answered. They mainly include background and other related information and the circumstances of the adoption. A full completion and understanding of self is not possible when there are gaps or 'holes' in the knowledge about one's individual biography (Brodzinsky *et al.* 1992; Haimes and Timms 1985; Triseliotis 1973; Walby 1992). The adopted person's family of origin and ancestry, and, as we shall be saying later, race and ethnicity, represent only one aspect of social identity but nevertheless a vital one that cannot be ignored. To accomplish the task of identity-building satisfactorily, adopted people need to have answers to questions such as:

- Who am I?
- Where do I come from?
- Why was I put up for adoption?
- Who were my birth parents?
- What did they look like?
- What kind of people were they?

Studies in adoption with contact have found that it is of great value if the adopted child and the adoptive parents have the opportunity of meeting the birth parent(s) and are able not only to have a physical view of each other, but also to share and obtain direct information (see Triseliotis, Shireman and Hundleby 1997: ch. 4). In a case before him, Judge Simon LJ., as if quoting from research, referred to the importance of contact for the long-term welfare of the child by saying: 'it can help children realise that their parents still love them and care about their welfare; it can help children to attach to their new family knowing that they have the 'seal of approval' from their birth parents; and it can help give the child a sense of family continuity and personal identity' (FLR 146, 1994, pp.154H–155B). He could also have been echoing Giddens' (1992) words:

> it is the self as reflexively understood by the person in terms of her or his biography. Identity here still presumes continuity across time and space; to be a 'person' is not just to be a reflexive actor, but to have a concept of a person as applied both to self and others. (Giddens 1992: 53)

Barbara Hardy (1968) captures the importance of continuity in life by her reference to the 'narrative' of life: 'We dream in narrative, daydream in narrative, remember, anticipate, hope, despair, believe, doubt, plan, sense, criticise, construct, gossip, learn, hate and love by narrative' (Hardy 1968).

How to assist those who are unable to find background information or meet with members of their birth family, such as many of those who are adopted inter-country, still poses problems.

The acknowledgement of difference

As far back as 1964 Kirk rightly concluded that, for successful adoptive parenthood, parents had first emotionally to acknowledge, instead of deny, the difference between biological and adoptive parenthood. This is an acknowledgement that the child was not born to them and that psychosocial parenting has similarities with, but also differences from, biological rearing. Kirk's theory could be expanded, this time in relation to the adopted person, by suggesting that a failure to acknowledge the difference between psycho-social and biological parenting, or its exaggeration, limits the adopted person's potential for reaching full identity integrity and resolving identity issues, though the timing of such acknowledgement may differ from individual to individual.

Those adopted inter-country or transracially have the added task of acknowledging not simply their adoption and origins, but also their different ethnic background and heritage. In effect they have to acknowledge two instead of one difference. In the same way that there can be different levels of intensity in a search for origins and, where relevant, ethnicity, there can also be different levels of acknowledgement and of thinking about the biological or ethnic connection.

Why adopted children and some adults deny or are intensely preoccupied with their origins and, in the case of inter-country and transracial placements, with their ethnicity, is far from clear. We can assume that a basic identification or affiliation with the adoptive family and the 'host' society is a sign of attachment and of successful adaptation, while emotional denial or intense preoccupation is the opposite. Denial, or 'difference blindness', could signify the adopted child's desire to feel at one with the adopting family or 'host' society, perhaps being fearful of separation, difference or rejection. Both denial and preoccupation could also signify strong internalized anger about the original parting and/or be a statement on the quality of experiences inside or outside the family, including the experience of racism and discrimination.

We seem to know somewhat more about preoccupation than about the denial of the importance of origins, because most studies have concentrated on adopted people who search for their roots. The relationship between excessive preoccupation with one's adoption and impaired mental health was first reported in my 1973 study (Triseliotis 1973), later to be confirmed by Sachdev (1989). Based also on their study of adolescents, Stein and Hoopes (1985: 65) ascribe excessive genealogical concern either to 'an impoverished relationship within the adoptive family' or to a 'felt lack of similarity to the adoptive parents'. They too found that open styles of communication about adoption produce significantly higher identity scores among adopted adolescents. Wrobel et al. (1996) carry the debate further by adding that the more curious children in their study were about their origins, the lower their self-worth, especially among boys. Curiosity was also negatively related to the level of satisfaction with their circumstances, except in fully disclosed adoptions. As Quinton and Selwyn (1998) also observe, this links unhappiness with the situation, for whatever reasons, to their feelings of self-worth and to greater curiosity about their origins.

A similar relationship, this time between preoccupation with ethnicity and failure to identify with the 'host' society, was reported by Irhammar (1999). Irhammar found that almost nine out of ten adopted adolescents indicated a Swedish ethnic self-identity and, more important, that those who did so had higher levels of mental health than the rest. Detailed analysis, though, between different levels of identification was missing when these provisional findings were reported. The conclusion is that those adopted inter-country cannot function positively in their new country without a basic identification with its institutions. Doing so need not involve a denial of the duality of their ethnic heritage.

Achieving a duality of ethnic identities, not necessarily in equal proportions, cannot be easy for inter-country or transracially adopted children, many of whom come to feel wanted and loved by their adoptive families, but rejected and discriminated against by sections of the 'host' community (see Bagley, Young and Scully 1993: ch. 13; Botvar 1999; Dalen and Saetersdal 1987; Rorbech 1991). Botvar (1999) puts at 20 per cent the number of inter-country adoptees who experienced high levels of negative discrimination within Norwegian society to 'the serious detriment of their mental health'.

As with other aspects of development, interest in biological origins or ethnicity is not static and can change over time. Equally, the boundary line between acknowledgement, natural curiosity, denial and overstressing the difference can be a very thin one and difficult to separate or measure accurately.

The sense of loss and rejection

However it is put, awareness of the adoptive status and of what it means raises, as we have found, strong feelings of loss and rejection (Triseliotis 1973). Much has been written on the subject since then, though we still understand little of how these feelings are expressed or operate. Like understanding the meaning of adoption, so too the sense of loss and rejection does not usually start until after about the age of 5, reaching greater intensity with adolescence.

Loss is an inevitable part of adoption. The loss and its accompanying grief are most probably about the original family and in the case of inter-country adoption, also ethnic heritage. Overall, the sense of loss seems to generate anxiety about the past and about possible future losses, especially of parental figures. However, studies so far are uncertain about what exactly is being mourned and how, and about its exact impact. The element of loss is real in another sense in that some people are often absent from an adopted person's conception of genealogical family. As an example, some adopted children's paintings have been found to have gaps representing people missing from their lives such as birth fathers or grandparents or siblings (Owen 1999).

Alongside the sense of loss, and irrespective of the circumstances that lead to parting with a child for adoption, a further realization, arising from the understanding of what adoption is about, is the sense of rejection which usually accompanies most parent–child separations. Even though most birth parents love and care for their children before they part with them, nevertheless, the sense of rejection, of not being wanted or of being 'a cast-off', seems to undermine the children's sense of self-esteem and self-worth.

Irrespective of how adoption has worked out, it does not stop some adopted people from asking why this has happened to them. We have no precise knowledge of how strong such feelings are and how they vary between individuals.

Far from clear also is the fantasy that accompanies feelings of rejection, for example, whether it is associated with being bad, demanding, or not likeable. Whatever the fantasy, it can be accompanied by sadness or anger about what has happened. This is why one of the first things adopted people often ask or want to know is: 'Why was I given up for adoption?' Behind this question usually lies a more important one, that is whether the adopted person was wanted before being given up. Similarly, the knowledge that a parent kept one child but not them was experienced as more hurtful. As some would say: 'If she could keep one, she could keep two.' An interesting question arising from the increasing number of currently contested adoptions is whether the children at the centre of the disputes will, in years to come, view this as a demonstration of their birth parents' love or feel angry towards their new parents for persisting with the adoption.

The conclusion arising from a number of studies is that feelings of loss and rejection can be healed depending largely, though not always, on the quality of the adoption experience. Where this is empathic and secure, then healing appears more likely. Fear of and actual new losses can rekindle new feelings of loss, abandonment and rejection. As with attachment theory, there are also situations in which, irrespective of what the adoptive parents do, such feelings may persist.

Identity formation and the adopted person

At its most basic, identity is about what we feel about ourselves and how we think other people see us. How individuals experience and explain themselves and how they are perceived by the wider society are abstract qualities and therefore difficult to define. The ultimate aim, though, of the processes described so far is that their positive resolution will contribute to the formation of a strong identity with an increased sense of self-worth. One writer refers to identity as a self-structure – an internal, self-constructed, dynamic organization of drives, abilities, beliefs, and individual history (Marcia 1980). Depending on how well this structure is developed, individuals can come to feel whole and unique or confused and different. Erikson (1968) describes a positive identity as 'a sense of psychological well-being, a feeling of being at home in one's body, of knowing where one is going, an inner assuredness of anticipated recognition from those who count' (Erikson 1968: 165).

Social identity (self)	Physical identity (self)	Psychological identity (self)
Awareness of our relations with others	Awareness of one's body (how it looks, feels, sounds, smells)	Capacity for making relationships
Awareness of how others see us	**In relation to adoption**	Ability to control impulses
In relation to adoption	Physical reality of birth parents	Ability to have empathy for others
An accepting community		Our view of our intelligence
Absence of stigma		**In relation to adoption**
Racial, ethnic and cultural awareness		Genealogical information
		Answers to questions, e.g. why given up
		Opportunities for contact

**Whole identity or self
(self-esteem, self-worth)**

Figure 6.1 The major identities in relation to the whole self and the role of adoption in each. Adapted from Thoburn, J. (1994) Child placement.

More recently a number of writers have been putting forward the idea of a plural, rather than a single, identity (see Brodzinsky *et al.* 1992; Tizard and Phoenix 1993). In other words, instead of a single identity, the self is made up of a number of them such as personal, social, physical, genealogical, racial or ethnic. At the same time this plurality must add up to a coherent whole. Brodzinsky *et al.* (1992) use the term 'self', instead of identity, and refer in their writings to the 'psychological', the 'social' and 'the physical self' (see Figure 6.1). As an example, the centrality of physical identity is illustrated by the fact that for many of those who set out in search of a birth parent, one of their main wishes is 'to see what she/he looks like' (Triseliotis 1973).

The importance of community attitudes and their impact on the social identity of those who were adopted was highlighted in earlier studies (Triseliotis 1973; Triseliotis and Russell 1984). The reported experiences of adopted people in my 1973 study and of recent experiences by a significant number of inter-country adopted people in western Europe confirm Goffman's (1969) writings on role theory and spoiled identity. Goffman highlights how part of the roles we take on in life include the attitudes and views that others have of us by learning to see ourselves through their eyes. He then adds that as a result of this social process we may come to perceive ourselves as 'best' or 'second class' or 'bad' or 'dull.' A sense of 'spoiled identity' usually develops from the receipt of consistently negative messages from those around us (Goffman 1969).

Though in some respects we can intervene in the process of self-building and resist attempts by others to affix to us a certain identity, this is difficult for children because they are in a formative stage of development and have less power to resist consistently negative messages. Being made to feel different or 'second class' or not accepted was also not an unusual experience of in-country adopted people who featured in our earlier studies. Besides school, countless other situations in life seemed to stress their difference and a lower status: 'When my in-laws heard that I was adopted they said they didn't expect that and had to think about it, as if I was different just because I was adopted' (Triseliotis 1973: 67).

Studies from some northern European countries report disquieting, if not altogether surprising, findings about racism and discrimination directed at inter-country adoptees (Botvar 1999; Dalen and Saetersdal 1987; Rorbech 1991). The racism is of course less related to the fact that the children or adults are adopted and more to their being visibly different. Similar rejecting attitudes are also directed towards immigrant groups who are equally visibly different. Even those of Greek origins adopted in the Netherlands did not, apparently, feel fully accepted there because of their appearance. It was only when they visited Greece that they felt 'fully at home' and as having found a place where they felt they belonged and were accepted (Storsbergen, Hoksbergen and Itjeshorst 1997).

As said earlier, in-country adopted children or adults who are not visibly different have developed the coping strategy of choosing with whom to share the fact of their adoption. For those who are visibly different this choice is not open to them, but a few, apparently, try to cope by stressing their adoption as a way of distinguishing themselves from those who are 'only' immigrants (Irhammar 1999).

An organizing concept

Brodzinsky *et al.* (1992) view self-esteem as the overriding, evaluative component of the self that integrates the psychological, social and physical self. They go on to add that 'this represents our judgements about whether aspects of our selves are good or bad, likeable or dislikeable, valuable or not' and that 'self-esteem plays a major role in patterns of psychological adjustment' (Brodzinsky *et al.* 1992: 13), thus disputing claims that self-esteem and mental health are not necessarily related (e.g. Botvar 1999).

A hierarchy of identities?

A difficult and still largely unanswered question is whether there is a hierarchy of identities operating and to what extent identities change in importance depending on circumstances such as the strength of individual needs at a particular time. Genealogy, heritage and roots have been found to be essential ingredients to the formation of self and identity, but not the only ones (Triseliotis and Russell 1984). My studies suggest that during early childhood the overriding developmental consideration which contributes to the core of identity formation is the quality of children's relationships and attachments to their primary carer(s).

A realignment of identities in hierarchical order, not necessarily in a linear form, seems to take place depending on age, new needs, events and circumstances in people's lives. For example, in adoption, biological origins begin to assume greater importance with increasing age and understanding and at times these come to dominate and override most other considerations and needs. The same process seems to be followed by most children who are transracially or inter-country adopted. As they grow older, and especially with the onset of adolescence, they become much more aware of their racial and ethnic roots. The importance of the past will again begin to recede when the needs and demands associated with this part of the self are satisfied, including possible contact with members of their birth families.

An equally related, but unanswered, question is how far identities can compensate for each other. For example, would gaps in one identity, such as genealogical or ethnic awareness, be compensated for by strengths in other identities, for example high quality relationships and a strong sense of belonging? And how far would high levels of self-esteem acquired as a result of the quality of experiences within the adoptive home be able to withstand consistently negative messages from outside? If so, it would help to explain studies which claim to have found no connection between self-esteem and ethnic identity (McRoy and Zurcher 1983) or that bullying and discrimination do not significantly affect self-esteem but seriously affect mental health

(Botvar 1999). But then can measures divorce self-esteem from mental health, when poor mental health is so often associated with low self-esteem?

The search for roots and reunions

The search for roots is one of the major characteristics of the 1970s, 1980s and 1990s. It seems to have been brought about and made respectable mainly by minorities wishing to assert their ethnic identities and by adopted people wanting to establish a more complete self.

The distinction between different levels of thought about one's adoption or ethnicity and its relationship with different types of quest has only partly been explored so far. Furthermore, thinking and even a preoccupation with one's origins or ethnicity does not always lead to a quest. Based on my calculations, I estimate that around 300,000 out of around 800,0000 adopted people in Britain have so far embarked on some kind of a quest concerning their original family. When adopted people are asked what they are looking for, the answers that emerge are mostly to do with identity, self-worth and relationships, as one would possibly expect, including:

- information on genetic and genealogical heritage
- explanations of why they were given up for adoption which raises issues of self-worth
- the physical appearance of members of the birth family which relates to the issue of physical identity
- the possibility of developing a new relationship.

As with my 1973 study, present studies confirm that different outcomes can follow from the search for the adopted person including:

- satisfaction from simply having more background information
- because nothing can be found the 'vacuum' remains
- face-to-face contact established
- nothing further happens after one or two meetings
- agreement to keep in touch, which may or may not happen
- face-to-face contact fading out after a period of time
- one party wishes for more contact but not the other
- more enduring relationships established.

The above outcomes with regard to face-to-face contact need not surprise us. Very often the two parties go in with different expectations, such as the one seeking a parent–child relationship while the other wanting only a single meeting and information. The baggage from the past that each of the protagonists brings to the contact is such that it can generate powerful feelings and expectations which cannot always be fulfilled. As a result, accounts, especially of reunions, refer to many successful new relationships being established, but equally to many disappointments (see also Feast *et al.* 1998; Iredale 1998).

Some three-fifths of adopted adults seem uninterested in an active search, though the wish to search or not can change depending on new experiences and new circumstances in the adopted person's life. Why some are interested and others not, we do not yet fully understand. Most of the conclusions reached so far on the relationship between identity formation and the adopted person's quest for origins have been based on those who search. Studies with controlled samples of searchers and non-searchers have largely been missing. A new study, though, by Howe and Feast, which does this, should appear in 2000.

Some explanations were offered earlier in relation to those who are either intensely preoccupied with their origins or not interested at all, but the relationship between mental health, self-esteem and interest in searching is still a disputed one. Neither is there evidence yet which links those who are uninterested in a search as having an incomplete or 'frozen' identity, though Irhammar (1999) suggested the possibility of impaired mental health.

Equally elusive is an understanding of the full meaning and attraction of the 'blood relationship'. Are there, for example, genetic and social factors operating which pull people together? Does the relationship which starts in the womb explain why more women are interested in a search? The paradox with adoption is that almost all studies support the success of psychosocial parenting, while at the same time a great number of adopted people search for their roots or seek reunions. New relationships, though, which are established through reunions, are mostly seen as additional to the ones already in place, rather than as a replacement for the adoptive relationship. As many of them would say: "'I have a family"; "I have parents"; "I have a mum"; or "parents are those who rear you'" (Triseliotis 1973: 146).

Sachdev (1989) found that the predominant type of relationship that developed after reunions was that of friendship, with almost one-fifth claiming to have established a mother–child relationship. Schaffer (1990) pointed out that both children and adults are capable of relating satisfactorily to more than one set of people at the same time.

Concluding remarks

The adopted person's construction of self is mainly bound up with the quality of family relationships, prevailing community attitudes towards those who are brought up differently from the rest, and with how they have accomplished a number of additional tasks associated with the adoption experience. Besides their adoption, those adopted inter-country or trans-racially have to accomplish further tasks associated with their ethnicity and their being visibly different. In spite of all these additional hurdles, most studies point to high levels of satisfaction with the adoption experience and to the reality of this form of psychosocial parenting.

There is still much that we do not understand about the psychosocial processes involved in adoption and the formation of identity in adopted and other people. Some things perhaps we will never come to know about, while others have to be revised continuously because adoption is bound by time and context. For example, there is no shortage of evidence linking the importance of origins to identity formation and to aspects of mental health, but the exact relationship between mental health, self-esteem and levels of thought about one's adoption or ethnicity and levels of search is still a disputed area. Some other areas requiring further study include how con-cepts of loss and rejection operate in adoption, whether there is a hierarchy of identities and how far identities can compensate for each other. We also need to understand more about the exact impact of racism and discrimination on the mental health and self-esteem of those who happen to be visibly different. Finally, we need to establish the exact meaning and significance of the blood relationship. Until now, definitional and measurement problems have made the search for more insights into all these questions problematic.

Some readers could be wondering why we should be so concerned to ensure that children are helped to develop full and complete identities when postmodernity seems to suggest that identity is a dated concept with 'diminishing' returns. In postmodernist language nothing seems more positive than fractured and disunited identities and a belief in 'dynamic instability'. Either way, for postmodernism the search for self and for genealogical information, including contact and reunions, would possibly be viewed as a useless activity. However, anyone who has worked or interviewed people who lack a core identity and feel fragmented knows how stressful this can be for them. With this in mind, adopted people possibly have the best script for the construction of self.

References

Bagley, C., Young, L. and Scully, A. (1993) *International and Transracial Adoptions*. Aldershot: Avebury.

Bohman, M. and Sigvardsson, S. (1990) 'Outcome in adoption: lessons from logitudinal studies'. In D. Brodzinsky and M.D. Schechter (eds) *The Psychology of Adoption*. New York: Oxford University Press.

Botvar, P.K. (1999) 'International adoptees from adolescence to adulthood.' Paper delivered at the International Conference on Inter-Country Adoption, Oslo, 6–8 May.

Brodzinsky, D.M. (1984) 'New perspectives on adoption revelation'. *Adoption and Fostering 8*, 2, 27–32.

Brodzinsky, D.M. and Schechter, M.D. (eds) (1990) *The Psychology of Adoption*. New York: Oxford University Press.

Brodzinsky, D.M., Schechter, M.D. and Henig, R.M. (1992) *Being Adopted*. New York: Doubleday.

Craig, M. (1991) 'Adoption: not a big deal'. Unpublished report. Edinburgh: Scottish Adoption Society.

Dalen, M. and Saetersdal, B. (1987) 'Transracial adoption in Norway'. *Adoption and Fostering 11*, 4, 41–6.

Erikson, E.H. (1968) *Identity: Youth and Crisis*. New York: W.W. Norton.

Feast, J., Marwood, M., Seabrook, S. and Webb, E. (1998) *Preparing for Reunion*. London: Children's Society.

Giddens, A. (1992) *Modernity and Self-Identity*. Cambridge: Polity.

Goffman, E. (1969) *The Presentation of Self in Everyday Life*. Harmondsworth: Penguin.

Grotevant, H. and McRoy, R. (1998) *Openness in Adoption: Exploring Family Connections*. Thousand Oaks, CA: Sage.

Haimes, E. and Timms, N. (1985) *Adoption, Identity and Social Policy*. London: Gower.

Hardy, B. (1968) 'Towards a poetic fiction'. *Novel 1*, 2, 5–14.

Howe, D. (1997) *Patterns of Adoption*. Oxford: Blackwell.

Howe, D. and Feast, J. (2000) *Adoption, Search and Reunion*. London: Children's Society.

Iredale, S. (1998) *Reunions*. London: HMSO.

Irhammar, M. (1999) 'Meaning of biological and ethnical origin in adolescent adoptees born abroad'. Paper delivered at the International Conference on Inter-Country Adoption, Oslo, 6–8 May.

Kirk, D. (1964) *Shared Fate*. New York: Free Press.

Lambert, L. and Streather, J. (1980) *Children in Changing Families*. London: Macmillan for National Children's Bureau.

McRoy, R. and Zurcher, I. (1983) *Transracial and Inracial Adoptees*. Springfield, IL: Charles C. Thomas.

McWhinnie, A.M. (1967) *Adopted Children: How They Grow Up*. London: Routledge and Kegan Paul.

Marcia, J.E. (1980) 'Identity in adolescence'. In J. Adelson (ed) *Handbook of Adolescence Psychology*. New York: Wiley.

O'Connor, T.G., Bredenkamp, D. and Rutter, M. (1999) 'Attachment disturbances and disorders in children exposed to early severe deprivation'. *Infant Mental Health Journal, 20*, 10–29.

Orbach, S. (1997) 'Family life'. In D. Kennard and N. Small (eds) *Living Together*. London: Quartet.

Owen, M. (1999) *Novices, Old Hands and Professionals: Adoption by Single People*. London: British Agencies for Adoption and Fostering.

Quinton, D. and Selwyn, J. (1998) 'Contact with birth parents in adoption: a response to Ryburn'. *Child and Family Law Quarterly 10*, 4, 349–63.

Rorbech, M. (1991) 'The conditions of 18 to 25-year-old foreign born adoptees in Denmark'. In H. Altstein and R. Simon (eds) *Intercountry Adoption*. London: Praeger.

Sachdev, P. (1989) *Unlocking the Adoption Files*. Toronto: Lexington Books.

Schaffer, H.R. (1990) *Making Decisions about Children*. Oxford: Blackwell.

Seglow, J., Pringle, M. and Wedge, P. (1972) *Growing-up Adopted*. Windsor: National Foundation for Educational Research.

Stein, L.M. and Hoopes, J.L. (1985) *Identity Formation in the Adopted Adolescent*. New York: Child Welfare League of America.

Storsbergen, H.E., Hoksbergen, R.A.C. and Itjeshorst, M. (1997) 'Adopted Greek adults in the Netherlands'. Paper delivered at the Conference on Adoption, Athens, June.

Thoburn, J. (1994) *Child Placement*. Aldershot: Avebury.

Tizard, B. (1977) *Adoption: A Second Chance*. London: Open Books.

Tizard, B. And Phoenix, A. (1993) *Black, White, or Mixed Race? Race and Racism in the Lives of Young People of Mixed Parentage*. London: Routledge.

Triseliotis, J. (1973) *In Search of Origins*. London: Routledge and Kegan Paul.

Triseliotis, J. and Russell, J. (1984) *Hard to Place: The Outcome of Adoption and Residential Care*. London: Gower.

Triseliotis, J., Shireman, J. and Hundleby, M. (1997) *Adoption: Theory, Policy and Practice*. London: Cassell.

Walby, C.M. (1992) 'Adoption: a question of identity'. MSc thesis, University of Wales.

World Health Organization (WHO) (1992) *The ICD–10 Classification of Mental and Behavioural Disorders: Clinical Descriptions and Diagnostic Guidelines*. Geneva: WHO.

Wee Adopted Girl

There was the time
when I was only four
my auntie Bridgie
took me shopping at the local Co

Some oul dears are standing
at the counter
watching the world go by
they are the kind
that never miss a thing
the kind with eagle eyes

Says one to my auntie
'My oh my
who's this wee lassie then'
before my auntie Bridgie
can open her mouth to reply
I step up and look
the oul biddy in the eye
'I'm our Davie's wee adopted girl' says I

'The lord bless us and save us'
says she looking at me
'Would you listen tae that.
Would you look at her size'

I left that oul biddy
standing there
with her mouth hanging open
catching flies

7

Whose Identity Problem?

The Dynamics of Projection in Transracial Adoption

Barry Richards

The evidence has not fared well in the debate about transracial adoption. In the polemic against transracial placements, the evidence from a number of studies (see, for example, Bagley 1993; Gill and Jackson 1983; Prynn 1999; Simon 1994; Tizard and Phoenix 1994) that such placements do not systematically or intrinsically harm children has been set aside or traduced. What might be called the evidence from daily experience has been turned on its head; the common-sense assumption that a child is better off permanently placed in a loving and secure family than in care has been seen as an attack upon the child.

Those of us wishing to defend transracial placements therefore face a dilemma. Do we confine ourselves to patient reassertions of the need to look carefully at the evidence? Or do we decide that since the evidence is always to a degree plastic, and that anyway people will believe what their broader values require them to believe, then we had better get stuck into the politics of it and challenge the values and beliefs which support dismissive attitudes towards the evidence? This chapter will show that between a bland empiricism on the one hand and the clash of polemics on the other there is a domain of analytical work which can change the terms of the debate by creating a shared understanding of its origins and why we are engaged in it.

In a highly charged area such as this, it is all too easy to concentrate on attacking the untruths or weaknesses in the opposing position. It might be useful instead to find what there is in our opponents' views which we can agree with, and work forward from there to where the differences between us emerge. There is one major theme in the arguments against transracial placements with which I personally can agree, despite my intellectual and visceral rejection of these arguments as a whole. This theme is the insistence that the whole history of racial oppression, of colonialism and racism, is relevant to our experience of race issues in adoption today. Every white adopter of a non-white child should be aware of this. In many public settings, the appearance of two white parents with a non-white child evokes for everybody concerned the history of white domination. This is because the position of the adopters is assumed to be one of material and social security, while that of the adoptee is known to have been one of deprivation or need. This matches, or at least partially reflects, the historical position of white peoples relative to non-white peoples in general.

The appearance of one white parent with a non-white child may have the same evocations, though in most actual instances these parents will be the biological ones. (What the arguments about 'identity' used against transracial adoption imply for the many single parents with children of a different colour from themselves is one of the questions for which proponents of those arguments do not have a good answer.) In these cases a related but different set of historical associations may come into play, often involving strong feelings about interracial sexual relations. Where however the visual parent/child difference is great, it is possible that, whatever the actual relationship, some observers may assume that the child is adopted, and the history of domination will be evoked.

Of course there are more than just historical reverberations. This relationship of security to whiteness and of insecurity to non-whiteness continues, and indeed is the main reason why we are much more likely to see white rather than black adoptive parents with black children. Of course black parents can and do become adopters, but those who do are like gold dust for social workers, because black people have been underrepresented in the secure social strata from which adopters usually come. Furthermore, the other main reason for the lack of black adopters relative to the numbers of black children needing adoption is the overrepresentation of those children in care. There are also some cultural resistances to adoption, but the racialized distribution of security in British society is the main factor. The same historical legacy thereby generates two forces – the limited availability of black adoptive parents and the large numbers of black children in care – that converge to produce transracial placements, at least when policy and practice have allowed. The parents in each family so constituted must then silently announce themselves to the world thus: 'We, being white, are comfortable and secure; you, if you are black, may not be.' The adopted child's presence with a white parent similarly says something like: 'I was in need because I am black' and 'There were no black people to look after me'.[1]

Prospective white adopters should consider how they feel about these messages which they will inevitably be seen as giving off, and how they will deal within themselves with their emotional and possibly social consequences. Those involved as academics or practitioners in debates about adoption also should consider how they respond to these messages from the history of racism and its persistence into the present.

Two main groups were responsible for the articulation and influence of the 'anti-racist' opposition to transracial placements: one comprised the academics and political activists who initially defined the issues, the other consisted of the social work practitioners who embraced and tried to practise a same-race policy. These two groups have overlapping but different agendas, but in each case their emotional responses to the racialized inequalities intrinsically flagged up by transracially adoptive families will have formed their emotional investments in the debate.

Intellectual proponents of same-race placements only seem to respond to the image of a transracial family by perceiving it as a concrete re-enactment of historical oppression. The comment that transracial adoption is 'one-way traffic', while statistically true, could imply that a forcible transfer of resources is taking place, a socio-economic bleeding of black people by acquisitive whites. The reality of transracial adoption – which is, to put it bluntly and without any fastidious fear of cliches, that a child may be saved – is lost; what is seen instead is an image of oppression. The evocation of colonialism is mistaken for its enactment; the pain of the historical relationships evoked is so intense that thinking becomes simplistic and concrete: 'If this family reminds me of that oppression, it must be a part of it.' The social task we all face, of creating new forms of relationship while living under the shadow of old ones, is thus abandoned.

This may the case for white commentators as much as black; the racial identity of participants in this debate is not crucial, since we can all identify with other groups and feel their pain as if it were directly our own. In this case a large and well-known repertoire of painful feelings is active, including rage at the brutal past, resentment of continuing inequalities, shame (however inappropriately felt) at the failure of the 'black community' to provide for its

---

1   There is an irony here in that historically, through the institutions of slave and domestic labour especially in the USA, it is probably the case that far more white children have been cared for by black adults (women) than vice versa.

own, and empathic concern for the child who so obviously is embarking on life from an experience of loss or abandonment.

There were various other forces in the wider social and political environment of the 1980s that created a favourable context for the advancement of same-race policies. The power of black activists and their constituencies was making itself felt, especially in local government, and creating space for debates such as that around adoption. However, the emotional dynamics of the same-race policy, involving a confusion between what transracial adoptive families remind us of and what they actually are, must also be taken into account.

What of the very large numbers of social workers who either actively pursued these policies in childcare work, or lent them support? Arguing for a particular line in committee meetings or in writing articles is one thing, making a decision about a child's life is another, and one might have thought that the practitioners faced with the emotional consequences of a same-race policy would have been less than zealous in pursuing it, even if they felt they had to agree with it. Fortunately for an unknown number of children, this has indeed been the case, as some practitioners have conceded that white parents are better than no parents and have placed children accordingly. However, for an unknown number of others, any opportunity of emotional security has been denied or delayed too long by adoption apartheid.

We are dealing here with a phenomenon which, at least in its more extreme forms, has a quality of perversity, in the sense of a transposition of good and bad (Grayson 1991; Waddell and Williams 1991). The goodness of the wish to parent, the nurturant impulse, is seen as worse than just misguided good will, but as something actively bad, as the evil of racism. Fair is foul. And foul is fair: arranging for years of institutional care or shifting foster homes, when permanent placements are available, is seen as acting in the best interests of the child.

How can this have come about? How can thoughtful and responsible people have become caught up in such an inversion of values? Two broad reasons can be suggested. One relates to the emotional demands of adoption work, and the other to inter-group dynamics on the societal stage.

The defensive location of the pains of adoption in transracial placements

Where placement policy has been flexible, this suggests that the adoption workers have been able to confront the emotional demands of their work, and to maintain their core identification with the child's needs. Where it has not, the adoption workers have found in the political agendas a defensive way of dealing with some of the more painful aspects of their work. This brings us to the point that the political debates around transracial adoption must be understood in relation to adoption in general. In any adoption, whether same-race or transracial, there are powerful and contradictory feelings aroused in all parties. The birth parents may feel both envious hatred of and some gratitude towards the adoptive parents. The adoptive parents may feel contempt for the birth parents on the one hand, and compassion and gratitude on the other. Guilt can run high on both sides: for having given away or for having taken away a baby or child; for being incapable of parenting; for being better off than others. And of course the pains of loss are ever-present: the birth parents are losing a child, the adoptive parents may have to accept their own loss or lack of procreativity, and may also identify strongly with the grief of the birth parents. All this is documented in the literature of adoption practice (see, for example, Lousada, Chapter 4, and Golberg, Chapter 13 in this volume).

Social workers and other professionals involved in adoption work inevitably participate in these feelings, and identify with both the positive and negative emotions on both sides. One of their main tasks in this work is to disentangle themselves from these feelings and to try to contain them, enabling the other parties, the birth and adoptive parents, to experience them in ways that do not subvert the placement, nor deposit in the mind of the child a legacy of envy, contempt or guilt. The containing activity of the professional, through which these feelings are acknowledged but not allowed to dominate the proceedings, can enable all the parents and children involved to come to terms with the pains of adoption. It can also enable the wider society to take a thoughtful and supportive attitude towards the whole process of adoption and all those involved in it. In this way social work can strengthen and develop the fundamentally nurturant and creative feelings that are embodied in adoption as a social institution.

In the field of transracial adoption we have an important example of the failure of the social work profession as a whole to contain the negative feelings involved in adoption. Despite the admirable work of some individual practitioners, the public stance of the profession as a whole, as measured both in numerous individual cases and in public policy statements, has been based on a failure to tolerate the pains of adoption. Instead of working to contain feelings of envy, resentment and guilt, social work has sought to defend against them, and has thereby inflamed them.

The process can be described as follows. In the context of transracial adoption, social workers have focused heavily on the negative dimensions of adoption — the guilt, the envious rage and so on. Moreover they have regarded these bad feelings as both justifiable and uncontainable. In this scenario, the only way to deal with the feelings is to abolish the situations that give rise to them. Thus social workers have ended up promulgating a counsel of despair, according to which transracial adoptions are doomed to failure, and should not be entered into.

Emotional difficulties that are at root common to all adoptions have been seen as of relevance only to transracial adoptions. Rather than seeking to confront and neutralize the difficult feelings in the context of these adoptions, the professional response has too often been to evade them by seeking to avoid the whole context, a defensive strategy for which the political arguments provided a rationale.

The projective location of identity problems in the transracial adoptee

The second reason for opposing transracial adoption appears to lie in a mistake, in a faulty understanding of what identity is and how it is formed. This issue is dealt with in contributions to the volume edited by Gaber and Aldridge (1994). Tizard and Phoenix (1994) argue that the ethnic labels that children apply to themselves bear little or no relation to their mental health, to their basic degree of self-esteem and their capacity to face life. In a similar vein I argue that the distinction between social and personal identity is an important one to maintain here. It is not an absolute distinction. Social categories such as class reach deeply into the heart of personal identity, and we might expect that a social category such as 'race', which is hooked on to a bodily characteristic such as skin colour, will have an even stronger influence on someone's sense of the person they are. But still, in the domain of early attachments and of relationships with care-givers, personal identity is forged in the encounter between the infant's needs for nurture and the emotional qualities of the care-givers. While framed by macrosocial categories, past and present, this encounter is not wholly constituted by them (Richards 1994).

In claiming that transracially adopted people will suffer identity problems, the critics of transracial adoption collapse personal identity into social identity. Of course the transracially adopted will have particular difficulties to negotiate around their social identities, and this was painfully so for many of those adopted into racist cultures, especially in the USA, in the early phase of transracial adoptions. But those with secure personal identities, founded in the quality of early emotional relationships with others, are well equipped to deal in creative ways with the sort of difficulties likely to arise in a society such as contemporary Britain. The critics of transracial adoption fail to address the issue of personal identity and the foundations of mental health, and so cannot meaningfully analyse the problems of social identity, which are negotiated with whatever resources of personhood individuals have at their disposal.

But why should this faulty understanding of identity have developed, and in this particular field? Several considerations are relevant to understanding the origins of the debate about transracial adoption, and some of them lead us back to the question of identity. 'Identity problems' are not, or should not be, the main issue in thinking about transracial placements. Yet issues of social identity are important in understanding why there has been such controversy in this field. However, the identities at stake are not those of transracial adoptees, but those first of social work, second of many black people in Britain, and ultimately of all of us.

If we turn our attention to the history and sociology of social work, we see a profession which has been chronically suffering an identity crisis. Caught historically between medicine and the law, and unable to match the institutional or cultural power of those old professions, social work has never had a secure base. The responsibilities heaped upon it by the welfare state have not made good its inner lack of certainty, though they have provided some concealment of this. The power of the profession in the delivery of welfare services has been as great as its intellectual weakness and the thinness of its skills base. The profession has always had to look outside itself for its knowledge base and its values, no matter how many proclamations have been made by its professional bodies. It has therefore been vulnerable to all sorts of incursions and hijacks. On being offered the identity of anti-racist vanguard it accepted with relief, especially since this was at a time when considerable numbers of black people were entering the profession.

The ban on transracial placements served therefore to alleviate the identity crisis of social work. It also enabled white social workers to deal with their guilt, both their general guilt about being white and also the specific practice-related guilt which anyone involved in adoption work would feel. They could deal with this latter kind of guilt by imagining it to relate only to one type of adoption, that in which it might be most poignantly symbolized, namely transracial adoption, and then deciding that adoptions of that kind must stop.

The ban also helped to deal with an identity crisis among black people, inside and outside the welfare field, who were most sensitive to the tensions of being black and British during a period of major transition in British culture. This transition, which is still taking place, is from a culture based on homogenized class blocks, all with white self-identities and broadly the same gender code, to one in which class influences are fragmented, gender codes

diversified and ethnic differences established within the boundary of British-
ness. While the transition is an incalculable improvement on the old
imperialist culture, it is at times a very painful and disorienting context in
which to live. White racism seeks to fix the causes of this pain in certain
groups of people, whom it may then imagine it can expunge. Within a black
experience, the notion that identity crises are being imposed upon transracial
adoptees gave a similar opportunity to fix, to limit and to abolish a pervasive
condition; the condition of not knowing how where you have come from, or
where your parents came from, relates to who you are.

Alongside the term 'identity', another unexamined rhetorical category in
the literature is 'heritage'. Transracial placements, it was argued, destroy
heritage, or take it away from the child. Although it is a notion of 'black'
heritage which is being referred to, this term makes it clear that the issue of
transracial adoption can serve for all of us, black or white, social worker or
not, to represent the problem of our contemporary identity, which is in part a
problem of heritage, of what we have lost and what we can preserve.

We can project into the scenario of a non-white child taken into a white
parental home not only all the feelings of loss, anger and guilt which
adoptions of any kind may evoke in us, but also the whole problem of who we
are. How people can make a good way for themselves in a society where the
past may seem to count for very little, how none the less the past may be
carried into the present in ways we do not well understand: these are
questions we all have to face. We know that 'heritage' is important, though
we may be sceptical of a 'heritage industry' as a means of preserving it for us.
What 'heritage' anyone may want to claim from the past, or should be able to
expect to find preserved for them, is a question for everyone; the situation of
transracially adoptive families is but one of a very large set of vicissitudes of
identity, or variations upon the theme of what has been called the postmodern crisis of identity. Defenders of transracial adoption need to acknowledge this as much as anyone else; the 'loving and secure' family, while not
mythological, is not a no-go area for deep problems in both personal and
social identity, and should not be a repository for defensive idealizations
which simply invert the denigrations of the other side.

In what is now fortunately a more favourable climate for rationality in
policy and practice, arguments about transracial adoption can perhaps be
conducted and policy developed with more recognition of the defensive and
projective processes which have fuelled antagonisms in the recent past.

Acknowledgements

Part of this chapter was originally written for a seminar on transracial adoption organized by the UEL Centre for Adoption and Identity Studies at the Tavistock Clinic, London, 19 October 1995.

References

Bagley, C. (1993) *International and Transracial Adoptions.* Aldershot: Avebury.

Gaber, I. and Aldridge, J. (eds) (1994) *In the Best Interests of the Child: Culture, Identity and Transracial Adoption.* London: Free Association.

Gill, O. and Jackson, B. (1983) *Adoption and Race.* London: Batsford.

Grayson, G. (1991) 'Fair is foul and foul is fair: perversion and projective identification in Macbeth'. *Free Associations 22,* 214–48.

Prynn, B. (1999) 'Family building in adoption'. PhD thesis, University of East London.

Richards, B. (1994) 'What is identity?'. In I. Gaber and J. Aldridge (eds) *In the Best Interests of the Child: Culture, Identity and Transracial Adoption.* London: Free Association.

Simon, R. (1994) 'Transracial adoption: the American experience'. In I. Gaber and J. Aldridge (eds) *In the Best Interests of the Child: Culture, Identity and Transracial Adoption.* London: Free Association.

Tizard, B. and Phoenix, A. (1994) 'Black identity and transracial adoption'. In I. Gaber and J. Aldridge (eds) *In the Best Interests of the Child: Culture, Identity and Transracial Adoption.* London: Free Association.

Waddell, M. and Williams, G. (1991) 'Reflections on perverse states of mind'. *Free Associations 22,* 201–13.

8

Race, Ethnicity
and Transracial Adoption

Ravinder Barn

The recruitment and selection of suitable permanent substitute families for children in the public care system is a difficult task. Issues and concerns facing carers and children are many and complex. Traditional social work practice has been to find families that best match the child's needs and background in order to increase the odds of placement stability. 'Race' and ethnicity present added variables for consideration in societies which are deeply racially divided. Historical and political discourse on 'race' and racism plays a significant role in the development and formulation of social policy.

Britain as a multiracial society is home to many and disparate ethnic groups. The two most predominant minority ethnic groups[1] include those of African Caribbean and Asian background, the latter originating largely from the Indian subcontinent (see Table 8.1).

The census figures do not as yet collate information about those of mixed racial and ethnic background. However, estimates suggest that there are about 350,000 individuals of mixed ethnicity, who make up a significant proportion (11 per cent) of the combined ethnic minority population in

---

1   The terms 'minority ethnic', and 'Black' are used interchangeably to refer to those who are disadvantaged and discriminated on the basis of 'race', colour and ethnic origin in Britain. These terms generally refer to those of African and Asian descent, who constitute the largest minority population in Britain.

Britain. Over 80 per cent of the mixed population are UK born and over half are under the age of 15 (Haskey 1997).

Table 8.1 United Kingdom population by ethnic group, 1991		
All ethnic groups	**54,889,000**	**100.0**
White	51,874,000	94.5
Ethnic minority groups	**3,015,000**	**5.5**
Black groups	891,000	1.6
Caribbean	500,000	0.9
African	212,000	0.4
Other	178,000	0.3
Indian	840,000	1.5
Pakistani	477,000	0.9
Bangladeshi	163,000	0.3
Chinese	157,000	0.3
Other groups		
Asian	198,000	0.4
Non-Asian	290,000	0.5

NOTE: Individual percentages add up to more than 100 due to rounding.
Source: UK Census 1991

Historical overview

Since the 1960s, minority ethnic children being looked after by local authority social services departments have been placed in transracial settings, that is, in white substitute families. White children have not had to experience similar upheaval at a time of separation and loss from their birth family. Cheetham (1981) found that social workers were reluctant to place white children in black families even when such families were available. The one-way traffic of minority ethnic children in white substitute families has been such that the term 'transracial' has come to be equated with this practice. Thus, although in theory, 'transracial' may mean 'across racial boundaries', in practice it has meant only one thing – the placement of minority ethnic children in white homes.

The placement of minority ethnic children into white adoptive homes began at a time when concern about their numbers and the difficulties of finding families was being highlighted. The political and ideological discourse around assimilation and integration of newly arrived minority ethnic 'immigrants' led to thinking around racial harmonization. Social work as an agency of the state was influenced by such political and ideological discourse. The praxis of such racial ideology within social work meant that attention was focused upon minority ethnic children in the public care system. Social work professionals believed that social work as a government agency could help contribute to a racially harmonious society. The placement of minority ethnic children in white adoptive homes was considered to be a positive step forward in mixing the 'races', and creating a racial utopia. De-segregation and the civil rights movement in the USA during the 1960s played a major part in British thinking about the British race situation. The low supply of suitable white babies for adoption was another major factor that resulted in white couples adopting black children (Divine 1985; Hall 1985). The number of adoptable white babies fell from 14,000 in 1968 to 2000 in 1974 and probably to less than 1400 in 1984 (Jasmine Beckford Inquiry Report 1985).

Longitudinal studies

The high numbers of minority ethnic children in residential care had been documented as early as 1954, four years before the arrival of the *Empire Windrush*, a ship associated with marking the beginning of a significant arrival of Caribbean people from the West Indies. This period also generally marks the significant arrival of African Caribbean and south Asian people into Britain. Katrin Fitzherbert (1967) in an anthropological study of African Caribbean families and social services highlighted the high numbers of Caribbean children in the care system, and advocated a 'tough casework' approach to curb this flow into care. Social work agencies were becoming increasingly concerned with the 'hard to place' children, a significant number of whom included minority ethnic children. Others included older children, sibling groups, children with disabilities and those with behavioural problems.

In the 1960s, the British Adoption Project (BAP) concerned itself with the question: 'Can families be found for coloured children?'. Within the context of 'racial harmony' ideology, it is not surprising that the vast majority of families found by this initiative were white families. The initial placement involved fifty-three babies of African, African Caribbean, Asian and mixed parentage background. These children were placed with fifty-one couples, the majority of whom were white. Three longitudinal studies evaluated the success of these placements (Gill and Jackson 1983; Jackson 1976; Raynor 1970).

Black children's best interests were perceived from political and ideological perspectives to the detriment of many such children who have had to grow up in a racial and cultural vacuum. The historical background of the 'melting pot' philosophy which believed that racial integration was best achieved by taking black children into white homes has been discussed elsewhere (Barn 1993; Rhodes 1992, Kirton 2000).

Since the early 1980s, the negative and highly disturbing experiences of black children in transracial settings have come to light (Black and In Care (BIC) 1984; Divine 1983; Gill and Jackson 1983). In the context of a transracial setting, it has been asserted that the denial of the reality of the black child in a white family or environment would eventually create identity confusion/conflict in that child (Small 1984). Indeed research studies of black children in white substitute families who are isolated from black communities demonstrate that these children have failed to develop a positive racial identity (Gill and Jackson 1983). Research studies into inter-country adoptions in the USA paint a similarly bleak picture and warn of the severe damage to a child's racial and ethnic identity (Koh 1988; Wilkinson 1985). These children have grown up believing or wishing themselves to be white, and have internalized white values, norms and attitudes of significant others. Gill and Jackson (1983: 137) recognized the identity confusion experienced when they stated that 'these black children have been made white in all but skin colour'.

Gill and Jackson (1983) made a study of the children in their adolescent years to explore this period of identity confusion (Erikson 1968). The findings show that the majority of the thirty-six families were living in areas that were either entirely white or in which there was only a small proportion of black residents. Eighteen families had no black friends. Adoptive parents showed little appreciation of the child's culture, but expected the child to have an automatic pride. Gill and Jackson (1983) stressed that these parents adopted their children at a time when not highlighting their child's racial background was regarded as the appropriate approach. They found that the way in which these parents were bringing up their children seemed consistent with the melting-pot approach of the 1960s. With regard to children's perceptions of their ethnic origin the researchers concluded:

> The evidence ... paints a picture of children who, although not directly
> denying their racial background, perceived themselves to be 'white' in
> all but skin colour ... There was little evidence of a positive sense of
> racial identity. (Gill and Jackson 1983: 81)

Despite evidence to the contrary, Gill and Jackson presented their central
argument as one of support for the continual practice of transracial placements: 'we feel confident in using the term "success" to describe the
experience of the majority of these children' (Gill and Jackson 1983: 132).

John Small, the then president of the Association of Black Social Workers
and Allied Professions (ABSWAP) and former assistant director of Hackney
Social Services, at an ABSWAP conference in 1983 argued that this desig-
nation of the adoptions as 'successful' might come implicitly from an
integrationist position so that the fact that the children do not see themselves
as black is seen as good in so far as it facilitates the creation of a genuine
multiracial society where 'colour' is irrelevant. This suggests that the stance
adopted by the researchers of this study is akin to the melting-pot era of the
1960s. In their own words, Gill and Jackson stated that they did not want to
'give undue emphasis to racial background or to emphasise the differences
between parent and child' (Gill and Jackson 1983: 13).

In their research design and interpretation of findings the researchers
adhere to a narrowly defined social class analysis whereby success is
measured according to the child's middle-class background and educational
attainment. The ethnicity of the child is reduced to a level of non-signifi-
cance.

Much of the Gill and Jackson (1983) study revolves around the elusive
concept of identity. Identity is seen as something that exists almost in a
vacuum. The research fails to move beyond the set parameters of identity to
observe the wider impact of societal and global issues on race and ethnicity.
There is little conceptualization of the position of black people in British
society except a passing remark which led one black practitioner to state that
the research was 'defective, hypocritical, and patronising' (Divine 1983).
Having given no regard to the problems faced by black people throughout
the research, Gill and Jackson stated in their conclusion:

> Transracial adoption over the past two decades has illustrated and
> highlighted the disadvantages of blacks in white society ... The black
> community has every justification for seeing itself as a 'donor' of
> children for white couples. Such a perception can do little for the dignity
> and self-determination of that community. To have a system which
> through 'benign neglect' in effect systematically removes black children

from black homes and places them in white homes without any traffic in the opposite direction can hardly be beneficial for the black community. (Gill and Jackson 1983: 137)

Divine (1983) argued that comments such as the above are no more than mere lip-service, and serve only to add to the hypocrisy of the researchers. He noted the damaging effect of the research on social work policy and practice:

> Having relegated ethnic identity as an irrelevance which is the effect of not including it as one of the crucial ingredients to be noted in the 'successful' placement of a black child, one cannot turn around and argue as an afterthought almost, about the 'dignity' and 'self determination' of the black community and expect child care agencies and our communities to take it seriously. (Divine 1983: 4)

The most notable finding of the Gill and Jackson study is that transracial placements are successful. Yet in their conclusion Gill and Jackson argued:

> Nevertheless, in our view, there are strong arguments for saying that wherever possible black children needing a permanent substitute home should be placed in black rather than white families. (Gill and Jackson 1983: 139)

Considering the fact that Gill and Jackson (1983) rejected all the arguments put forward by the opponents of transracial placements and view such placements as successful, it is ironic that they recommended black families for black children. Their lack of explicit emphasis upon issues of race and ethnicity within their methodological framework and their subsequent interpretation of their findings hailing transracial placements as successful (in spite of the difficulties experienced by the vast majority of the study children around issues of racial identity) points to the assimilationist/integrationist philosophy of Gill and Jackson (1983). Such 'empirical dissonance' around actual findings and contradictory ideological conclusions is unhelpful and does much to obfuscate the issues.

Other studies

Barbara Tizard (1977) compared three groups of children who originally spent some time in nursery care and then were adopted, fostered long term or 'restored' to their natural families. Tizard (1977) focused upon eight mixed parentage children, all of whom were adopted after the age of 2 and followed up to the age of 8. She found the placements to be extremely problematic. The families were said to be living in predominantly white areas and the children were experiencing immense difficulties in acknowledging their mixed racial origins and in forging links with black children.

Tizard (1977) also commented that the majority of the adoptive parents did not themselves have a positive feeling about the child's origins. She suggests that the transracial adopters in her study were trapped by an unconscious racial prejudice. Many of them saw 'race' as akin to mental or physical handicap, including one placement where the parent spoke of the child as having

> certain traits in his character which are definitely the traits of a coloured person. There's his lack of concentration. Also, he'll suddenly switch off if he thinks you're going to tell him off – he'll just go into his own little world. This is a thing that the coloured races do – one notices these little things. (Tizard 1977: 181)

Such thinking where the perceived characteristics of a racial group come into play has been explored by Robert Miles (1982) in his study of migrant labour. The idea introduced by Miles is of relevance here, that is that we are dealing with a situation where qualities of individuals are perceived to be representative of a wider collectivity (Miles 1982: 125). Thus if the individual is deemed to possess the criteria that designate membership of such collectivity, he or she is evaluated by the perceived qualities of the collectivity rather than the perceived qualities of the individual (Miles 1982: 126). Such negative labelling of an entire ethnic group points to the deeply embedded notions of racial superiority and inferiority.

Tizard (1977) found that, by the age of 8, only four of the eight children had been told that they were of mixed origin. This suggests that the concept of race could not have been discussed in those particular families. Despite her own evidence which suggests the contrary, Tizard argued that only one of the eight children is a 'cause for concern'. This child, who had been adopted at the age of 7, continued to identify with a group of black children in his previous children's home. The fact that the child actually saw himself as black is seen as 'cause for concern'. This example also serves to illustrate the importance of going beyond a narrow, family-based focus on identity.

The ideological thrust of Tizard's work is revealed when she suggests that the problems involved in transracial placements are not surmountable by 'same race' placements. Her commitment to the practice of finding permanent families for children in care leads her to suggest that social workers are unusually obsessed with blood ties. She argues that many social workers seek to return mixed parentage children to unsatisfactory natural families or to black extended families that do not want the children, rather than place them in a white adoptive family where they would be wanted. Without having conducted any research into the rehabilitation of black children into their natural or extended families, and without the availability of any such evidence it is not clear what leads Tizard to make such sweeping statements. Like the BAP studies, Tizard's (1977) work has been conceived in terms of one issue, whether or not transracial placements have been successful. This success has been measured by various methodological tools, including social work judgements, supposedly 'objective' psychological tests, and portraits of the 'experience' of families.

Tizard and Phoenix (1989) argued that there is no conclusive evidence to suggest that transracial placements are psychologically damaging for black children. Unlike Wilkinson (1985) and Koh (1988), they perceive identity in technical terms and fail to see a relationship between it and self-esteem. Indeed Tizard and Phoenix (1989: 432) assert that: 'it may be that young black people can have negative feelings about their racial identity, and yet have a positive self-concept'. Thus they perceive racial identity and self-concept as two distinctly independent variables. Nick Banks, an African American clinical psychologist, questions this 'implausible' distinction. According to Banks (1992), 'an integrated personality involves one having a stable concept of self as an individual as well as a group (Black) identity', whereby 'Black identity becomes an extension and indeed is part of the child's self-identity' (Banks 1992: 21). Banks maintains that the Eurocentric psychological perspectives require a significant perceptual shift to even begin to be relevant to considering the identity needs of black children and adolescents (Banks 1992).

In a study exploring the identities of a group of mixed origin children, Tizard and Phoenix (1993) point to the positive self-identity of these children. While this, in itself, is a significant finding, it is important to discuss it in its context. That is, these children were not in the care system, but came from stable home environments in multiracial areas that inculcated a healthy and positive identity. It is inappropriate to draw parallels between these children and those others whose identities are shaped by the negative experiences of the Eurocentric care system (Barn 1994). Such a deductive approach to research serves to negate the issues and concerns of vulnerable black youngsters in the care system.

Tizard and Phoenix (1993) argued that 'having a positive racial identity was not associated with living with a black parent'. While the impact of other influences such as peer group, schooling and the media is highly plausible, the contribution of parents cannot be dismissed. Recent research into permanent family placement for black children has pointed to the strengths of black families, and has found that most white families were aware that they could not meet the needs of a black child as well as a black family from the same ethnic and cultural background as the adopted child (Thoburn, Norford and Rashid 2000). Bagley and Young (1979) in a study of the identity and adjustment of transracially adopted young people suggested that children with 'racially aware' parents had a lower level of negative stereotypes of black figures and a higher level of black identification.

Other research into parental perspectives and child-rearing shows that while black partners in interracial relationships retain a strong sense of identity with their people, considerations of self-identity and of the identity of their birth children are a new experience for their white partners (Rosenblatt, Karis and Powell 1995). This US study shows that while the African American respondents believed it essential that the children should learn to identify as African American and to cope with racism, having their children defined as black or African American was not always easy for the white partner. Thus it would appear that the input that black and white carers can make towards children's racial identity stems from their own personal experience and understanding of race and racism.

Controversy over transracial adoption

In the 1970s, growing awareness of the high numbers of black children in the care system, and the low recruitment of black substitute families, led to some initiatives such as the Soul Kids Campaign. This campaign was designed to raise the numbers of appropriate black substitute families. Although the campaign is generally now regarded as a failure in that it was unsuccessful in recruiting sufficient black families, it nevertheless was significant in highlighting the issue of high representation of black children in the care system, and the need to recruit suitable black families. The failure of the campaign also taught important lessons around the ethnic composition of professional social work staff, and the Eurocentric nature of assessment procedures, and rigid criteria.

Britain, in the early 1980s, witnessed inner-city disturbances, national inquiry reports into British race relations, and the emergence of equal opportunity policies at local government level. Also, the formation of ABSWAP, national conferences organized by groups such as Black and In Care, the publication of transracial adoption research (Gill and Jackson 1983) and the corresponding criticism levelled at this study led to a re-evaluation of fostering and adoption policy and practice.

In 1983, the Association of Black Social Workers and Allied Professions made a strong attack upon the practice of transracial placement:

> Transracial placement as an aspect of current child care policy is in essence a microcosm of the oppression of black people in this society... The most valuable resource of any ethnic group are its children. Nevertheless, black children are being taken from black families by the process of the law and being placed in white families ... It is in essence 'internal colonialism' and a new form of the slave trade, but this time only black children are used. (ABSWAP 1983: 12)

Local authority social services departments (SSDs), particularly in inner-city London, took steps to recruit suitable black substitute families. It was soon realized that success in recruiting black families was largely dependent upon the resourcefulness and creativity of black social workers. One local initiative, 'New Black Families Unit', set up jointly by Lambeth Social Services Department and the Independent Adoption Society, demonstrated that there were families in the black community who were willing to adopt and foster if provided with the information concerning the need and if accorded the respect to which they were entitled (Small 1982). The impact of this initiative was profound in terms of restimulating practitioners and academics into looking afresh at the positive aspects of black family life.

By 1987, British Agencies for Adoption and Fostering (BAAF) had re-evaluated its position on transracial placements. In its policy statement on the placement needs of black children, the organization stated:

> BAAF believes that all children need families in which to grow and thrive. There are many thousands of black children in this country, children who come from minority ethnic groups, principally from African, Caribbean, Indian, Pakistani and Bangladeshi backgrounds. For the vast majority of black children – as with all children – the best place for them is within their own family. It follows that agencies should provide appropriate services which will enable these families to stay together or to be reunited quickly.
>
> In the small number of cases where children cannot be brought up within their family of origin, we believe that a substitute family should be sought urgently. We further believe that the placement of choice for a black child is always a black family. Agency policy and practice should therefore be geared to ensuring that an adequate number of black staff and of black substitute families is recruited to meet the needs of the black children in their care. (BAAF (1987) Policy statement on the placement of black children, Practice Note 13)

Since the 1980s, research studies have shown that some agencies have made tremendous efforts to recruit black families for black children, albeit largely in the field of fostering (Barn 1993; Barn, Sinclair and Ferdinand 1997). The vigour with which agencies have pursued the goal of recruiting black families has varied considerably. In the absence of national ethnic breakdown data, it is not possible to document the variations. Broadly speaking, areas with high numbers of black populations, coupled with political willpower and adequate resources, have been highly successful. The attacks from the media and campaigns such as 'Children First' have been quick to denigrate efforts in this area by exposing some poor decision-making on the part of social work practitioners (Toynbee 1985). In some cases, it has been asserted that in the absence of black substitute families, black children are languishing in residential care and being denied placement opportunities in white families (Dale 1987).

A Department of Health (DoH) audit report by the Social Services Inspectorate (SSI 1997) summarizing seven local authority inspections in 1996 found that placement patterns for minority ethnic children were varied. The report documented that local authorities were not rigidly pursuing same-race placement policies. In fact, the majority of minority ethnic children were placed in white families (see Table 8.2).

Table 8.2 Placement of ethnic minority children		
Placement	**Number of cases**	**Percentage of total**
Placed with white families	30	53.5
Placed with dual race heritage families	7	12.5
Placed with ethnic minority families	19	34.0
Total	56	100.0

Source: SSI 1997: 27

In line with the requirements of the Children Act 1989, the report stated: 'All things being equal, the preferred placement for a child from an ethnic minority is with a family with the same racial and cultural background' (SSI 1997: 28). With regard to transracial placement of minority ethnic children, the report placed the onus upon SSDs to establish that the placement choice is the preferred one. It is curious that, although the government's own audit highlights that the majority of adoptions in the case of minority ethnic children are transracial, Paul Boateng, the former junior health minister, should have attacked local authorities for pursuing same-race adoptions (Boateng 1998). The former minister's criticism of social work agencies resulted in a Local Authority Circular (LAC (98)20) highlighting the government's impatience with the 'race' principle. While reinforcing the underlying ethos around race and ethnicity embedded in the Children Act 1989 (section 22(5)(c)), the circular linked into the delay findings of the SSI report and stated:

> The Government has made it clear that is unacceptable for a child to be denied loving adoptive parents solely on the grounds that the child and adopters do not share the same racial or cultural background. (Department of Health 1998: 4)

The placement needs of minority ethnic children have, hitherto, been debated within the political framework of the day. The political ideology of the 1960s set the scene within an integrationist framework where the ultimate goal was one of racial harmony. Research evidence about the upbringing of transracially adopted minority ethnic young people informs us about the one-way and parochial nature of such thinking. Minority children were welcomed into white homes, but they were expected to think and behave as the adoptive family, and not see themselves as racially different. Lack of contact with people of their racial and cultural background, with little or no input about their racial and cultural heritage, meant that these youngsters grew up believing themselves to be 'white in all but skin colour' (Gill and Jackson 1983: 137). The outcome of such a cocooned upbringing meant that as children, and later as adults, these individuals were culturally bereft and ill-equipped to deal with race and racism in society.

Since the 1980s, there has been a political shift within the social work profession. The accompanying legal framework stresses that the ideal placement for a minority ethnic child is one with a racially and culturally similar family. Research evidence informs us that while some agencies are successful in finding racially and culturally appropriate foster families, there is still a chronic lack of suitable adoptive families (Barn *et al.* 1997; SSI 1997).

Future directions

Research evidence suggests that black children have an excellent chance of being placed within a substitute family setting (Barn 1993; Barn *et al.* 1997). We know that the majority of black children in the public care system are African Caribbean and of mixed White/Caribbean origin. Both of these groups continue to be placed in foster family settings; however, the latter present major difficulties for social work practitioners in placement decision-making. Overall, these children are no longer languishing in residential care. The fact remains that these children are placed in foster family situations, and have a low likelihood of permanent placement in the form of adoption (SSI 1997). Short-term fostering may be the appropriate placement for some of these children. For others, it is possible that long-term placement in a black family provides the child with security, and ongoing contact with their own birth family (Barn 1993; Thoburn *et al.* 1998). There is insufficient research evidence to understand the effectiveness of long-term foster care against that of adoptive placements.

The low socio-economic position of some minority ethnic groups continues to be documented by research studies (Modood *et al.* 1997). It is possible that poor housing, overcrowding, unemployment, low incomes and poverty exclude some black families from being considered as suitable adoptive families. While it is absolutely crucial that the best placement choices are made in the interests of the child, it is equally crucial that agencies re-evaluate their recruitment and assessment criteria for its possible bias which may militate against potential black adoptive families. Social work practitioners and policy makers must make decisions in the long-term interests of the black child, and act accordingly. The introduction of a generous adoption allowance would provide the financial security to families best placed to care for black children.

Black children in the public care system are subjected to a reality of isolation, alienation and marginalization. Such children are particularly vulnerable in the absence of the black family and community. This is further compounded by cultural ignorance and various forms of racial prejudice and discrimination on the part of a system that purports to provide a caring environment.

The debates around transracial and 'same-race' placements will continue as long as society remains racially divided. The importance of security, stability and psychological well-being of children must be given precedence over political and ideological thinking about the best way to achieve racial harmony in society.

References

Association of Black Social Workers and Allied Professions (ABSWAP) (1983) *Black Children in Care: Evidence to the House of Commons Social Services Committee.* London: ABSWAP.

Bagley, C. and Young, L. (1979) 'The identity, adjustment and achievement of transracially adopted children: a review and empirical report'. In G.K. Verma and C. Bagley (eds) *Race, Education, and Identity.* London: Macmillan.

Banks, N. (1992) 'Techniques for direct identity work with Black children'. *Adoption and Fostering 16,* 3, 19–25.

Barn, R. (1993) *Black Children in the Public Care System.* London: Batsford/BAAF.

Barn, R. (1994) 'Review of *Black, White or Mixed Race? Race and Racism in the Lives of Young People of Mixed Parentage.* Tizard, B. and Phoenix, A. (1993), London: Routledge'. *New Community 20,* 3.

Barn, R., Sinclair, R. and Ferdinand, D. (1997) *Acting on Principle: An Examination of Race and Ethnicity in Social Services Provision for Children and Families.* London: BAAF.

Black and In Care (BIC) (1984) *Black and In Care, Conference Report.* London: Blackrose Press.

Boateng, P. (1998) Speech given at an International BAAF Conference, 'Best Practice in Europe for Children Separated from their Birth Parents', Bradford, April.

British Agencies for Adoption and Fostering (BAAF) (1987) *Child Placement Policy.* London: BAAF.

Cheetham, J. (1981) *Social Work Services for Ethnic Minorities in Britain and the USA.* London: Department of Health and Social Security.

Dale, D. (1987) *Denying Homes to Black Children: Britain's New Race Policies.* Social Affairs Unit (SAU), Research Report 8. London: SAU.

Department of Health (DoH) (1998) *Adoption: Achieving the Right Balance,* Circular LAC (98)20. London: DoH.

Divine, D. (1983) 'Defective, hypocritical and patronising research'. *Caribbean Times,* 4 March.

Divine, D. (1995) 'No problems'. February/March.

Erikson, E. (1968) *Identity, Youth and Crisis.* London: Faber and Faber.

Fitzherbert, K. (1967) *West Indian Children in London.* London: Bell and Sons.

Gill, O. and Jackson, B. (1983) *Adoption and Race.* London: Batsford/BAAF.

Hall, T. (1985) *Submission to the Jasmine Beckford Inquiry Report.* London: British Agencies for Adoption and Fostering.

Haskey, J. (1997) 'Population review (8) the ethnic minority and overseas-born populations of Great Britain'. *Population Trends 88,* 13–30.

Jackson, B. (1976) *Family Experiences of Interracial Adoption.* London: Association of British Adoption Agencies.

Jasmine Beckford Inquiry Report (1985) *A Child in Trust.* London: Brent Borough Council.

Kirton, D. (2000) *'Race', Ethnicity and Adoption.* Buckingham: Open University Press.

Koh, F.M. (1988) *Oriental Children in American Homes: How do they Adjust?* Minneapolis, MN: East-West Press.

Miles, R. (1982) *Racism and Migrant Labour.* London: Routledge.

Modood, T., Berthoud, R., Latey, J., Nazros, J., Smith, P., Virdee, S. and Beishon, S. (1997) *Ethnic Minorities in Britain: Diversity and Disadvantage.* London: Policy Studies Institute.

Rashid, S. (2000) 'The strengths of black families, appropriate placements for all.' *Adoption and Fostering 24,* 15–22.

Raynor, L. (1970) *Adoption of Non-White Children: The Experiences of a British Adoption Project.* London: Allen and Unwin.

Rhodes, P. (1992) *Racial Matching in Fostering.* Aldershot: Avebury.

Rosenblatt, P.C., Karis, T.A. and Powell, R.D. (1995) *Multiracial Couples: Black and White Voices.* Thousand Oaks, CA: Sage.

Small, J. (1982) 'New black families.' *Adoption and Fostering 6,* 3, 35–9.

Small, J. (1984) 'The crisis in adoption'. *International Journal of Psychiatry 30,* spring, 129–42.

Social Services Inspectorate (SSI) (1997) *For Children's Sake, Part 2: An Inspection of Local Authority Post-Placement and Post-Adoption Services.* London: DoH.

Thoburn, J., Norford, L. and Rashid, S. (2000) *Permanent Family Placement for Children of Minority Ethnic Origin.* London: Jessica Kingsley Publishers.

Tizard, B. (1977) *Adoption: A Second Chance.* London: Free Press.

Tizard, B. and Phoenix, A. (1989) 'Black identity and transracial adoption'. *New Community* 15, 3, 427–37.

Tizard, B. and Phoenix, P. (1993) *Black, White, or Mixed Race? Race and Racism in the Lives of Young People of Mixed Parentage.* London: Routledge.

Toynbee, P. (1985) 'Care?' *The Guardian,* 2 December.

Wilkinson, S.H.P. (1985) *Birth is More than Once: The Inner World of Adopted Korean Children.* Detroit, MI: Harlow.

Knock Knock

Knock Knock

Pleased to meet you
how do you do
you don't know me
and I don't know you
but I'm the skeleton
in your cupboard

That's what I would say
if I ever went there
to the house where
my mother kept her secret
me
under her own lock and key
in her chest tightly
tucked away

I would come knocking
on her door
like a guyser at Halloween
looking for my due
'you don't know me
and I don't know you'

I would come
spooky as a spectre
rattling my chains
baring my bones
and their complacencies

Let me in. Let me in.
I am your kin
your blood runs
underneath my skin
Let me in

Knock Knock
Who's there
it's no joke
it isn't fair

9

Towards the Reality of Reunion

An Adoptive Mother's Journey through the Fantasies and Realities in Adoption and Birth Mother Reunion

Alison Benton

After nearly two decades of child-rearing, I can now look back over a great range of experiences within my daughter's adoptive childhood, and in the reunions that have followed. There were thirteen years of delight yet increasing concern in prime-time adoption, and three years of anguish and separation during her adolescent rejection of us and her return to foster care. Then there were the two reunions, first hers with us, then hers with her birth mother, culminating in all of us meeting up together. This was all before she was 18, and felt like a crash course in survival and permanence. There was an essential interconnectedness and continuity about all these stages in the journey, each stage growing despite many setbacks out of the stages before – all part of my 'honesty and reality' policy throughout adoption, of which eventual birth mother reunion was an integral part.

Before the days of post-adoption support, it was perhaps inevitable that much of my own parenting journey was taken up with attempting to secure professional help for this troubled child. So it has not always been easy to separate my own journeys through these fantasies and realities from those of my child. Nor is it possible within this chapter to include the roles played by the rest of the family, who were also essentially part of all these journeys; nor do I wish to leave any impression that the whole of our adoption was directly or exclusively focused on these issues of fantasy, reality and reunion.

Adoptive parents can be at risk of becoming subsumed by the forces of rage and rejection we have taken so unsuspectingly and unsupported into our homes. Adoptive mothers particularly are often targeted with the fall-out of hostility from the child's pre-adoption pain and loss, and early mothering experiences – or lack of them. Many such children need the defence of perpetuating and replicating the chaos and crises, confusions and rejections, of their earliest experiences. All this is now widely known, but while living it, I was 'learning on the job'. Discovering how much one's best efforts at adoptive mothering are subject to so many throwbacks from the child's earlier traumas is an ongoing trauma in itself. Discovering how little most of the professionals in our experience were aware of these past influences on the present, and able or willing to work with them, and therefore how damaging to the adoptive family were most of their interventions (and non-interventions), felt like having insult heaped on top of injury.

Starting the journey

Louise was 17 months old when she came to us in June 1980. The adoption world was at that time starting to move from its old 'clean break with the past' approach, towards more 'open' adoptions involving the concept of 'trusteeship'. Adopters began to be given more background details about the child's past life and family, to hold in trust for her to draw on while growing up and developing her need to know about herself. So I saw myself as a substitute mother, guardian of this child's past, and trustee for her future. She had had an uncertain number of carers, at least six, before she came to us. Her birth mother had finally relinquished her six weeks earlier, on starting a new relationship in May 1980. This was after several changes of mind about adoption before and after the birth, and several absences from Louise in the earliest months. No ongoing contact with her during childhood was envisaged, but I was glad to provide the photo of Louise in her new environment which she asked for.

Two important factors influenced how I saw some of the key realities before and after Louise was placed with us. The first was my own earlier social work training, including much from Bowlby and Winnicott. The latter gave lectures about the utter dependence of the infant on its mother, its corresponding utter devastation if separated from the mother in the early months, and the development of the crucially symbiotic early relationship between the two. He delivered these lectures pacing the floor, cradling an imaginary baby in his arms, a picture which has stayed vividly with me. My ensuing hospital social work career and life experience in general had also served me well in meeting much loss and grief, and in fine-tuning my hearing of 'cries unheard' around loss and separation.

The second involved facing the reality of our presumed infertility. I remember being asked about that during our adoption assessment in the mid-1970s, and replying that it was

> like being held up on a country road by a horrible accident ahead ... having to slow right down and see lots of dead bodies laid out on the grass verge waiting to be taken away ... trying desperately to avoid seeing any of this, but knowing you just had to face it and go right past it, to get on with the rest of your journey.

I know it was important for me to face, as it were, the 'dead bodies' of the children I might myself have given birth to, before I could get far in being prepared to adopt.

Part of this facing of infertility, I came to realize, meant being ready to adopt a child for its own sake, rather than to fill a gap in my life. An old friend, an experienced adoption social worker who was to become one of Louise's godmothers, said 'the thing about adoption is you've got to get to the point of positively wanting to raise someone else's child'. This was not what I wanted to hear at the time, while still hoping for my *own* child. But I came to see that it is in fact 'someone else's child' that adoption is all about; that is the underpinning reality of adoption, and of reunions too.

Later on, once Louise was with us, we discovered how fortunate we all were to have been given full information about her roots, and her own and her birth mother's early experiences, however challenging it might prove to pass on appropriate information at the right time for the child. With hindsight I realize that I could not have survived this adoption, or the separation and reunion which followed, without having had the background information from the outset.

But there was the sting in the tail of an otherwise empowering adoption assessment. As our assessing social worker bowed out of our lives, she said just what at the time we most wanted to hear: 'Well, there you are! Congratulations, you're out on your own now, just the same as any other parents!' In reality, of course, we were not at all the same as 'any other parents', and the child we were raising had her own very special needs and losses that made her unlike 'any other' child. It took us many years to realize how many additional and different parenting skills were needed. But that handover comment, well meant though it was, encouraged us to fight long and hard in the fantasy that we could cope, and to deny that we needed help in raising this precious, damaged and challenging child.

Thus were we sucked into the most dangerous of adoption fantasies – the one that pretends that the memory of anything before placement rapidly diminishes, if the placement is 'right'; with enough love and with rose-tinted spectacles firmly in place, it says, the past will disappear without trace in no time at all – 'and anyway, she's so young she won't even have noticed'.

There were two further realities I knew I had to take on board before I could go ahead with adoption. I made two deliberate decisions. The first was to become Louise's substitute mother, not another note-taking social worker, and deciding that six changes of 'home base' in your first seventeen months were more than enough for anyone, and the buck had to stop with us. So, we made this 'vow of commitment' never to have her moved on again in her childhood. The second decision was never to lie to her. Whatever she asked about her origins we would reply honestly and with age-appropriate detail. We felt liberated to make this decision by the birth mother's own dictated letter to us forwarded at handover, in which she gave us her full permission to pass on any of the details as given, as and when we felt fit.

But there was a little fantasy hiding away among those realities. Even though I knew with my head that a child with Louise's background was bound to find family life difficult, I determined with my heart that I alone would prove the theory wrong. I would be such an all-aware, all-caring and all-successful substitute mother, that I would succeed in meeting her needs, healing her pain and facilitating her full discovery of her own identity and potential. It just never occurred to me that any of us would need any professional help in the process. Most of the rest of this chapter is about my own process of discovering this reality, helped as it was at some of the more difficult times by psychotherapy to unravel the intertwined identities, pain, and losses involved.

The pre-school years: on the freeze / dazzle roller-coaster

There were three big realities about those lovely early years, once Louise had begun to thaw and open up a bit. First, there was the dazzling charm, her articulate and endearing conversations, and her sheer resilience. We came very quickly to love her deeply and irrevocably, and to admire and respect her enormously. She had the same effect on all the family and friends she met – a real winner. From very early on we could see such dazzling potential, her great giftedness and capabilities shining out. Discovering her musicality was one of the early joys; it was greatly satisfying both to know of the birth-parent roots it came from, and to identify it as a talent we were well placed because of our interests to help her develop.

Second, we soon realized that quite a lot of her mind was elsewhere, trying to sort out the past rather than concentrating for long on the here and now. In the main, we were the only ones who saw the 'shadow side'. However much we denied it in those early years, she could switch off all that dazzle like a light and withdraw into private pain and fantasy. Not to be wondered at after all her upheavals and losses, we thought, she is bound to grow out of it. Years later, when we tried to get help, that is what the professionals said too, though they did not even acknowledge the upheavals and losses. We also began to realize how much of her early flair and competence was a sort of learned self-care, to ensure her own survival when those around her had had other preoccupations. This, too, is something Louise has grown into rather than out of, and she still feels safer relying on none but herself, not having learned trust from those around her in her earliest months.

Third, there was the joy of creating her first life story album, from the wealth of background information we were given. This album (which proved to be the first of seven) included her birth mother's letter and hopes for Louise's life, some early photos and drawings, and her family trees – both of her birth parents as the roots she grew from, and of us as the branches she was growing into. There was also an account and photos of her arrival with us, the many connections between places in her past life and our own, and in a wallet at the back of the album all the cards sent to us at her arrival, and a list of all her presents from our family and friends. Her appropriating of this story as her own, and as favourite bedtime reading with me, was a joy to experience and share; it seemed to be an important part of her becoming anchored in the dual reality of past and present. She knew it by heart long before she started school, and came back to it intermittently throughout her schooldays and later.

The middle years of childhood: juggling with pain

The uppermost reality of these years was the two-way pull between building belonging in her new family, and not discarding the old. We were all living with the long-lasting effects of the old and its loss, but we had to keep faith with it for the future. We all, including Louise herself, had increasing concerns about her violent outbursts of hate and hurt. 'Why me?', she would weep in their wake. Through her tears she would explain (one minute, but deny it the next), that 'I'm only being horrid to you because you're here and the others aren't, so I can't be horrid to them.'

For me, it felt like being a performer switching rapidly between all sorts of circus acts, sometimes one after the other, sometimes several at once, and rarely being the ringmaster. Louise always had a hidden agenda, and it was sometimes a matter of running to catch up. I was constantly juggling past and present, while all the time working for a future that might somehow encompass both. There was much juggling in the present, too, around the varying needs of adopted daughter and born son (born to us after adopting Louise), not to mention the needs of self and husband as well. A major part of my endeavour in this great circus ring was to maintain the safety net under the high wire on which she spent so much of her childhood, suspended between past and present up there beyond our reach. From below I picked up the bits of discarded props and costumes that fell, helping to shift the balance between all her component parts as and when needed. There were also her raging lions to be kept caged when there were young children in ringside seats.

Louise was 7 and starting junior school before we accepted that her distress was not going away, and that she needed something more than we could reach unaided. The Post-Adoption Centre (PAC) in London provided our first lifeline, and for many years the only one. I remember the relief in discovering there that all this was usual in the circumstances, and no reflection on us. With their support, I was able to go on coping by using more of the same openness and honesty, as well as firmness about what was acceptable behaviour. She needed lots of love, yes, but 'tough love' with 'reality plus consequences'.

The Christmas after that first visit to the PAC we had an early glimpse of the real sadness under the brave, resilient exterior. Walking back from the shops past our town prison had always led to searching questions, since she knew of the drugs and prison past of her birth father at least (though I had deliberately delayed filling in the counterpart in her birth mother's story until she had had longer to play with her Barbie dolls in the nightclub costumes she knew her mother used to wear). That Christmas, as we got back home and Louise was helping me make mince pies, an uncharacteristic 'real' tear rolled down her cheek. 'It is horrid', she confided, 'to know your own father did drugs and had to go to prison'. She even tolerated me giving her a hug of commiseration, but then she switched back to the pastry.

There were other times in those junior school years (often, with hindsight, around key anniversaries) when my 'tough love' approach led to tears, and left me emotionally wrung out. She would sometimes claim that the 'bad behaviour' or sad finger-sucking or whatever, were continuing only because 'I just want to be a baby again but in this family now, and out of your tummy...'. Every now and then she expressed a fear of being teased at school about her adoption: 'I'll *never* be happy', she sometimes said.

A few years later she had reached more of an understanding about each of her birth parents and their relationship. I remember a particularly angry and tearful outburst after which she said with great feeling:

I can understand why she couldn't keep me when she was on her own, but what I can't understand – and shall *never* forgive her for – was her getting rid of me just when she was getting married to someone else. How dare she choose him rather than me!

There was no answer to that, given that hugs were not her favourite currency, but I felt relieved it was out rather than in, and that she had been able to share it with me.

Inner pain and outer denial

All the realities of her happy/sad childhood concerned pain and loss to some extent (lying, stealing, violence, friendlessness, underachievement, cutting of clothes and body, binning of best presents from us, love/hate, love/hunger, rejection, and so on). There were happy and achieving times, and we obviously tried to boost these – we still saw so much dazzling potential – but they nearly always ended prematurely, and were increasingly overtaken by sadness, anger, and transferred hate and destruction.

For us, it was the unpredictability of her behaviour and the switches between so many different realities that we found hardest to live with, particularly when these changes bore no relation to the current external circumstances. It would almost have been easier if she had been consistently unreachable, rather than intermittently so, with so many tantalizing glimpses of how lovely she could be even in her sadness in between times.

For Louise, this was her way of coping with being torn in two between her two worlds, partitioning the pain and hurt into separate compartments where it might be more manageable. Even with these splitting and dissociative defences up and running (and I mean running), a lot of her pain and chaos from her past did get mixed up with the present, and spilled over into the family. She desperately wanted to belong and was at the same time desperately afraid of it, therefore hostile to it. The sheer contrast and difference between her two worlds was enormous, and we tried to minimize this early on, wanting to avoid putting her heritage in a 'bad light'. Gradually we came to see these differences for what they were, and that some of them had to be faced as such.

As the adoptive mother, a big difficulty for me was in confronting her inner pain and helping her to do so too, without being overwhelmed by it myself. For years I was the only one she would acknowledge it to explicitly. Much as I valued her confidence, I had to find ways of not taking it into myself, yet assisting her to reach professional help to deal with it in herself. This was doubly difficult because of her need to keep it so thoroughly wrapped up and hidden when with professionals, which contributed to professional help being well-nigh unreachable. With them she reverted to the 'no problem with me' line, so I was written off as an 'overanxious mum' and 'seeing problems where none exist'. My recurring pleas for it to be seen as pain rather than problems fell on deaf ears. I was even told by one professional that my daughter had no problem but me, and that it was 'fanciful and over-analytical' of me to see any link between current behaviour and pre-adoption experiences.

If I had begun to have doubts that there was indeed such a link, these were swiftly dispelled when Louise first ran away from home. This was soon after her move to secondary school; transitions were always difficult for her. Although she was gone only for a matter of hours, the incident arose out of much distress and caused more. When I finally found her, leaving the house of an old primary school classmate, her frenzied rage began to give way to distracted sobs. In the holding and sobbing that always followed the rage and yelling, I eventually asked her where she would have gone if I hadn't found her: 'To find Mary,' she sobbed ... 'I'd have gone to a phone box and got her number from Directory Enquiries.'

We talked through the possible difficulties of that approach, and realized together that the time had come for another visit to the PAC. It was there that the run-up to the birth mother reunion began. The PAC made it clear that Louise's distress and near-rejection of us was likely only to worsen, until and unless she could begin to face more directly the realities of her own origins and her birth parents' 'rejection' of her.

Breakthrough to the birthplace

The burden that fell away from us in the aftermath of that PAC visit was as palpable as the burden we had been carrying in loco parentis all those years. Louise was now ready to respond positively to the PAC's suggestions for implementing this move towards reality. The first step was to contact the placing agency, just to express a potential interest in any updated birth family information initially, but with a view to taking it further and tracing if and when appropriate.

The second step was for us to revisit her birthplace city with Louise. She was 12 when we did this at the next half-term; she was wide-eyed at the impact of it all, particularly the shock of inner-city deprivation. We drove past the maternity hospital, and some of the addresses in her life story album. A bonus was finding and being welcomed at the day nursery she had attended around her first birthday; we even recognized the same curtains from those in the birthday photos in her album! That was a very identity-affirming experience, and the whole trip was to be a turning point for her. She even thanked me for having adopted her out of that environment; this was not actually the response I was looking for, but new realities were beginning to dawn for her.

Next, there was the reply to our letter to the placing agency. It turned out that the current Family Placement Team manager was none other than the senior social worker who had supervised Louise's own social worker in the early months and who could actually remember Louise and both her birth parents. This felt like manna from heaven to me, and eventually came to be very important to Louise too. She was invited to write in with the questions she would like to ask about her birth mother and her own early months, which had great value even then, but she did not feel ready to take it further for some years. For me, the greatest value was the acknowledgement from a professional that we were in reality an adoptive family still with a role in maintaining permanence, and that we were personally remembered, with our daughter, from the very start. It was so helpful, too, to have this social worker pass on to us the panel's reasons for choosing us for Louise all those years ago, and to have her encouragement and validation.

All this was a major factor in me regaining my optimism about Louise's potential for becoming happier and finding more of herself, and about our own potential to survive. Above all, we were back in partnership with the original Family Placement Team, albeit on the other side of the country, but with the PAC in the background we could continue working together towards reunion and a more fulfilled identity.

Adolescence: re-run of toddler rejection

Even though we knew that an adolescent 'blow-out' was a likely culmination of a troubled toddlerhood, knowing was no preparation when it hit us. Louise had never had one toddler tantrum, doubtless too fearful of further moves to risk anything but being 'too good to be true' at the time. If the middle years of her childhood were chaotic and convoluted, adolescence was volcanic, as if all those toddler tantrums that had never happened now fused into one 'father and mother' of an explosion.

I had had a warning that something was about to happen, when Louise shared one of her dreams just a few weeks before she disappeared. She dreamt, as she often did, that the house was burning down. She assured me this was 'not a nightmare any more, just a dream'. But this time she was the only one who could get out in time; the rest of us were lost with the house. She was apologetic and regretful about it, but that was how it was. I asked her how she had been able to get out herself, and she replied: 'My little girl ghost

came and led the way downstairs – she told me I'd be all right if I just
followed her and put my feet in her footsteps, so we just walked out and I had
to leave you all asleep'.

She was 14¼ when she left us, on a sunny Sunday in May. The horrendous
hate-filled explosion in which she left was appalling. Only later did we come
to connect up the dates, and realized it had been the exact thirteenth
anniversary of her birth mother's final relinquishing of her to the pre-adoption foster carer. Essentially relevant though we could see this was, it was not a
view shared by the professionals. This new family explosion was seen as final,
and as our failure. (I even had teenagers removed from my caseload at work –
'as your daughter has seen fit to run away from you'.)

Once we began the initial recovery from the violence and horror of her
final frenzy, we realized she would need more than a short-term cooling-off
period, and the 'help to sort out my angry feelings about you all' that she was
by then asking for. We were eventually able to get some valuable mental
health input, but the minimal cooperation of other professionals with this we
found shocking and distressing. Family restoration or even contact with
either adoptive or birth family were just not on their agenda. Thirteen years'
hard work, and home and family for Louise, were discarded in as many
minutes.

Professional attitudes and Louise's own became entrenched as the months
went by, feeding off each other in an horrific anti-parent and anti-reality
collusion. Together they were denying the reality and relevance of any
adoption-related issues, and going off on a rather macabre jaunt down
fantasy lane, pretending an 'ordinary teenager' of 14 has no need of any
family, either adoptive or birth. There was no thought given as to how she
might ever be able to contact us without loss of face, or how the rest of the
traumatized family could survive to be there for her in the future. Having our
role in raising Louise thus far, and our understanding of her pain and her
needs then and now, denied and rubbished by the professionals was
unimaginably hard. The three years of that denial were the longest and most
painful of our lives. It felt as if a very complicated piece of knitting to which I
had devoted thirteen years of my life had been unravelled with a single tug
and obliterated, discarding the irreplaceable pattern I had felt was nearing
completion.

Survival: the place of poetry in healing heartache and reaching reunion

One of the ways I survived the early shock of realizing Louise had gone was to write it all out in a long 'poem'. I had this need to affirm the positives of her childhood with us, that it had not all been wasted, and that some good might yet be salvaged from it. I also needed to affirm the links between her own eruption out of home and family now, and all that she (and indeed her birth mother before her) had suffered at the hands of home and family before our time. I needed to acknowledge, potentially also for her, the pain that we knew she had been suffering, and that we loved her through it all and willed her freedom from it.

I entitled this poem 'Anniversaries: a Farewell to Louise', because of the extraordinary way so much in her life was happening on the anniversary of something else. I offered it to social services to lodge on the file for potential use with her, but it was returned as 'inappropriate – too personal'. It did, however, come into its own a few years later, just before she was to be moved, under a different team, from her last foster home to a hostel. I had pushed for a last meeting with her before this move, expecting an even longer gap after it. So we met for lunch, in a trattoria where we had often had special birthday meals. It happened to be just before Christmas, so I also had a few little presents with me, and was pleasantly surprised to be greeted by presents from her to us all. There was a special one which she insisted I opened straight away – a framed poem she had written out for me. She hoped it would help us understand why she had had to leave us, and why she had now dropped out of education – 'just too much on my mind', she said. It was one of the most poignantly beautiful gifts I have ever received:

> A thought that spans a million dreams,
> This image provokes a million screams,
> Across the void it comes for me,
> The nemesis that only I can see.
> The blight that feeds on life's free wealth,
> My deepest fear is of myself.
>
> (quoted with Louise's permission)

It was chilling confirmation that, as I had long feared, she had throughout childhood felt too 'blighted' by her past to benefit much from 'life's free wealth' that had come to her by being adopted by us. But the clear pull towards reunion realities was the biggest breakthrough of the whole long process, the best vindication yet of what all my adoptive mothering had been about. I was much encouraged that Louise could be so explicit about her inner world again, and with me even after the long separation, and felt that it boded well for her future healing.

At the end of our lunch she expressed interest in seeing the 'Anniversaries' poem I had cautiously mentioned having written for her. She lapped it up, insisted on having a copy, thanked me, and seemed almost as moved by it as I had been by hers. 'No one has ever understood me as well as you do, Mum,' she said, and 'if ever I have to see another ****ing shrink, all I'll need to do is show him this and he'll know everything he needs to.'

There were other key developments during those traumatic re-accommodated years of separation that had a major bearing on my survival. One was my joining of what was then PPIAS (now Adoption UK), a life-saving mutual support network of adoptive parents. Another was the visits they arranged, with the PAC, of the American attachment therapists, Greg Keck and Regina Kupecky, from 1994; Louise's blow-out from us in 1993 had coincided with the first UK featuring of 'Reactive Attachment Disorder'. Despite the professional scepticism this met, it felt like a weight rolling off me to discover there were names to Louise's pain and reactions to it, strategies for parents to survive it, and even (potentially) for professionals to treat it. A comment made to me by Regina Kupecky, in a consultation I was fortunate enough to have with her in 1994, was the first affirming comment about my parenting I had had from a professional:

> Staying at home full-time with Louise for her second eighteen months was probably the best thing you ever did … you might not be able to alter much about her *relationships*, having not been around in her first eighteen months, but you were there when her *values* were being laid down.

And another was the great benefit I discovered at this time of the Christian healing ministry, a major resource for me. I began to realize how deep and ingrained is such early damage in these children, and I had to relinquish the last of the dreams I had had for her.

Apart from that amazing poetry-sharing lunch, the downward spiral of Louise's last accommodated months was gathering momentum. As I had half predicted, she disappeared off into the wide blue yonder, the archetypal vulnerable care-leaver with no family contacts. The professionals were busy driving their last nails into our coffin, with such tender farewells as: 'She's never coming back to you … she's voted with her feet … you've just got to accept that her relationship with you is over.' When I said to the Team Manager at the last meeting with him, while Louise was still missing, that I would not be surprised to find she had gone back to the city of her birth, he replied with true professional ignorance to the end: 'Why on earth would she want to do that?'

In what must be to the professionals the infuriating way that mothers who actually understand their children do have of seeing these things, it was precisely to her birthplace that she did gravitate, within a matter of months. But what even I had not expected, or ever dared hope – particularly after the 'encouragements' just quoted – was that she would involve me first and ask for my help in bringing this about.

Young adulthood: birth mother reunion, sandwiched between two stages of adoptive parent reunion

Louise's disappearance from the hostel, and her remaking of phone contact with us, both happened on key anniversaries – one sixteen years on from her birth mother's relinquishment of her to foster care and, six weeks later, the other which was sixteen years on from her placement with us. The significance of the dates was not lost on her, either; we had always celebrated the 'anniversary' of her joining us. It was a most profound 'joining up' experience for me. But her anguish, and then ours, in living through these six week gaps had been indescribable, and there was yet another to come. 'Nightmare' was the word she kept coming back to.

When Louise and I did actually meet and talked the day (and the lost years) away on the anonymous safety of a London park bench, there were tears and regrets, and wishing things had been otherwise. It was a great bonus to discover also how much thinking she had been doing, and how far she had already moved on from the old displaced anger and rejection.

'Do you still have the phone number of that social worker who's got all my details?' she asked. 'And would you mind if I went to see her, and see if she could help me find Mary?' She continued: 'I know I'm never going to get sorted and make anything of my life till I've faced her ... I've come to the end of myself and I know I can't go further till I've faced my past.'

Everything fell into place rapidly after that. Within a month, thanks to close collaboration over the phone between us and the original placing social worker, Louise had returned to the city of her birth and met several 'significant others' from her early months. One of them even put her up in her home and was, with the social worker, instrumental in her meeting several members of the wider birth families, and later in arranging the actual birth mother reunion. They handed over to an ecstatic, yet newly awed, Louise some beautiful photos and a box made for her by her birth father before he died, with the photo of Louise herself in our garden that I had supplied for

Mary, set into the lid. They were all most generous with their phones, and I was kept in daily contact and given a hug-by-hug account of each new meeting, both by Louise herself and the others there. It was extremely fulfilling (to put it mildly) to hear the jubilation and sheer childlike exuberance in Louise's voice, filling in so many gaps.

Within another month, everybody had met up with everyone else, including aunts and uncles and all the half-brothers, in a great spiral of delight. Mary had not initially been willing to meet Louise, unhappy to hear from the social worker of how Louise had left us at 14. 'If I'd wanted you to have druggy dropout boyfriends', she said later, 'I'd have kept you with me, then they'd all have been like that'. Nor was Mary happy about Louise meeting up with her half-brothers, but this was an important part of the reality for Louise, even though her insistence in doing so was also a factor in the premature ending of their reunion.

I revelled in hearing Louise's excitement about all the special meals Mary had prepared for her, the clothes she had bought her, the likenesses they talked about, the cuddles they had tried, and their sharing of photo albums. Then came the phone call suggesting I might actually talk with Mary on the phone, and fix a date for us to come over and meet them – 'if you can cope, Mum', added Louise with welcome concern. But this was the moment of ultimate reality in our adoption, presenting Louise back to her birth mother and fulfilling the trust placed in me. I had not slept more soundly for a long time than I did that week, in between all the phone calls. Mary repeatedly said that it was I who was and would remain Louise's 'real mother'. Mary said she had merely been the biological mother and was 'not cut out for mothering anyway'. This was very moving, and the fact that Louise was on the extension echoing her agreement to it all, made it even more amazing.

We had in reality now come full circle. With so many fantasies evaporating like the morning mist, we were on the threshold of a new era. I knew that the placing social worker had been pivotal to this whole process, and I was particularly grateful to her for sounding me out beforehand on my views on this reunion. I remember asking her to be there to prepare Louise and pick up any pieces afterwards. And I remember saying how much we would love to be included in some way; I knew that if this high point of Louise's whole childhood were to happen without us, being the culmination of the reality I had so long worked for, I would find that more painful than any of the other exclusions from her life we had already suffered.

So here we were fixing dates and details for a meeting like none other, and there we all were a week or two later, sharing a drink, a photocall, and lots of laughing and talk about likenesses and temperaments. Yet somehow the bubble of excitement seemed already to have burst, and there was a lot of tension around, probably inevitably. In the very act of unloading Louise's remaining black bin liners (from the hostel she had disappeared from) into her new bedroom in Mary's flat, we sensed that the joys of the honeymoon were beginning to wear a bit thin.

We discovered weeks later that it had been by then all over bar the shouting, and there had been some of that too. But at the time, our drive back home across the middle of England was for the two of us, like no other. I too felt almost as old as the century, but marvellously completed. It was harvest time, which I remember thinking was particularly appropriate as all was now 'safely gathered in'.

Post-reunion sequel

Three years on, the new relationship of adult reality between Louise and us has taken root. We marvel that this has been possible, given the enormous amount of additional pain and rejection she has had to suffer since finding her birth mother. Mary's sudden disappearance, as the honeymoon of their reunion faded, was an added trauma that Louise could have done without. She needed more than six weeks' wound-licking time after that. She went to ground again, but emerged some months later, bloodied but unbowed, in true survivor fashion. But, she says, even with all that she is profoundly glad she did meet Mary: 'It's only now that I can know where I came from, and where I don't want to go to – and start making something of my life.'

Fantasy gives way increasingly to reality, but much of that reality is extremely difficult. She can at least have an enormously more real relationship with us, in a new semi-detached sort of permanence at a distance. She is able to make more rational decisions and plans about education, boyfriends and lifestyles, directions and goals, and much more besides. Much of Louise's life is still on a roller-coaster, the difference being now that the rage and fury have gone, and she knows we are still there for her. She wants to keep 'touching base' every week or so and invites us over every few months to see the progress on her new flat, and meet her new friends. This is rich reward after all the pain and hurt, and we are proud of her. I now know that we have made a difference to her life; she has more options open to her now to find her own identity and fulfilment than she ever would have done without us and the reunions.

Note

1. 'The dawn of a new realization: taking a long view in adoption' is the title, quoted from Louise, of my article updating the post-reunion developments (*Adoption Today 88*, February 1999). Through the support group I help run within Adoption UK for other adoptive parents in similar situations, I am also aiming to raise professional awareness and working towards earlier specialist intervention to meet these children's needs and preserve challenged adoptions.

2. 'Louise' has had her first name changed in order to preserve her anonymity. She has seen a draft of this chapter and endorsed it, commenting that it was 'too important to cut' and, 'the more people who realise the anguish of it all the better.'

Wee Bardy Bones

From 'The Making of Wee Bardy Bones'
A theatre piece performed by The Skin You're In

It wasn't easy hanging on in there at times. Talk about knowing when you're not wanted. Have you ever felt crushed. Did you ever feel like you were invisible, like people were ignoring you, pretending you weren't there. Well that's how it was. I kept trying to attract her attention, trying to amuse her, take her mind off things, help her see the funny side of things, but she didn't want to know. I would do all kinds of tricks like cartwheels and somersaults and 'look no hands'. But she would just ignore me or else she'd vomit.

I tried changing, turning into other things. I figured if she didn't want a baby, she might like a fish or a frog, or maybe a tortoise or something but nothing I did could make her happy so in the end I just let her be and got settled in for the journey. It was a rough crossing I can tell you. Talk about going down the Clyde in a banana skin, talk about paddle your own canoe. What with eh? I was well and truly up the creek with no paddle, no compass and no map.

> Row Row Row your boat gently down the stream
> merrily merrily merrily merrily life is but a dream

There I was balancing between life and death so I was. Between the devil and the deep blue sea, between one thing and another, between one wave and the next, between seagulls swooping down to peck my eyes out and the big fish popping up and gobbling at me. Between all the pushing and the shoving, the to-ing and fro-ing, the coming and the going, all the grunting and the groaning. All the doctors and the nurses and the nuns with bad tempers and bad habits and none of them knowing what it was like having babies or making them for that matter.

And then I popped out like a wee pearl from the oyster shell and it was a perilous journey I can tell you.

Everybody was dressed in black. You would have thought it was a funeral, born into a wake I was. When I saw her face she looked so sad it might as well have been a funeral. After all the trouble I had getting there, you might have thought she'd be pleased to see me but no.

One big happy family. Well it was big. There were loads of sisters. They were the ones in black. I couldn't tell if they were my sisters or hers and I couldn't see my daddy anywhere. Then I heard one of the sisters say, 'Come in Father.' So I thought 'this must be my daddy.' He was all dressed in black too. I thought he might be pleased to see me. I was expecting him to pick me up and give me a cuddle maybe. But he stood there waving his hands in the air and muttering funny words I couldn't understand so I said, 'Are you my daddy?' They all fainted clean away. I was only trying to be friendly. Some welcome eh.

10

Lesbian and Gay Parents as Foster Carers and Adoptive Parents

Damian McCann and Fiona Tasker

'Adoption by gay men and lesbians is an intensely emotional topic that polarises groups of people on the basis of their values and beliefs' (Sullivan 1995: 21). Perhaps not surprisingly, the translation of these values and beliefs into the practice of placing children for adoption with lesbians and gay men often results in confused thinking. On the one hand, there is a recognition that lesbians and gay men are legitimate carers for children in society, witnessed in the decision by some local authorities to open their assessment processes to homosexuals. On the other hand, many prospective lesbian and gay adopters face bureaucratic resistance and a variety of strategic manoeuvres on the part of adoption agencies, designed to deter them from applying. Some agencies make no secret of the fact that they operate a complete ban on gays and lesbians adopting children. Equal opportunities policies also appear to afford little protection in regard to the assessment and eventual placement of children for adoption with lesbians and gay men (Hicks 1996), since some groups appear to be more equal than others.

In order to decode the logic of such muddled thinking and practice, one has to return to basics. For instance, although there is clear evidence of an increasing diversity in family forms and family life, emphasis continues to be placed on the primacy of the heterosexual dual-parent nuclear family. This is both reflected in government policy and reinforced at other levels of society. The odds are stacked against those lesbians and gay men who wish to parent. Questions are raised not only about their right to parenthood, but also about the damaging effects their parenting will have on the children in their care. Also, in a climate where homosexuality and paedophilia are sometimes viewed as one and the same, suspicions are raised about the motives of lesbians and, particularly, gay men wishing to care for children in their homes. This level of scrutiny could be justified on the basis that, within the context of fostering and adoption, the best needs of the child must prevail. However, the questions and objections raised about prospective lesbian and gay male adoptive parents may be motivated more by homophobic reactions than by the best needs of the child.

There should be little doubt that the placement of children for adoption is a serious business that, as Brown (1991) suggests, has lifelong consequences. For that reason, it is imperative that strenuous efforts are made to ensure that a prospective adoptive placement, irrespective of sexual orientation, can meet the needs of the child. The extent to which lesbians and gay men can offer such care will provide the focus of this chapter. Finding a space to think in the hotly contested political minefield of rights and needs is not an easy task. However, the arguments for adoption by lesbians and gay men will be evaluated in the light of existing research and issues relating to the assessment process will also be highlighted.

Routes to parenthood and the legal framework

Lesbians and gay men may come to parent children in a variety of ways. First, they may have children in the context of a heterosexual relationship or marriage. Second, lesbian women may give birth to a child following sexual intercourse with a man, or by means of donor insemination. Third, gay men may enlist the help of a surrogate mother. Fourth, lesbians and gay men, using any of the above means, may together decide on a co-parenting arrangement. Fifth, homosexual men or women may apply to become foster or adoptive parents.

It has been suggested that the motives for adoption by lesbians and gay men may be less connected to childlessness and failure to conceive biologically, than to a wish to start a family in the context of relationships becoming more established, work and home lives feeling secure and a growing awareness by lesbians and gay men themselves of having something valuable to offer such children (Hicks and McDermott 1999). Attention has also been drawn to the fact that black children need adoptive parents and a wish to provide homes for such children may provide further motivation for black lesbians and gay men in applying to become adoptive parents. For those who wish to adopt, the Adoption Act 1976 carefully sets out the grounds on which this is possible. In essence, the Act privileges legal marriage over other forms of couple relationships. Section 14(1) states: 'an adoption order shall not be made on the application of more than one person except in the circumstances specified in subsections (1a and 1b)'. Essentially, this means that only one partner in a homosexual relationship may apply to become an adoptive parent. Although attempts have been made with regard to lesbians and gay men to clarify the ruling contained in the 1976 Act, the long-awaited review of adoption law published by the Department of Health in 1993 leaves the original ruling untouched. The review did, however, acknowledge the existence of lesbian and gay relationships and even went as far as recommending that 'where the applicant is in a steady homosexual relationship, his or her partner should be vetted as part of the process of determining suitability' (DoH 1992: 16.14). As we shall see later in this chapter, additional obstacles may be encountered by lesbians and gay men who 'come out' or acknowledge a lesbian or gay partnership in the context of an adoption assessment.

It is possible for the non-adoptive lesbian or gay male partner to gain parental rights in relation to an adopted child or young person by means of a residence order (referred to in the Children Act 1989, section 12.2). Essentially this gives the non-adoptive parent equal parental responsibility in relation to, for example, decisions about the child's schooling, emergency medical treatment and such like. In the event of the adoptive parent dying, it also allows the non-adoptive parent the right to retain parental responsibility, or in circumstances where partners separate, it provides a recourse to the court to determine with whom the child lives. Nevertheless, lesbians and gay men often feel cautious about using the legal system, knowing that it operates within other larger social and political systems that may discriminate. It is true that some recent landmark rulings give grounds for optimism, but in spite of acknowledgements, such as those contained in the Adoption White Paper (DoH 1993), that lesbians and gay men can make good adoptive parents, often they are viewed as a resource that should be used only in exceptional circumstances.

A further component in the legal framework relating to adoptions is the Adoption Agencies Regulations (1983). These regulate the creation of adoption panels for the purpose of considering applications for adoptions and making recommendations to the agency decision-maker. They also impose a duty on agencies to consider the particular circumstances of each case and empower the agency decision-maker to veto an application if it is believed that the proposed adoption is not in the best interests of the child. They must consider the recommendations made by their adoptive panels, taking into account the competing needs of any interested parties, if these exist. For instance, the need to safeguard the welfare of the child throughout his or her childhood takes precedence. In fact, the Inter-governmental Working Group, whose recommendations formed the basis of the Adoption

Review Paper (DoH 1993), advocated that on attaining 12 years of age the child should be given a power of veto. Nevertheless, it must be recognized that the child's views are only one of a number of factors. Birth parents should also be consulted where possible and their agreement should be sought in support of a proposed adoption. It is possible to dispose of parental consent under section 16(2) of the Adoption Act 1976, assuming that the child's needs outweigh the birth parent(s)' objections and it is deemed that they are unreasonably withholding their consent. However, as Sandland (1993: 323) points out: 'It is unlikely that a court would hold a refusal to consent by reason of the applicants homosexuality to be unreasonable'. This is particularly pertinent given the push towards partnership with birth parents and the whole question of contact in 'open' adoption.

It is therefore imperative that agencies and courts, when considering applications for adoptions from lesbian and gay men and when dealing with contested applications, have at their disposal accurate information to guide their thinking and judgements. Views such as that it is wrong to place a vulnerable child in an 'immoral' or stigmatizing environment, or those held by Whitefield (1991) that 'The role model of gay and lesbian households is simply not appropriate for the developing child and adolescent', will inevitably deprive children and young people of the valuable resource that some lesbian and gay carers can provide. The extent to which either prejudiced view informs decisions, or the extent to which agencies and courts rely more on existing research evidence to assist in balanced and fair judgements remains unclear. Before considering the research evidence in detail, attention will now be focused on the assessment procedure and the questions raised by this particular aspect of the process.

The assessment procedure

All prospective adoptive parents are required to partake in a full and comprehensive assessment conducted by a qualified professional working on behalf of an approved adoption agency. The primary task of such an assessment is that of determining the appropriateness of the applicant or applicants (if legally married) in relation to meeting the needs of a child or young person requiring adoption. The fairness of such a procedure for prospective lesbian and gay male adopters rests entirely upon the agency's policies, procedures and beliefs as to the value of such individuals in meeting the needs of children in society. Some adoption agencies, as mentioned earlier, operate a blanket policy of non-cooperation with homosexuals. Others, within the context of equal opportunities, may feel obliged to undertake such an assessment, but subsequently fail to place children with lesbians and gay men, or alternatively only place disabled children or those who would not otherwise successfully be placed elsewhere. Hicks (1996) highlights the irony of placing children with greatest needs with carers who are otherwise dismissed as lacking appropriate parenting skills.

The British Agencies for Adoption and Fostering (BAAF) helpfully provide a lead when they say:

> Agencies should be open in their approach to potential applicants, to reflect the wide variety of children needing families. Applicants come in many guises: single people, married or unmarried couples, people with disabilities, lesbian and gay people. Stereotyped notions of the ideal family should be examined critically. (BAAF 1991: 2)

Sullivan (1995) reinforces this point by suggesting that what is being assessed in prospective fostering and adoption applicants is not whether they 'fit a particular ideological notion of the family', but rather 'their capacity to meet the needs of particular children'.

Two contrasting positions emerge in relation to the assessment itself. One school of thought pushes in the direction of uniformity where all applicants are treated the same irrespective of sexual orientation. The other emphasizes a more individualistic approach based on the unique circumstances of each individual case. For instance, Brown (1991) suggests that when assessing prospective lesbian and gay foster and adoptive parents, the assessor should inquire about the individual's personal and family developmental processes in relation to his or her sexual identity. She also suggests inquiring about the level of comfort with one's sexual orientation and strategies that have been employed to manage homophobia in society. Other avenues for investigation might include asking the prospective adoptive parent about his or her current relationships and how they would help a child or young person negotiate and manage the interface between home and the outside world. The rationale for such an in-depth assessment is, according to Brown (1991: 16), 'a need to know if they [lesbians and gay men] have adequately coped with difficulties relating to sexual orientation'. The counter-argument is, of course, that it is unfair to hold homosexual adoptive applicants to different or higher standards and that dealing with psychosexual development is something that all applicants should be questioned about.

A key consideration in the assessment process is the willingness of the applicant to disclose his or her sexual orientation. Although many favour absolute disclosure (Brown 1991; Sullivan 1995), potential applicants need to be aware of the dilemmas of disclosure. For instance, some applications in process have been halted as a result of a lesbian or gay male informing the practitioner undertaking the assessment that they are homosexual. Others have noticed a change in attitude towards the applicant after disclosure and, in one case cited, the applicant and his partner were required to see a psychiatrist before a decision could be made regarding their suitability as adoptive parents (Hicks and McDermott 1999).

There are reports of some practitioners undertaking the assessment choosing to ignore the fact that an applicant is lesbian or gay, on the basis that an acknowledged disclosure will unnecessarily complicate a process that should be focused on the ability to parent effectively. Another difficulty seems to be the agency's fear of attracting unwanted press and media attention and being made to account for its unwillingness to entertain or even support such applications. Silence also offers the practitioner the chance to avoid having to convince a reluctant birth parent that it is in the child's best interests to be placed with a lesbian or gay male carer. Adoption agencies must take seriously the need for practitioners involved in the adoption process to have a clear lead from the agency itself. For instance, it is essential that agencies open to applications from lesbian and gay male carers demonstrate support both for lesbian and gay carers and their adoption workers when faced with homophobic reactions from elsewhere.

Appropriate training and a sound knowledge base are prerequisites to responding appropriately to prospective lesbian and gay male adoptive parents. After all, the individual practitioner's own prejudices about lesbian and gay men as adoptive parents may inform the outcome of such an assessment. However, the extent to which agencies provide such training is open to question. Yet, without appropriate training, practitioners may lack the necessary understanding of the particular qualities that some lesbian and gay adoptive parents bring to a child's life. They may also fail to recognize the range of families within the lesbian and gay communities, and generally lack the confidence to work with lesbians and gay men. This may account for the majority of lesbian and gay respondents in Hicks's (1996) research feeling that it was their responsibility to raise issues relating to sexuality in their adoption applications, and noticing that, even when they did disclose, practitioners had little or no real understanding of lesbian and gay lifestyles. One small example will highlight the issue in action. Although the application form that guides the assessment interview emphasizes kin relationships, it is imperative that practitioners apply a broader framework to the relationships of lesbian and gay people if they are truly to capture the patterns of relating and support networks that exist within lesbian and gay communities. This is because specific networks have evolved in response to homophobic reactions from within families and the dominant heterosexual community, and for some gays and lesbians these have actually replaced the family of origin as the primary source of connection and relationship (Weeks, Donovan and Heaphy 1996; Weston 1991). Without this understanding, lesbians and gays, if assessed solely on the basis of relationship to family of origin, may be viewed as isolated and sad individuals who could not possibly offer a child a full and integrated family setting.

Ultimately, prospective lesbian and gay adoptive parents must be assessed on the basis of their ability to meet a child's need in the long term. Some agencies have used them initially as foster carers while assessing a particular applicant's ability. Although effective in one sense, practice of this kind runs the risk of reinforcing the divide between heterosexuals and homosexuals if it is not applied evenly. Jenny and Susan's story will be used to illustrate this and other points raised in relation to the assessment process.

Jenny (aged 29) and Susan (aged 33), a white British couple, had, at the point that they decided to adopt, been living together in the West Country of England for some three years. The decision to adopt came mainly from Jenny although Susan was also enthusiastic about raising a child. As a couple they had considered the possibility of donor insemination, but Jenny was not in favour of this and Susan, following the onset of an illness six years previously, which involved lengthy chemotherapy, was believed to be infertile. Finances were not a problem and both women agreed to share the care of their adoptive baby.

Jenny first made contact with her local social services department, but was disappointed to learn that the likelihood of her being offered a baby for adoption was remote. Furthermore, Mary, the social worker she spoke to on the telephone, was of the opinion that as Jenny had no previous childcare experience, a short-term foster placement was by far the best option to begin with. If this went well, then her case for adoption would be strengthened. Jenny did not at this point disclose her sexual orientation but did indicate that she would need to discuss the situation further with her partner.

Following lengthy deliberations, Jenny and Susan decided to proceed in the direction advised by Mary, but felt that it was important to emphasize their wish for a long-term foster placement with a view to adoption. This was discussed in greater detail when Alan, the allocated social worker, visited them at home. Jenny was pleased that Alan did not seem perturbed by the fact that she and Susan were a lesbian couple, but they were a little surprised at the amount of attention Alan seemed to devote to Susan's lymphatic cancer, which as far as she could determine was in remission. Alan justified his interest in Susan's illness in terms of the local authority needing to be sure that they, as a couple, could cope with the demands of a child, particularly as they had little previous experience, as well as clarifying whether they would be in a position to provide care for a child until she or he reached independence.

Alice (aged 8) was eventually placed with Jenny and Susan. She was a child who had been taken into care when she was 6 years old, following the death of her mother from an overdose of amphetamines. Information about the first six years of Alice's life was patchy, although it was believed that she had endured a number of different carers, some of whom were known drug-users. Her previous placement with an experienced foster mother had come to an end and the local authority, in the absence of any suitable carers within Alice's extended family, were seeking a more permanent arrangement.

Alice was initially unsure of her new carers, but after a couple of weeks she settled surprisingly well. She seemed to like the organized feel of the placement and responded well to the attention she received from Jenny and Susan. In fact, things were going so well that Jenny and Susan decided, after twelve months, to apply for adoption. The local authority felt confident in undertaking the assessment, but the process was severely interrupted when Susan collapsed and was rushed into hospital. It quickly became apparent that Susan's lymphatic cancer had recurred and there was some uncertainty about her prognosis. Jenny was distraught and Alice too was beginning to show signs of distress. The local authority offered what help they could, but became increasingly alarmed at Alice's disturbed behaviour which she was now exhibiting both at home and at school. For instance, she had started smearing faeces and was seen to be masturbating in public. Given Jenny's preoccupation with Susan's deteriorating condition and the fact that she seemed to be turning to Alice for comfort, the social workers thought that it would be best for all concerned if Alice were offered a respite placement. This decision, however, had profound implications. Shortly after the move, Susan's condition improved and she eventually recovered and returned home. Alice, however, continued to exhibit disturbed behaviour and she never returned to the care of Jenny and Susan, since her behavioural difficulties had become so unmanageable that she required intensive therapeutic care in a specialist residential resource.

This painful example is presented as reminder of the complexities involved in the assessment process. In essence, the local authority, like Jenny and Alice, felt overwhelmed and instead of facilitating a 'working through' of the issues, actually contributed to the break-up of the system. Alice's reaction was perfectly understandable in the context of her early traumatic history, involving disrupted attachments and the eventual death of her mother. Like Jenny, Alice also needed help, but attempting to care for Alice by sending her away only served to reinforce the pattern of broken attachments and her sense of being unmanageable. A solution would have been to hold the family together and to work with them as a unit rather than separating them. The decision to use respite care actually deprived Alice and her prospective adoptive parents from reaching any real solution together. The extent to which Jenny and Susan's sexuality contributed to the eventual decision to remove Alice from their care remains open to interpretation, but it is arguable whether Jenny's increasing preoccupation with her partner's deteriorating condition provoked a higher level of anxiety in the workers than might have been the case were Jenny to be caring for a male partner.

Because of the complexities involved in negotiating the application process, the Lesbian and Gay Foster and Adoptive Parents Network was established in 1988. It exists to provide support for lesbians and gay men who are thinking about becoming, have applied, or actually become foster or adoptive parents. Those using the service have been empowered in the often fraught and mystifying process of applying to become an adoptive parent and have been helped in not giving up. With this in mind, what then are the questions that continue to trouble agencies and their practitioners in being truly responsive to applications from lesbians and gay male adopters? A central question seems to be concerned with the effectiveness of lesbian and gay parenthood.

Can lesbians and gay men be effective parents?

Arguments raised against lesbians and gay men as carers revolve around the questionable assumption that lesbians and gay men are less able than heterosexual women and men to parent effectively. Currently only a limited number of case studies exist on children fostered or adopted by lesbian and gay carers: consequently, it is not possible to examine the potential advantages or disadvantages of lesbian and gay carers. However, the issue of effective parenting has been extensively debated within the wider arena of whether lesbians and gay men should be able to become parents through access to new reproductive technology such as donor insemination and surrogacy.

What are the 'qualifications' for effective parenting? Three main issues have been identified with respect to children with lesbian and gay parents: the quality of family relationships; the extent to which the child is stigmatized through association with their parent's sexual identity; and the psychological well-being of the child, including his or her own psychosexual development. Traditional theories of child development have claimed that children of lesbian and gay parents will be disadvantaged on one or all three aspects (see Patterson 1992). However, there is a growing body of empirical research which finds that children of lesbian and gay parents do as well as children of heterosexual parents in these respects (see reviews by Parks 1998; Patterson 1992; Tasker 1997, 1999).

The quality of family relations

The research literature on the quality of family relationships experienced by children growing up in lesbian-led families indicates that in general these children experience as much support in their families as do children brought up by heterosexual parents. One national British study of primary-school-aged children raised in planned lesbian (single or two-parent) families assessed the quality of the mother–child interaction and found that the children raised by a lesbian mother had closer relationships with their birth mother than did the children in two-parent heterosexual families (Golombok, Tasker and Murray 1997). Analyses of children's data further suggested that the children in the lesbian mother family group were more likely to have a secure attachment style compared with children in the two-parent hetero-sexual family group.

Children in two-parent lesbian-led families could also possibly be at an advantage in terms of the generally greater involvement of non-biological mothers in childcare compared with involvement of most fathers in hetero-sexual two-parent families (Tasker and Golombok 1998). This greater involvement of co-mothers in childcare is likely to be achieved through a more equal division of household labour in lesbian couples (Dunne 1998).

To date there has been limited research on parenting by gay men. Data have mainly come from surveying gay men themselves about their parenting practices. Nevertheless, the studies that have been conducted suggest that gay fathers are considerate as parents. Bigner and Jacobsen (1989) concluded that divorced gay fathers generally seemed to be more responsive to their child's real needs, and yet were able to set more consistent limits for their children compared with divorced heterosexual fathers.

Two specific issues have been identified for gay men to overcome in their applications to be foster carers or adoptive parents (Hicks and McDermott 1999). First, there is the tendency to view bringing up children as 'women's work'. Second, there is the mistaken confusion of homosexuality and paedophilia. There is no evidence that lesbians and gay men are more likely than heterosexuals to commit sexual crimes against children (Strasser 1997). Research evidence also suggests that gay fathers in fact may be more cautious than heterosexual fathers in expressing physical affection to their partners in front of their children (Bigner and Jacobsen 1989).

Effectively supporting children within the family often involves considering family relationships beyond the immediate home environment. It is often suggested that relationships between lesbians and gay men and their families of origin may have been complicated by hostility during the 'coming out' process, although many lesbians and gay men do have good relationships with at least some relatives (Cramer and Roach 1988). Research also suggests that many lesbians and gay men develop effective social networks within the lesbian and gay communities, which function as 'families of choice' with mutual obligations of emotional, practical and/or financial support (Weeks *et al.* 1996; Weston 1991). One study on children in planned lesbian-led families has shown that most of these children had regular contact with other adults not in their immediate household, including their grandparents, other relatives, and male and female friends of their family (Patterson, Hurt and Mason 1998). Furthermore, children in regular contact with unrelated adults rated themselves more positively on general psychological well-being, and those in regular contact with their grandparents were rated by the mothers as having fewer behaviour problems with other children.

It therefore seems that lesbians and gay men can effectively parent children. It is the quality of the parenting that is paramount for children, and this needs to be assessed irrespective of parental sexual orientation. In certain circumstances, being brought up by lesbian or gay carers and the reassurance of safety in a same-sex household may in fact fit better with the particular needs of some children who have been fostered or adopted because of prior experiences of abuse within heterosexual family units.

Prejudice against children with lesbian and gay parents

Considerable attention has been devoted to the issue of whether children of lesbian or gay parents are more likely than children of heterosexual parents to experience teasing and bullying at school. Interviews with the adult offspring of lesbian mothers participating in the British Longitudinal Study of Lesbian Mother Families (BLSLMF) revealed that they were no more likely than the sons and daughters of heterosexual mothers in the comparison group to have experienced teasing or bullying during their schooldays, either in general or specifically in relation to their mother's sexual identity, although a slight trend in the data suggested that they tended to be more likely than the comparison group to recall being teased about their own sexuality (Tasker and Golombok 1997). These data suggest that children in lesbian-led families are no more likely than other children to be subject to peer victimization, but that they may be more sensitive to homophobic

remarks because of their identification with their family. How to deal with
the possibility of their children experiencing prejudice is a matter of major
concern for many lesbian mothers (Lesbian Mothers Group 1989) and the
sons and daughters of the lesbian mothers in the BLSLMF were generally
protected from prejudice because of the way their families managed and
negotiated the interface with the world outside the home.

Gay fathers also report considerable concern that their children may be
stigmatized at school (Wyers 1987). However, in the same survey only
one-fifth of the gay fathers reported that any of their children had actually
experienced any prejudice because of their father's sexual identity. Bozett
(1988) lists a variety of strategies that the gay fathers and children whom he
interviewed successfully used to deal with or avoid the possibility of
homophobia: from maintaining boundaries between the privacy of the
family and the public world of school to selectively disclosing to others to
pre-empt negative reactions.

Hicks and McDermott (1999) suggest that when lesbian and gay carers
are able to be open about their sexual identity in discussion with their
fostered or adopted children, they also might be in a better position to
discuss ways to prevent children from being harmed by stigma. If a carer is
not 'out' to them, children may unknowingly 'out' their carer(s) and then be
uncertain about how best to deal with a prejudiced response. In these
circumstances children may be more likely to experience teasing and
bullying, but may also wish to protect their carer by not telling them.

Well-being and psychosexual development

Recent research on elementary schoolchildren born through donor insemination to lesbian and heterosexual parents in single- and two-parent families
found that neither parental sexual orientation nor family structure influenced
children's psychological adjustment (Chan, Raboy and Patterson 2000).
Irrespective of family structure or parental sexual orientation, increased levels
of parenting stress, parental conflict and relationship dissatisfaction were
associated with higher levels of psychological problems among these children. No studies of gay men have systematically examined the psychological
well-being of the children; nevertheless, qualitative studies give no reason to
suppose that problems exist. After reviewing their interviews with the
children of gay fathers, Barret and Robinson (1990) conclude: 'They are like
all kids. Some do well in just about all activities; some have problems, and
some are well adjusted' (Barret and Robinson 1990: 168).

Issues of concern about adequate provision of gender role models often
arise for lesbian and gay carers in fostering or adoption assessments. It has

been suggested that lesbian and gay carers are often under greater scrutiny than heterosexual carers concerning their attitudes towards the opposite gender and opposite sex friends (Hicks and McDermott 1999). However, studies of children in planned lesbian-led families suggest that lesbian parents generally do not have restricted social circles (Patterson *et al.* 1998) and that these children are not confused about their gender identity and have typical gender role behaviour for children of their age (Patterson 1994). The large majority of the sons and daughters of lesbian mothers in the BLSLMF identified as heterosexual (Tasker and Golombok 1997), although they were more aware than young adults in the comparison group that lesbian and gay relationships were possible. Again compared with young adults in the comparison group, more of the sons and daughters growing up with lesbian mothers in this study were able to communicate effectively with their mother about their own relationships.

Research on the sons and daughters of gay fathers has focused on the sexual identity of these young adults. Bailey and colleagues (1995) found that the majority of sons of gay fathers in their survey identified as heterosexual with only 9 per cent identifying as gay or bisexual, a percentage that the authors argue is congruent with evidence of slight genetic inheritance. Other research studies that have interviewed the adult sons and daughters of gay fathers find that a large majority identify as heterosexual (Bozett 1987; Miller 1979).

From these research studies it seems that lesbians and gay men are able effectively to parent sons and daughters who grow up to be heterosexual. This should be no surprise as many lesbians and gay men grow up in heterosexual families. Nevertheless lesbian and gay carers can often give particular support to lesbian, gay and bisexual young people, and schemes such as the Albert Kennedy Trust support this.

Existing evidence would therefore suggest that there is no reason why children fostered or adopted by lesbian or gay carers should fare any worse than the biological children of lesbian and gay parents who feature in the studies reviewed here. Although it has sometimes been argued that fostering and adoption is regarded by heterosexual parents as 'second best' and considered only because infertility makes a biological basis for parenting impossible, it may be high on the list of preferences of lesbians and gay men for starting a family. Given the difficulties of arranging to have a child through surrogacy, fostering or adopting a child is likely to be a first choice for gay men in particular. For both lesbian and gay couples, fostering or adopting a child gives both partners in the couple a clear opportunity to have an equal parenting connection with the child from the start. In contrast having a child through donor insemination gives a genetic connection to only one parent. Over half of the contributors to a collection of essays written by lesbian and gay carers on their own experiences of parenting referred to fostering and adoption as their first choice in their consideration of ways to have children (Hicks and McDermott 1999). These authors also emphasize the importance for fostered or adopted children of hearing a clear story about how they came to be in the family. Lesbians and gay men often have particular skills in this respect because lesbian and gay parents have always faced questions about how they had children and how to give an effective answer to the children themselves is a topic to which many devote considerable attention (Mitchell 1998). Many children with lesbian or gay carers will also see a variety of family forms and support networks within the wider lesbian and gay community.

These points notwithstanding, some children who are fostered and adopted by lesbian and gay male carers will experience difficulties just as some children who are fostered and adopted by heterosexual parents also experience difficulties. Peter (aged 14), adopted by David and Martin, will be used to illustrate the point. Peter had initially been fostered by David and Martin when he was 7 years old. Although he had a disrupted childhood with few boundaries and an emotionally abusive mother, he settled extremely well into his new home and this reinforced his carers' confidence in being suitable parents for him. The placement was supported by the social workers involved in the assessment and by Peter's mother, who continued to have contact with him on a fortnightly basis. Although she had talked of having Peter home this was not considered appropriate or realistic in the long term. Gradually it became apparent that Peter would not be returning to the care of his mother, who by now had decided to move to the USA with her new partner, and a greater emphasis was therefore placed on David and Martin caring for Peter on a more permanent basis. They became increasingly interested in adopting Peter and he too welcomed this idea. His mother took some months to admit that this was in Peter's best interests and the adoption eventually went through when Peter was 10 years old.

For the first twelve months things remained settled and the placement was regarded as a great success. However, on transferring to secondary school, Peter became very unsettled and his behaviour challenged the status quo. David and Martin, although prepared in one sense, were not expecting the degree of challenge they received from Peter, which for the first time since he was placed with them included homophobic remarks. Not surprisingly this threw David and Martin's trust in Peter into doubt. They became quite reactive towards his abusive remarks and gradually they began to lose their confidence and perspective. Although they needed some assistance to stabilize the situation, they were reluctant to seek outside help as they felt that this would only reinforce the belief that gay carers cannot properly care for children. They also feared being blamed by the outside world and thought that they risked losing Peter. Instead, they decided to resolve the problem from within by continuing to confront Peter about his behaviour and his prejudice. However, this failed to contain matters and proved disastrous for the placement.

Peter became increasingly provocative in his behaviour, staying out late at night and drifting into trouble with the police and his school. When confronted by his form teacher he attempted to justify his actions by complaining that he was being brought up by '****ing poofs' who did not understand him and who were far too strict. Not realizing the situation at home, Peter's teacher questioned him further. On discovering that his carers were gay men, she became anxious and decided to speak to the head teacher. David and Martin were contacted at home and invited to a meeting at the school. On hearing what Peter had said they became angry and upset. David went on the defensive, insisting that Peter be confronted. The head teacher advised a different route, namely that they contact social services emphasizing the need for help in re-establishing their parenting of Peter, who was believed to be spiralling out of control. Social services were duly contacted and a duty social worker visited them at home. Peter refused to join the meeting but was later interviewed alone by the social worker. The social worker was instrumental in normalizing Peter's behaviour within the context of adolescence, a change of school, and his difficult and distressing childhood history. He also tried to assist David and Martin in thinking of ways in which they could regain their position as parents who had much to offer Peter. The issue of their sexuality was not ignored nor was it viewed as the most relevant aspect of the work. David and Martin's own sensitivity about their sexuality essentially played into the evolving dynamic and left them exposed. The pain and upset they felt in relation to Peter's offensive remarks gave him the ammunition he needed to attack. In subsequent conversations with him, Peter spoke of missing his mother and was able to put into words his own discomfort with David and Martin being gay. With the continued help of the social worker, all three were able to consider Peter's own pain and upset as well as his questions and concerns about being raised in a gay male household. The fact that Peter's own sexuality was now on the agenda did not go unnoticed but David and Martin were also forced for the first time to consider aspects of their relationship in relation to Peter. Eventually things settled down and Peter resumed his attendance at secondary school.

Conclusion

This chapter has discussed a number of issues facing lesbians and gay men wishing to become adoptive parents. At the same time, it has highlighted the challenges facing the heterosexual community and the institutions that rely on heterosexist assumptions in placing children for adoption. The development and implementation of equal opportunity policies which provide lesbian and gay men with equal access to a full and comprehensive assessment undertaken by properly trained and qualified practitioners remains an issue. Bridging the divide between those who, on the one hand, continue to question the validity of lesbian and gay men as adoptive parents and, on the other, boosting the morale and confidence of lesbian and gay carers themselves, is no easy task. Although this chapter provides a statement of how things are at present, it seeks to challenge the outdated notion that lesbian and gay men have little if anything of value to offer this and future generations of children.

Acknowledgements

The authors would like to thank Lois Williams for her helpful comments on this chapter.

References

Adoption Agencies Regulations (1983)

Bailey, J.M., Bobrow, D., Wolfe, M. and Mikach, S. (1995) 'Sexual orientation of adult sons of gay fathers'. *Developmental Psychology 31*, 124–9.

Barret, R.L. and Robinson, B.E. (1990) *Gay Fathers.* Lexington, MA: Lexington Books.

Bigner, J.J. and Jacobsen, R.B. (1989) 'Parenting behaviours of homosexual and heterosexual fathers'. In F.W. Bozett (ed) *Homosexuality and the Family.* London: Harrington Park.

Bozett, F.W. (1987) 'Children of gay fathers'. In F.W. Bozett (ed) *Gay and Lesbian Parents.* London: Praeger.

Bozett, F.W. (1988) 'Social control of identity by children of gay fathers'. *Western Journal of Nursing Research 10*, 550–65.

British Agencies for Adoption and Fostering (BAAF) (1991) *Form F: Information on Prospective Substitute Parent(s).* London: BAAF.

Brown, H.C. (1991) 'Competent child-focused practice: working with lesbian & gay carers'. *Adoption and Fostering 15*, 2, 11–17.

Chan, R.W., Raboy, B. and Patterson, C.J. (2000).'Psychosocial adjustment among children conceived via donor insemination by lesbian and heterosexual mothers'. *Child Development 69*, 443–57.

Cramer, D.W. and Roach, A.J. (1988) 'Coming out to Mom and Dad: a study of gay males and their relationship with their parents'. *Journal of Homosexuality 15*, 79–91.

Department of Health (1992) 'Review of adoption law: Report to ministers of the interdepartmental working group'. London: HMSO.

Department of Health (1993) 'Adoption: The Future'. London: HMSO.

'Introduction: Add sexuality and stir: Towards a broader understanding of the gender dynamics of work and family life.' In G.A. Dunne (ed) *Living Difference: Lesbian Perspectives on Work and Family Life.* London: Haworth.

Golombok, S., Tasker, F. and Murray, C. (1997). 'Children raised in fatherless families from infancy: family relationships and the socioemotional development of children of lesbian and single heterosexual mothers'. *Journal of Child Psychology & Psychiatry 38*, 783–91.

Hicks, S. (1996) 'The "last resort"? Lesbian & gay experiences of the social work assessment process in fostering & adoption'. *Practice 8*, 2, 15–24.

Hicks, S. and McDermott, J. (1999) 'Editiorial essay'. In S. Hicks and J. McDermott (eds) *Lesbian and Gay Fostering and Adoption: Extraordinary Yet Ordinary.* London: Jessica Kingsley Publishers.

Lesbian Mothers' Group (1989) '"A word might slip out and that would be it" Lesbian mothers and their children.' In L. Holly (ed) *Girls and Sexuality: Teaching and Learning.* Milton Keynes: Open University Press.

Miller, B. (1979) 'Gay fathers and their children' *Family Co-ordinator 28*, 544–52.

Mitchell, V. (1998) 'The birds, the bees … and the sperm banks: how lesbian mothers talk with their children about sex and reproduction'. *American Journal of Orthopsychiatry 68*, 400–9.

Parks, C.A. (1998) 'Lesbian parenthood: a review of the literature'. *American Journal of Orthopsychiatry 68*, 376–89.

Patterson, C.J. (1992) 'Children of lesbian and gay parents'. *Child Development 63*, 1025–42.

Patterson, C.J. (1994) 'Children of the lesbian baby boom: behavioural adjustment, self-concepts, and sex-role identity'. In B. Greene and G. Herek (eds) *Contemporary Perspectives on Lesbian and Gay Psychology: Theory, Research and Application.* Beverly Hills, CA: Sage.

Patterson, C.J., Hurt, S. and Mason, C.D. (1998) 'Families of the lesbian baby boom: children's contact with grandparents and other adults'. *American Journal of Orthopsychiatry 68*, 390–9.

Sandland, R. (1993) 'Adoption law and homosexuality. Can gay people adopt a child?' *Journal of Social Welfare and Family Law 5*, 321–32.

Strasser, M. (1997) 'Fit to be tied: on custody, discretion, and sexual orientation'. *American University Law Review 46*, 841–95.

Sullivan, A. (1995) 'Policy issues in gay & lesbian adoption'. *Adoption & Fostering 19*, 4, 21–5.

Tasker, F. (1997) 'Children with a lesbian or gay parent'. In National Society for the Prevention of Cruelty to Children (NSPCC) (ed) *Turning Points: A Resource Pack for Children.* Leicester: NSPCC.

Tasker, F. (1999) 'Children in lesbian-led families: a review'. *Clinical Child Psychology & Psychiatry 4*, 153–66.

Tasker, F. and Golombok, S. (1997) *Growing Up in a Lesbian Family: Effects on Child Development.* New York: Guilford.

Tasker, F. and Golombok, S. (1998) 'The role of co-mothers in planned lesbian-led families'. *Journal of Lesbian Studies 2*, 49–68.

Weeks, J., Donovan, C. and Heaphy, B. (1996) *Families of Choice: Patterns of Non-heterosexual Relationships.* Politics and Social Science Research Report no. 2. London: South Bank University School of Education.

Weston, K. (1991) *Families We Choose: Lesbians, Gays, Kinship.* New York: Columbia University Press.

Whitefield, R. (1991) 'Don't give in to pressure'. *Community Care* 24 January, 16.

Wyers, N.L. (1987) 'Homosexuality in the family: lesbian and gay spouses'. *Social Work 32,* 143–8.

For Kathleen

Somewhere in the dark kitchen
you counted the days
brooding uncertain
it not being the custom in those parts
to know the body well
only a slight sense
of a distant star's tremor
and your growing unease

Where did you turn
on the dark isle
a slip of a girl
past the old eyes and nods
of the women folk
quick tongued and sure
well versed in the signs
of curse and carry on and cure

Past linking young girls
the children of Mary
murmuring fruit of thy womb
the size of a rosary bead
our joyful sorry mystery

Fearful of glances
in the aisles of churches
that smelt of incense and oak
cowed before images
your scared and sacred heart
with no comfort in strangers
how could you keep faith
with the men of dark cloth
for giving your sins

In the shadows of mountains
where secrets are kept
you held your superstitions
with the sadness of stones
the dark and handsome stranger
in a hotel room

an exchange of letters
and the call of blood
leaves in the cup
our bitter brew

So having planned
our little emigration
a crossing of water
stars and palms
you sank in the swell
while I wallowed in utero
dreaming of whale mothers with their young
they sang in deep waters
with a grace impossible on land
I sympathised.

They took you in upon arrival
awaiting mine
into their hands
these hold Mary maiden midwives
meek and submissive
you bowed to their ushering
down the pristine corridors and passageways
to your unorthodox novitiate

I wonder if you saw the remnants
of the gingham girls
who had been looked over once
and somehow overlooked
I'm sure I leapt in you
like some baby baptist in some book

There in a white room
you passed the days of your confinement
dutiful and dreamlike
you kept me clothed and cared for
and then you let me go
to the good and smiling couple
with correct credentials
and an eager home
not at first suspecting
that the spin of wheels upon the gravel
would turn your insides out
You stood breaking by the window
as we left

II

Pregnant Bodies
and Rational Parenthood

Sallie Greenwood

I am 48, an Englishwoman living in New Zealand. I once thought that you could leave painful memories behind like unwanted parcels in the post office. I have found since that they follow you, these cast-off packages, forwarded on by a kindly postmistress. We need these memories.

So, I am an Englishwoman. I am also the mother of four daughters. I used to say mother of three daughters. To be the mother of daughters is a wonderfully unsettling position. My mother had only daughters and her mother before her. I am positioned firmly in the feminine, a feminine I have essentialized. I take other positions, ones that are anti-essentialist. Contradictions. There is a piece missing, though, in this genealogical jigsaw: my first daughter. Anne was adopted into a closed stranger adoption thirty-two years ago.

When I say thirty-two years, I am aware that for some readers this means antiquity. 'What could an old experience from another time and place say to us today? We have moved on, become more enlightened. That was very sad then but it isn't what happens now.' I have echoed this same arrogance in my own reading of other narratives.

I want to ask some questions, explore some of the differences I see between the open and closed processes. I want to use the personal narratives of mother (myself) and daughter to frame my exploration. My obvious emotional connection to those accounts makes my view partial. I make no apology for that: how could it be otherwise? In a positivist world, such partiality renders my exploration of little value. Not so, the partial voice is a valid voice, an important contribution to the total picture.

The mother's story. Already my use of the word 'mother' complicates the issue at hand. In calling myself mother, I refer to my relationship with my second daughter rather than my first, who was adopted. I do not feel so entitled to use the word mother to describe my relationship with my first daughter. If I say 'birth mother', the ground feels surer. I will not be criticized for this nomenclature. I am claiming a relationship which is only part, the incubating part not the nurturing part. I am the body not the mind. I will say more of this later.

My story is not unusual; it concerns the loss of a child when the mother is still a child herself. I was a 16-year-old with fantasies of motherhood and the belief that my condition demonstrated my adulthood, my special connection to another person, a man, a boy really. My story is also a little different from others, in that my first grandchild has also been adopted. My daughter's story of adoption is quite different from mine.

This chapter is not another personal narrative of grief and loss. That story has been told many times. Western culture and those colonized by western cultures know it. Knowing the story has led us to examine our adoption practices. We no longer believe that it is a good idea to deny the existence of relationships that society has deemed crucially important.

The value of the parent–child relationship, how much should be known about both sets of parents and, perhaps more critically, who should know it, have been central concerns of the adoption process. I would like to share some reflections on two aspects of adoption; one looking inwards at the mother and the other looking outwards at society. The distinction is of course arbitrary: we cannot separate one from the other; it is really a matter of focus.

The first – looking inwards – is the concept of choice, in particular the idea of 'choosing' the parents who are going to replace you. The second – looking outwards – is how the situation of open adoption confronts us with two mothers. I suggest that to have two mothers is extremely unsettling, because they embody a splitting. They are fecund and empty, mind and body, desiring and resisting. These contradictions are held tentatively in place by the 'sanctioned' maternal body.

I am also comparing experiences across countries as well as across time. The things I have experienced in New Zealand may not be representative of Britain where my own adoption took place. I have experienced one as a middle-aged woman, vastly different from the girl who relinquished her baby. I will not juxtapose my experience of closed adoption with my daughter's experience of open adoption. Such a juxtaposition would nec-essarily obscure points of similarity. I would say, however, that there is huge potential in the idea of openness and negotiation which does not exist in a tightly controlled process.

One of the things which strikes me clearly is that accounts of closed stranger adoption are painfully uniform both within and between New Zealand and Britain. I suspect, from discussions with people involved and anecdotal evidence, that accounts of 'open' adoption are, at least here in New Zealand, more dissimilar from each other.

I want it to be clear from the beginning that I support the concept of open adoption with its recognition of complex human relations. Yet, I realize it is that complexity which is seen as problematic. The move towards open adoption has been rising in western culture for some time, in theory. In terms of practice we are only just beginning the journey; old ideas and fears persist and inform our attempts to do things differently. Open adoption will not be an easier option.

Western society has for decades seen fit to regulate human relationships as much as it is possible to do so; for example, at what age one can have a sexual relationship and with whom, restrictions on whom one can marry, and on who is entitled to receive financial support or inheritance determined by their mode of relationship. The list goes on and penalties are meted out for transgression. Additionally, society has its own moral codes surrounding relationships, codes which do not always reflect the legal position. Such moral codes serve to ensure that people will behave in ways which society finds acceptable. 'Good' behaviour is coerced by the subtle threats of marginalization and exclusion.

Adoption has been tightly regulated by western authorities and has been imposed on colonized societies, eradicating alternative systems that had existed for centuries. Adoption protocols have resonated with society's racial and class biases, containing the assumption that the adopted child is 'moving up' and thus is benefiting socially from adoption.

Adoption is not regulated merely because it is a social relationship. Rather, it concerns women's relationships within society, particularly their sexuality. 'Female sexuality is threatening if it is outside the circuits of reproduction or relatedness' (Flax 1993: 65). A young unmarried mother represents sexuality for pleasure, even though this may not be the case; she is thus outside control. Maternity itself is constructed as asexual: 'Images of maternity are de-sexualised' (Flax 1993: 66). As Whitford (1995: 154) suggests: 'maternity ... is not an identity as a woman, only as a mother ... It is not a sexual identity as amante – woman-as-lover' and yet the relinquishing birth mother is positioned as particularly sexual. She is a paradox. The construction of the relinquishing mother is transgressive in the extreme; hence the need to regulate her.

In contrast to closed stranger adoption, open adoption is not so amenable to regulation and so small groups of individuals appear to be wresting control from patriarchal authority; social chaos threatens. This sense of chaos is heightened by the apparent loosening of moral standards and the attendant freedom of behaviour this appears to offer. A strong backlash to this threat can be perceived in terms of the return to 'family values' espoused by mainstream politicians. For family values read an apparently self-regulated unit of two heterosexual parents and their children living in the same house. The authority inside this unit resides in the male body and woman remains under the authoritarian gaze. This view was clearly apparent in a national survey (Code of Social Responsibility 1998) conducted in New Zealand by Jenny Shipley's National (akin to the Conservative Party in Britain) government. The rhetoric which accompanied the survey was saturated with individual responsibility reproduced within a nuclear family.

A young woman relinquishing her baby is not outside culture; she also carries the culture's ideological notions of 'family'. Indeed, her inability to provide this family for her baby may be one of her rationalizations for seeking adoption.

There is some notion of 'choice' associated with the concept of open adoption. But at the same time there are many variables which inhibit the freedom and the agency we commonly associate with choice. I am here using the notion of choice not in the sense of full agentic control as imagined for men by the Enlightenment philosophers, but with the assumption that we have some autonomy – an assumption that is probably more imagined than real. I do think there are degrees of autonomy and that some subject positions are less circumscribed than others. There is a psychological power in believing we have some control which may paradoxically serve to permit others greater control over us. I have placed 'choice' in inverted commas to denote minimal choice. For example, the only choice might be how you do something not whether you do or do not do something.

Closed stranger adoption was in the past fully controlled by the adoption agencies. Everyone followed the same process because there were few, or no, other options. The discourse of unmarried mother was incontestable. The illegitimately fecund body was a sign of deviance and the punishment was exclusion from society with its accompanying loss of citizenship rights. The deviant woman was to submit unconditionally to the authoritarian gaze of all in the hinterland. While oppressive, this state of affairs ensured uniformity, and a relatively unproblematic transfer of babies. Unproblematic, that is, to the bureaucracies. Having said that, at the eleventh hour some birth mothers found the courage to refuse the process and would not relinquish their babies. This slight possibility informed the process so that protection of the adopting parents was the paramount consideration.

My own submission to the discourse meant that I 'chose' to know little of the adopting parents or what they looked like, even though I could have seen them. The people who adopted Anne brought their two small sons with them to collect my baby. The woman who supervised the home tried to encourage one of the boys to come to my room with her to get Anne. He declined. Nevertheless, these were signals of the family's unusual openness around the process. After Anne had been taken downstairs and I sat sobbing, my two room mates (themselves relinquishing mothers who a few weeks later decided to keep their babies) were looking out of the window. They encouraged me to come to the window to see the family leaving. To their amazement I refused. The rationale I offered to myself, and them, was that it would not be a good thing to recognize the family if I saw them out in the street with my daughter; that it would cause me more pain. This may have been true, yet I hear my enacting of the discourse of closed adoption too. I was a 16-year-old girl making 'choices' of a kind.

Western society has changed since then: 'girl power' has arrived, Barbie is now a vet or a dentist, the Spice Girls pinch the bottom of the future British sovereign, women become prime ministers. Sex between consenting people is rarely seen as deviant; shame does not appear to be a strong facet of young women's sexuality. (Clearly, I am not talking about coerced and non-consenting sex but about voluntarily sexually active women who do not consciously desire to become pregnant.) The picture of sexuality that I paint is not uniform. Within our societies are people of differing ethnicities, religious beliefs and familial expectations. Sexuality and reproduction represent diverse meanings. Fear and shame will be aspects of the experience for some women in some situations.

Abortion is more freely available and is an option for some women. It is likely that a greater number of women who continue with an unplanned pregnancy today have 'chosen' to do so, as my daughter did. While unplanned pregnancies continue to occur, western society has developed different attitudes to its social organization. Pregnant women no longer hide their bodies under voluminous clothes, young women are assumed to be sexual (even when they are not), individual rights are taken for granted (even though they are circumscribed), state bureaucracies have been critiqued and have lost influence and power. Although social agencies and lawyers attempt to control open adoption, there is more room for birth mothers and adopting parents to develop their own process. I do not wish to imply that people have absolute choices, only that the process of adoption has moved slightly towards the main players and away from the bureaucrats.

However, legal processes often lag behind social ones and indeed may get in their way. One of the biggest barriers in New Zealand and, I believe, Britain (although not all writers would agree) is the lack of legal flexibility. The legal agreement available to adopting families is either guardianship or adoption. If the latter is chosen, the birth mother effectively loses any legal rights and can be expelled from any personal arrangements made, without redress. Guardianship may not offer the sense of security that many adopting parents are seeking in their arrangements. Open adoption is then largely dependent on the good will of those concerned, whichever legal option is taken.

There seems to me to be a strong class bias related to open adoption as it stands now. The best opportunities for open adoption appear to be those where particular forms of communication are valued and fostered. These forms require people to be assertive, articulate, consistent, invested in 'truth', reflective, able to articulate their feelings and be empathetic: the communication styles and values of the white middle class. Additionally, the people involved have to be able to negotiate a whole raft of emotionally charged dynamics which are not constant. This may mean that the best opportunities for open adoption are where there is minimal class difference between the mothers. It is not popular in New Zealand to talk about class, the old colony having been built on egalitarian myths. Certainly it does not have the same resonance as in the UK. Nevertheless, there are differences of power and opportunity between citizens that can be understood as class. As in the UK, class is intersected by gender and ethnicity. Due to a range of factors, there is often a class difference between adopting parents and relinquishing mother, with the adoptive parents occupying a more powerful position. This significantly complicates the issue.

When you read the profiles of prospective parents they naturally enough present the very best construction of themselves that they can. The construction is that of a family waiting only for a child. Hence, the aspects that are foregrounded tend to be the home, a well-fenced, spacious home and section (grounds). Well-fenced is important; 'good' parents provide a safe environment. Often there are animals and surrogate offspring in the form of nieces and nephews or friends' children who visit regularly. The parents' relationship is a long-standing, supportive one and the mother is presently working in a job that is secondary to her desire to be a full-time mother. This couple in order to qualify as potential parents have had to construct themselves in the image of the ideal family as imagined by western society. That is not to say that these things are lies. They are facets of people who have survived the processes (barriers) to becoming adoptive parents. They are required to submit themselves to scrutiny because their desire, which normally resides in the private realm, has become public. Once in the public arena they are in the ideological gaze and must construct themselves as legitimately entitled to their desires.

In the open adoption process the relinquishing mother becomes part of the scrutinizing process. Even closed stranger adoption often involves the relinquishing mother in sanctioning the adoptive parents. The family I desired for my baby was an ideological template (I thought it was choice): a couple who had been married for some time who were financially comfortable, were non-conformist in their religious beliefs and who already had a child, preferably a son. This was the family that received Anne.

As the mother who relinquished her 9-week-old baby to strangers, my fantasy is always of the complete family that she grew up in. I perceive myself as lacking, partially fulfilled by my other daughters, but still lacking. The fantasy I hardly dare have, which lurks around the edges of my mind, is one of blissful reunion; completion. The notion that Anne's adoptive family has been less than perfect does not bear consideration; it too lurks in the further reaches of my consciousness. It is a bargain struck, this exchange: I will give you my baby but you must provide the perfect family for her.

Until I began writing this chapter I believed that this spectral notion of family was merely the ideal of social agencies who were interested only in the best interests of the child. I had not realized that this was my requirement of others. Have I required this of myself? I certainly did for many years, failing of course in the attempt (in a way that my baby's adoptive parents were not to be allowed to). Through the extraordinary experience of parenting I have discovered my flaws and, more recently, accepted them. I have also realized my own implication with ideology.

When my daughter was dealing with letting go of her child, I understood for the first time in twenty-nine tears (this was a typing error – I left it because it speaks) what my mother experienced when her granddaughter was adopted. My mother had been stoical, being strong for me I suppose; she never cried or spoke about her pain. Her behaviour signalled her expectations of me. I would never talk about my pain, never cry in front of others, no one would ever know that I had had a child.

When I became pregnant at 15, my mother (who was divorced) and I were distanced. I think she had some difficulties adjusting to a relationship with an adolescent instead of a child. For my part I felt that I had been a failure as a daughter and projected that right back at her. My boyfriend and my fantasies about forming a complete family sustained me; it kept at bay the sense of fragmentation which constantly gnawed at me. When my pregnancy was discovered, the fantasy (being made reality) shattered.

There were class differences between my boyfriend's family and mine which gave my mother the edge of legitimized control over his family. Once my pregnancy became public knowledge and I was the deviant one, I lost any sense that I could influence the chain of events that followed. Every encounter with authority, doctors, social workers, social welfare, the mother and baby home, reinforced my sense of myself as deviant and helpless. I would fantasize that somehow my boyfriend and I and our baby would form a little family, be our own authority, but I had no idea of how I could make that happen. I saw with regret that my 'man' could not be the authority and there was some level at which I did not want him to be either. I had more confidence in my mother's ability to manage things. And so I made the 'choices' I could, which were the ones already determined for me.

I lost the fantasies that had sustained me through a lonely and troubled adolescence. I became an adult, if that means confronting material realities. I regained my mother and so became a child, if that means feeling totally dependent and safe. Perhaps she became once again the phallic mother of my infancy. I have a sense of exchange, my daughter for my mother. My mother died tragically six years later. (There is another related story unravelling here which goes beyond the boundaries of this chapter.) The cultural fantasy of family sustained me again. Almost four years after her death I gave birth to my second daughter.

My daughter too had clear desires about the family she required to raise her son. Without the shackles of secrecy, I think her desires may have been tempered by realism but they are less ideologically bound. She seemed to be in full control of the process for a long time. She chose the adoptive parents and insisted, despite the Department of Social Welfare's resistance, on meeting them earlier than was usual so that she could get to know if they were the people she wanted to bring up her baby. My daughter was behaving as a rational autonomous being. She, and the adoptive parents, worked very hard at establishing a relationship of trust and respect and talked openly about their desires for the baby. They exchanged ideas about discipline and freedom, about encouragement and restraint, about education and health, and a great deal more. They found they had much in common.

The profile of my grandson's parents provided by the Department of Social Welfare did conform to the usual pattern. Barbara and Brian (not their real names) were typical in their stable, supportive relationship, financial comfort and child-friendly environment. Yet, they were also different, finding ways to present themselves as real people with flaws. Such a presentation says much about their integrity which has been borne out through the sometimes difficult processes of my grandson's adoption. I suspect it was this difference that attracted my daughter to them, a signal of ideological resistance perhaps. There were other profiles of parents who were more privileged, who had more money, who had other forms of status. My daughter's 'choice' was concerned with other priorities.

However, social processes do not take place in a vacuum; people working counter to the expectations of society have to mediate their desires through society's institutions. Although we perceive our choices as an individual matter, often, as exemplified by the American preoccupation with self-help, we are motivated by unconscious desires and our range of choices is determined by the culture and the desires of others who may occupy a more powerful position. My daughter's desire to control the adoption process was continually thwarted by staff in the maternity hospital. I still feel angry when I think about how they hurt her with their clumsy behaviour. The nurses and midwives acted from their fear and misunderstanding, relying on ideolog-ically determined beliefs. They simply ignored her choices and rights and she found herself powerless. My daughter's experiences in the maternity unit are a telling example of residual attitudes to adoption, in particular to open adoption. The story is worth relating to show that the exercise of power is often unintentional and that we are enlisted in the policing of society's tropes and imperatives by our own identificatory processes.

My grandson's birth was difficult and, medically speaking, he was at risk of dying or of being brain-damaged. My first look at him through the plastic of the incubator as they wheeled him out of the operating theatre revealed a baby stained with meconium, struggling to breathe. Yet, I knew the instant I saw him that we had no need to worry, he would survive. (He is 3½ now and shows no evidence of brain-damage.) My other daughters and his new parents accompanied him to the special care baby unit (SCABU). I remained with my daughter to be there when she came round from the anaesthetic and to reassure her that her baby would be fine. My daughter's planning and relationship with her baby's new parents had paid off. Even in the except-ional circumstances of his birth they had been fully included and the involvement of all appeared seamless. Neither my daughter nor I had anticipated that the health professionals involved would not be able to navigate these unusual waters.

Initially, things worked quite well. We all visited with baby through the day, making sure that not too many people were there at the same time. My daughter was able to visit him at night due to the kindness of one night nurse who would bring her down in a wheelchair when everything was quiet. I believe my daughter cherished this time alone with her baby. Nevertheless there were warning bells. The nurses muttered about our baby being held too much. We ignored them.

I saw so many emotions in my daughter at this time: tenderness for her son; tolerance of us all wanting to be involved with him when I believe her desire was to be alone with him more often; envy when his other mother handled him, which was reciprocated. The two women wanted to be kind to each other and they expressed an openness that allowed them to talk about their feelings and to negotiate ways of behaving. I witnessed huge generosity of spirit. Altruistic concern for her sick son prompted my daughter to express breast milk for him so that he could at least have a ten-day start with the balanced nutrients and immunity protection supplied in breast milk.

I understood for the first time the pain that my own mother had experienced at the loss of her granddaughter. There is something about birth that collapses the boundaries between the woman giving birth, her mother and her child. I experienced it with the birth of my second daughter and again with the birth of her son. I occupied a different position in the triangle this time.

Despite the initial appearance of acceptance displayed by staff, within a couple of days we began to notice small things that indicated their high level of discomfort, although they would never admit it even when they were given the opportunity to do so. It seemed to me that they could not cope with, and had no cognitive framework for understanding, the notion of two caring and involved mothers, and therefore they had no means of articulating this. To be fair, this is how many people feel when confronted with the reality of open adoption rather than just the principle. Ideas are clean, compartmentalized, rational. Behaviour is sullied with desire and conflict.

I believe that the relationship demonstrated by my daughter and Barbara challenged the notions of motherhood that the nurses and midwives held. They continued to cast the two mothers as 'good' and 'bad' and behaved protectively towards Barbara and in an increasingly hostile way towards my daughter. There were many incidents which indicated to us that the staff considered my daughter to be a 'bad' patient and a 'bad' mother. The breast milk carefully expressed by my daughter repeatedly lay in the SCABU fridge and her son was given formula. I found this one of the most interesting expressions of their discomfort. Was there a suspicion that bonding might somehow be contrived through the protein from my daughter's breasts? Was she perceived as the wicked queen transmitting a poison which would turn the baby away from the 'good' mother? Did the presence of a bodily substance tie her inextricably to the realm of the body, the unclean, the tainted, juxtaposed with the rational mother who would act in the baby's best interests? I think it was all of these and more.

My daughter's intention had been to remain in hospital for ten days with her baby, sharing his care with Barbara and Brian and creating memories for later. Instead, seven days post-op, leaking breast milk and devastated by the undermining of everything she had attempted to do in the adoption relationship, my daughter left her baby in the hospital. She and I returned two days later, rented a motel room, and discharged him from the hospital. We spent the day with him. Barbara and Brian collected him that night to take him home. The next day my daughter went to the lawyer to sign the preliminary papers and we had lunch with Barbara and Brian.

The nurses' and midwives' behaviour led me to think about splitting, which is the second focus of my reflections. The maternal is not a stable category and has been destabilized by technological changes that have permitted the splitting of maternal functions such as surrogacy, in vitro fertilization (IVF) and lesbian parenting (Ireland 1993). Yet the maternal body has been a particular signifier of female identity. As Jane Flax has said: 'mother represents the impossible borders, the confounding of the dualities of Western culture ... simultaneously nature and culture; subject and other' (Flax 1993: 64). However, the relinquishing mother is rejecting maternal desire. She is resisting the 'normal' desire of femininity to reproduce. She is not truly a woman. Such a subject cannot hold together the unstable, but hope is at hand. There is another, a woman who has embraced her femininity, who occupies all the desire but whose body refuses fulfilment. We have then two mothers, the body and the desire, who together form the maternal.

Western language and, thus, thought are characterized by Cartesian dualism. In relation to my discussion, the paired terms of male/female and mind/body are central. Moira Gatens (1988, cited in Longhurst 1996: 27) argues that: 'not only have mind and body been conceptualised as distinct in western knowledges but also the divisions have been conceptually and historically sexualised'. The body is associated with the feminine, and woman is the inferior term. Woman is the lack, the absence (Grosz 1994; Irigaray 1988; Kristeva 1980). The masculine is associated with the mind and rationality: the ideal. However, some female bodies are able to come closer to the ideal than others by operating within a model of rationality and suppressing emotionality. For example, middle-class women have more status than working-class women.

Walkerdine and Lucey's (1989) research exploring the parenting styles of the families of academically successful daughters found that middle-class daughters were 'trained' to function in a rational way, to suppress strong emotions and to talk through rather than act out problems. This style may also be seen as the masculine style of being. Privileging of rationality in the behavioural style of middle-class girls ensures that they are well positioned to enter professions that require a rational autonomous citizen. These women, then, achieve more status individually but are also more likely to be in relationships with successful men from whom they gain additional reflected status. My point is that women who adopt rationality as their preferred style of being are positioned as more powerful in society.

There is nevertheless a contradiction when we explore the positioning of pregnant women. Robin Longhurst's (1996) doctoral research suggests that pregnant women are more unequivocally positioned as the body in terms of mind/body dualism. Although some writers (Gatens 1991; Grosz 1989; Kirby 1992) suggest that women are always associated with body rather than mind (even when they take a rational approach), Longhurst (1996) asserts that pregnant women are 'conceptually more aligned with the body than either men or other women who are not pregnant ... women are represented as becoming increasingly irrational, forgetful, emotional, that is, less-mind as their pregnancies proceed' (Longhurst 1996: 176). Maternity is problematic in western thought and is managed so as to suppress aspects of female subjectivity. The maternal body represents a splitting between woman as body, and therefore sexuality, and the maternal, as defined in Christian thought as being the 'ideal or spiritual' (Whitford 1995: 149).

In the adoption triangle I suggest that the split no longer resides in the pregnant body of the birth mother. She can be all body and sexuality, she is rejecting the ideal by rejecting motherhood. Another woman, who cannot escape her association with the body either, because she is a woman, but who is less tainted by it, can more comfortably represent the ideal or spiritual in our imagination. Her body, like that of the Virgin Mary, is not marked by the sexual act. She represents maternal desire in a purer form. Yet, while we may derive comfort from this tidy separation we are not entirely at peace with it, something niggles at the back of our minds.

Despite my daughter's rational approach she was not taken seriously; her pregnant body contradicted her rationality and positioned her firmly as woman. In fact, her insistence on rationality was deviant inside the subjectivity of the maternal body. Her style of behaviour, which ordinarily might have gained her status, was distinctly outside the subjectivity clearly marked by her fecund state. Perhaps her insistence on rationality also invoked the dualism of mind/body signalling the absent father. Perhaps the staff 'chose' the only present father, the one accompanied by a desiring mother – a recognizably authoritative family.

The health professionals 'caring' for my daughter and grandson could do this more comfortably when they were presented with only one mother. Talking with Barbara, she experienced the same dynamic operating; staff were more comfortable and thus more helpful to her when she was the only mother present. So it seems that, at a conceptual level, society feels more comfortable about adoption when the two mothers stick to their roles in the split. Yet, when we are confronted with the two mothers at an operational level we are still unsettled. Is this because we are unconsciously reminded of the repressed aspects of the split which are culturally contained inside the maternal body?

To summarize: although I was a deviant female, I accepted the subjectivity that was demanded. I disappeared from the public arena and articulated the discourse of adoption as 'doing the best' for my child. This is the position expected of a woman: to suppress her own needs for those of others, especially her children. I did not disrupt the status quo. My daughter, on the other hand, remained in the public arena and spoke from a rational, autonomous position. She rejected the dominant discourse and adopted a counter-discourse which was that she had the right to determine outcomes. This was not a subjectivity available to her as a pregnant body. She thus became deviant by attempting to occupy a position she was excluded from. The more rational she attempted to be, the more deviant she actually became.

My daughter's subjectivity was indeed transgressive; as a relinquishing mother she was apparently rejecting the feminine, the nurturing role. Simultaneously she represented transgressive feminine sexuality, a sexuality which she controlled for herself. Yet perhaps the biggest challenge she presented was that she insisted on being rational. Her way of being radically threatened the social order; that is, the order of the Law. How then, are we to proceed towards formalizing different arrangements if the women who are able to construct subjectivities capable of such arrangements are immediately marginalized?

Note

In the course of writing this chapter I have recognized some aspects of my grief which are also about an anticipated reunion. I recognize that my fantasies of reunion were imbued with desires to reconnect with my baby; perhaps to do the performative mothering, to be her mother. My reunion, if it happens, will be with an adult woman like myself. I cannot be reunited with my baby; she has gone for-ever.

References

Code of Social Responsibility (1998) *National Survey of Attitudes to Social Responsibility.* Wellington, NZ: Department of Social Welfare.

Flax, J. (1993) *Disputed Subjects: Essays on Psychoanalysis, Politics and Philosophy.* New York: Routledge.

Gatens, M. (1988) 'Towards a feminist philosophy of the body'. In B. Caine, E. Grosz and M. de Hepervanche (eds), *Crossing Boundaries: Feminisms and Critiques of Knowledges.* Sydney: Allen and Unwin.

Gatens, M. (1991) 'Embodiement, ethics and difference'. Occasional Paper Series no.1. Department of Women's Studies, University of Waikato. Hamilton, New Zealand.

Grosz, L. (1989) *Sexual Subversions: Three French Feminists.* Sydney: Allen and Unwin.

Grosz, L. (1994) *Volatile Bodies: Towards a Corporeal Feminism.* Sydney: Allen and Unwin.

Ireland, M. (1993) *Reconceiving Women: Separating Motherhood from Female Subjectivity.* London: Guilford.

Irigaray, L. (1988) *Speculum of the Other Woman.* New York: Cornell University Press.

Kirby, V. (1992) 'Addressing essentialism differently ... some thoughts on the corporeal'. Occasional Paper Series no. 4. Department of Women's Studies, University of Waikato, Hamilton, New Zealand.

Kristeva, J. (1980) *Desire in Language: A Semiotic Approach to Literature and Art.* New York: Columbia University Press.

Longhurst, R. (1996) 'Geographies that matter: pregnant bodies in public places'. Unpublished master's thesis, University of Waikato, Hamilton, New Zealand.

Walkerdine, V. and Lucey, H. (1989) *Democracy in the Kitchen: Regulating Mothers Socialising Daughters.* London: Virago.

Whitford, M. (1995) *Luce Irigaray: Philosophy in the Feminine.* New York: Routledge.

12

Changing Practice in Adoption

Experiences and Lessons from East Sussex

Barry Luckock

By the mid–1990s concern was growing about the effectiveness of social work practice in adoption. As the principles and procedures of the Children Act 1989 took effect in child welfare practice, the implications for adoption were explored from a number of rather different perspectives within the policy community.

In the first place, the new statutory orientation towards shared parental responsibility for childcare though partnership and participation reinforced the case for openness and contact in child placement practice, including adoption. This case continued to receive powerful endorsement from reported experiences of adults adopted as children and their birth parents brought together as a result of legal provisions allowing access to birth records (Adoption Act 1976, section 51)) and registration of interest in contact (Children Act 1989, sch. 10, para. 2). An overarching commitment to, and belief in, the benefits for child well-being of kinship links informed this perspective on post-Children Act adoption practice (Ryburn 1998a).

A second account, in contrast, drew attention to certain dangers for child welfare arising out of the operation of the Children Act 1989 and its presumptions of restoration and contact. Delayed decision-making about protection (Department of Health 1992) and care planning was identified (Department of Health 1994a) and extended deliberations about contact were said to contribute to this trend (Department of Health 1994b). A sense emerged in some local authorities and in the Department of Health that such delays could reinforce historic tendencies in the care system towards drift and impermanence. In this context the significant fall in the numbers of children adopted from care in the first four years following the implementation of the

Children Act 1989 suggested that permanence planning may have become marginalized as well as delayed. Both these perceptions were given powerful endorsement by the Social Services Inspectorate in its report in 1996 on the performance of local authority adoption services (Department of Health 1996). It was this report, additionally, which gave official sanction to the view that children adopted from care were typically of school age, with troubled pasts and clear memories of their birth parents as well as having extended care careers resulting from a combination of delay through contested proceedings, lack of appropriate families and passive case management.

This latter allegation confirmed politicians in their view that social workers themselves and the departments they worked for were the cause of the identified fact that large numbers of children in need of homes were not being placed with equally large numbers of couples who were available and willing to care for them. Hesitant and cautious proposals to improve effectiveness through legislative reform (Department of Health and Welsh Office 1993, 1996) gave way to a political call for the transfer of the adoption agency role from local authorities.

Professional efforts to revive pre-Children Act 1989 plans for a comprehensive adoption service which addressed the new challenges of contact, delay and complex needs had therefore to be pursued in the context of an unchanged legal framework and fresh uncertainties about organizational arrangements for service delivery. These efforts began to focus both on the more effective and speedy use of adoption as a permanent placement option for children who could not return home and on the improvement of the social work and wider services to placed children and their families, both birth and adoptive. This chapter reports the experience of one local authority in 1996–7 as it attempted to put this latter commitment into practice in collaboration with a voluntary organization. Findings from an independent evaluation undertaken by the Centre for Social Policy and Social Work at the University of Sussex are used to inform the discussion and analysis. Important messages about the nature of social work decision-making and about the process by which it might best be influenced in adoption emerged from the findings.

A 'complementary' model of through-placement care and post-adoption services

During the post-Children Act 1989 period, East Sussex County Council maintained a relatively high rate of placements for adoption.[1] Despite this fact, there was a recognition that adoption work was perceived by practitioners to be marginal within children's services as a whole at a time when the work was increasingly complex and the risks of disruption of placements were rising. Managers responsible for Adoption Agency work at County Hall took a lead in confronting this problem by developing a more centralized strategic overview of practice and decision-making and by consolidating and reinforcing the expert role of specialist adoption workers in the area-based family placement teams. While responsibility for case management and childcare decision-making in adoption cases remained with fieldwork practitioners and their line managers, the specialist workers were given a leading role in aspects of service coordination and provision in the post-placement and post-adoption period. These included the development of a county-wide 'letter box' system, individual and group support for adoptive parents and birth records counselling. In common with other local authorities, East Sussex faced increased pressure to develop a model of 'through-placement care' (Department of Health 1995) which integrated assessment and decision-making for permanence (managed in the field social work role) with post-placement and post-adoption support (led by specialist workers).

In deciding to enter into a partnership arrangement with the London-based Post-Adoption Centre, the authority rejected two other approaches to post-adoption service development. On the one hand the contracting out of the work to a specialist voluntary organization would be likely to reinforce, it was claimed, the split between care planning and service provision and have no impact on practice knowledge and skills development in the assessment and decision-making process. Such an approach also appeared reactive and problem-led. On the other hand, a fully integrated 'in-house' service would imply the consolidation of through-placement care in specialist teams for which finances could not be made available and which would still be faced with the question of when to transfer the decision-making and case-management functions from the locality field teams. The authority chose a third way

---

1   In the year ending 31 March 1996, East Sussex placed 5.6 per cent of its looked-after children for adoption compared with a national rate of 4.52 per cent (see Department of Health 1997; Ivaldi 1998).

in the form of a 'complementary' contract with the Post-Adoption Centre (Burnell and Briggs 1995). The existing shared responsibility for adoption between the field worker, the adoptive family support worker and the specialists in the family placement teams would be underpinned by the independent professional advice and direct service provision of centre workers.

In respect of fieldwork decision-making and planning, new operational instructions were issued which required practitioners to consult either the specialist family placement workers or the Post-Adoption Centre at the point where recommendations were to be made to the Adoption Panel about the placement of a child with prospective adopters. The consultation should include considerations about the needs of the child, post-placement contact and through-placement support for birth and adoptive parents. The Centre was also contracted to provide training for practitioners and consultation on the establishment of the new letter box system. In respect of enhanced service provision, specialist centre advice and counselling was outposted on a surgery basis on two days each month to one of three locations in the county. Access to the London helpline was also available for East Sussex residents. Groups and workshops for birth mothers, adoptive parents and adults adopted as children were offered in the county. Findings from the research into this enhanced provision are not reported in this chapter. In keeping with the emphasis on complementarity, contract implementation was overseen by a steering group of key stakeholders. Chaired by the Principal Service Manager for Children's Service (who was also chair of the Adoption Panel) the group included representatives of the three main adoption self-help groups in the county, i.e. PPIAS (now Adoption UK), NORCAP (the National Organization for Counselling Adoptees and Parents) and Natural Parents Network in addition to Social Services Department staff from County Hall and from the family placement teams who were most closely associated with Adoption Agency work.

In these ways an attempt was made in one local authority in the mid–1990s to kick-start the process by which it was hoped the adoption work of the Social Services Department would be transformed. Championed by the chair of the Adoption Panel and the Adoption Staff Officer, the strategy sought to shift the focus of the work of the department in adoption towards a through-care perspective based upon improved assessment, better informed decision-making and more active care and contact planning. The 'Complementary Contract' seemed to provide a practical way forward for local authorities seeking to address the challenge of service development in contemporary adoption where 'the changing characteristics of children more likely to be adopted; the emotional links that some of the children continue to have with members of their birth family which has led to a shift in emphasis from closed to more open arrangements; and the trend towards a concept of adoption as a contract for care' (Department of Health 1995: 3) made the task increasingly complex.

Methodology

During the first year of operation of the Contract (1 January–31 December 1996) the Adoption Panel 'approved' fifty children for adoption. Contrary to the impression given at the time by the Department of Health (1996: 31), that almost half of all children being referred for adoption were 6 years of age or more, the East Sussex approvals included sixteen infants under 1 year and twenty-two toddlers aged 1–3 years. Only twelve children were 4 years or older. An analysis of the national profile of children adopted from care (Ivaldi 1998) confirms the fact that the large majority of such children are under 5 on placement. For the purpose of the evaluation of the effects of the Contract on social work decision-making, a sample was selected of twenty-seven children from twenty families, being all those children both approved and 'matched' with adoptive parents in 1996. This sampling method had the benefit of capturing all matching decisions on post-Contract approvals at the expense of over-representing infants and toddlers for whom such decisions were more speedily made. Data were raised through file analysis on each case and from semi-structured interviews with the child's social worker in sixteen of the twenty cases (twenty-two of the twenty-seven children). The findings from this study not only demonstrated the extent of the impact of the Contract on local practice but also illuminated the nature and dynamics of decision-making in adoption more generally.

Social work decision-making and the impact of compulsory consultation

As far as the process of compulsory consultation is concerned, the Contract was found to have had a limited impact on the process of social work decision-making during its first year of operation. Neither procedural requirements to consult, which went largely unheeded, nor panel policy on best practice, which was expected to be uncertain and unpredictable, had a significant impact on the way social workers used expert advice to reach decisions in the first year of the Contract. Social workers were pleased to have access to a new source of expert and independent advice, and were generally active in their use of consultation on both substantive and procedural issues but they were equally certain that it was up to their own professional discretion whether or not or when they consulted and to what extent the advice received influenced their decision.

So for example, practitioners used external consultation with the Post-Adoption Centre over matching, contact and post-placement support decisions in one-third of the cases and sought the advice of a specialist family placement worker in three-quarters of the cases. Their decision to do so, however, resulted from the exercise of their professional discretion rather than from their respect for any procedural requirement. Indeed, and unsurprisingly, social workers had a very varied understanding of their new obligation to consult formally. Instead when they sought advice they did so first because they felt personally and professionally responsible for the particular planning decision yet uncertain or ambivalent about the right course of action. Where cases were complex, and options contested, consultation with supervisors alone did not always contain anxiety and produce the confidence required to decide. Any inexperience of the practitioner or supervisor accentuated the impulse to consult. The primary role of consultation in these circumstances was to help the practitioner reach or confirm a substantive decision. Social workers reported in positive terms about the helpfulness of the advice of the Centre, the independence of which was particularly highly valued where proposals were contested, and they also appreciated the availability of specialist family placement workers. But they also chose other sources of professional advice in and beyond the department and in accordance with their own judgement about what help they needed at the time. Their combined sense of professional responsibility to decide and personal anxiety about getting the decision right, especially over questions of contact, was further amplified for social workers by their perception that the Adoption Panel deliberations on their recommendations in these matters would be unpredictable in their focus. Hence consultation played a role in the process of justification of a decision already taken as well as in providing advice about the substance of the decision itself. In these circumstances practitioners consulted the staff officer and specialist workers in order to be advised about how best to ensure that their recommendations were framed in accordance with the current predilections of the panel.

On the evidence of the early East Sussex experience attempts to bring expert opinion to bear on adoption decisions by social workers through procedural requirements to consult underestimate the complex process of substantiation and justification that characterizes the decision-making process.

Intuition and incrementalism in social work practice

While consultation helped social workers clarify and inform their deliberations about aspects of a case, the research found that it had a limited impact on both placement decisions and through-care planning. Intuitive and incrementalist approaches continued to characterize practice. Matching decisions were based on highly subjective considerations rather than on any method of calculation derived from the assessment of a child's needs and the capacity and commitment of prospective adoptive parents to meet those needs. Decisions about birth family contact and about post-placement and post-adoption support were not strategic in focus resulting in a general absence of agreed arrangements at and beyond placement. Consultancy itself was shown to have had a significant impact upon social work aspirations about contact, with practitioners being more likely to seek advice on this question than on others and in all cases making positive proposals for continued links of one kind or another after adoption by the time of the placement. To a lesser extent, recognition of the question of through-placement support was also increased, with general commitments to help being made in half the matching reports presented to the Adoption Panel. However, these signs of a shift in social work perception about the need to exercise through-care responsibilities were not translated into new approaches to the decision-making and case-planning task. Instead, the limited impact of consultancy exposed some significant structural dynamics which appeared to be inhibiting practice change in adoption.

In the first place, the dominance of intuitive over calculative methods in matching a child to prospective adopters was striking. Practitioners were as likely to embark on a sequential process of visiting eligible prospective adopters and selecting the first appropriate family as they were to visit all such adopters before then selecting the most suitable family. While they had prepared their own mental list of criteria prior to this selection process the actual decision itself was very often instinctive in nature with social workers speaking of using 'gut feeling' and of the particular parents 'feeling right'. There has long been recognition that individuals in organizations simplify decision-making over complex problems by reducing to the most salient the information used and then selecting the first option that satisfies the narrowed-down criteria (see e.g. Beach 1997). However, the social workers in the study used this 'bounded' approach to problem-solving within a wider decision-making framework which reinforced the potential for using their discretion to exclude as well as to distil relevant facts. Two main structural problems were apparent in this respect. First, the department was not, in 1996, making use of the 'Looking After Children' (LAC) materials and had no other standard means by which practitioners could assess and record the needs of children awaiting placement. Additionally, and of much greater importance, the assessments that were used to inform decisions about placement were normally made within the child protection process and for court or conference. As a result, decisions about adoption which concerned future care-taking needs were derived from assessments of current and past parenting harms and risks. The Adoption Panel scrutiny at the matching stage, notwithstanding the procedural improvements sought in the Contract, provided an inadequate counterweight to this retrospective and harm-focused assessment and decision-making process. A future-orientated, life-cycle perspective on what might be called the permanence needs of the child does not automatically emerge within current protection and care planning mechanisms.

The absence of an effective operational framework which demanded a strategic focus for placement choice and for contact and through-placement planning provided the context for incrementalist approaches to this work. These approaches were reinforced by three main practice dynamics. First, in contested cases social workers reported on the difficulty they faced in working collaboratively with birth parents over future contact and support plans. For the birth parents, matching and placement for adoption represent a final confirmation of the formal loss of their child. In some cases their response was to continue or escalate their battle with the local authority in order to sustain their interest in their children. In other cases parents retreated from any association with the social worker, sometimes by moving to another part of the country. In one case a mother tried to hang herself shortly after the placement. In these circumstances social workers were faced with the task of engaging angry, desperate or absent parents in plans for future contact with their children when grief and grievances remained unresolved. Strategic approaches to post-adoption arrangements require joint planning by practitioners and birth parents but there are intrinsic difficulties to confront. While the social worker is required to establish long-term child-centred plans from the earliest possible stage in the legal process,[2] the parents and other relatives will still be using that same process to fight the assumptions about their caretaking capacities and commitments upon which such plans are based. It is not entirely surprising in these circumstances that post-adoption contact

2   See Department of Health (1998) in which official policy went so far as to demand that a child for whom adoption was planned should be matched with prospective adopters prior to the final care hearing.

plans, in particular, and arrangements for their implementation were so rarely secured at placement.

Second, inherent problems could, however, be mitigated or compounded by the perspective taken by the practitioner on the question of contact in each individual case. In lieu of any authoritative professional or policy principles in relation to the issue, practitioners used their discretion to mobilize and manage contact plans and to make arrangements for support for birth parents. Both social work attitudes themselves towards the task of supporting the birth family link and the practice methods they used varied widely. The central importance of active and inclusive social work practice in creating and sustaining effective contact for children in care has long been identified (Millham *et al.* 1986). Similar practice dynamics may now emerge in respect of post-adoption contact. While the East Sussex study could not provide information on any correlation between levels of social work intervention and contact planning outcomes, there was striking anecdotal evidence of the way in which social work attitudes about birth parents could affect practice. In some cases the social work approach seemed to be based upon little more than commiseration. Practitioners spoke of their twin feelings of frustration and pity where birth parents had failed the child in question, especially where previous children had been removed. They felt sad about the lamentable position these parents were in and recognized their grief but they were not thereby persuaded that their own professional responsibility extended to the continued pursuit of parental involvement in care planning. In other cases practitioners spoke in terms of respect rather than regret when they explained how they had tried to continue work with birth parents through periods of conflict, anger and grief. This approach was more hopeful that something wider might be redeemed from the particular loss of this child and clear in its commitment that active practice was demanded.

Respectful, as opposed to merely regretful, attitudes to birth parents were not necessarily associated with the establishment of purposeful and specific contact plans which were generally absent at the placement stage when research interviews were undertaken. However, it is difficult to see how, without such a stance at this stage, sustainable plans of whatever degree or type of contact could be secured. Indeed, although social workers reported a positive commitment to post-adoption contact in all cases, including a hope that it would involve face-to-face meetings with birth parents in one-third of the cases (and with siblings in three-quarters of the sample), there was much continued uncertainty about who should or would be responsible for actually negotiating arrangements and for managing them over time. In half the cases parents were actually no longer in touch with their children at placement and the lack of any reliable means of re-engaging and supporting birth parents suggested that it would be difficult to realize. Even letter box contact seemed compromised by these facts.

Third, the final practice dynamic inhibiting strategic through-placement planning in adoption concerns the organization of responsibility for decision-making and direct practice following placement and the changing balance of power within the professional and family system. The East Sussex study did not include interviews with the adoptive families' social workers but the fieldwork practitioners holding case responsibility generally spoke well of their joint working relationship with these support workers. Their accounts were consistent with the findings of the Maudsley Adoption Study (Quinton *et al.* 1998a) in respect of the largely positive reports made about shared arrangements for initial post-placement visits and direct work with adoptive parents and newly placed children. The Maudsley study itself made no attempt to examine decision-making, planning and implementation mechanisms for contact and birth family support, giving the impression that these matters occupied little professional time. In East Sussex in 1996–7, while deliberations about these questions were far more salient for practitioners, there was still no formal protocol for the organization of the dual shift from field-based case management towards joint professional working, on the one hand, and from professional care planning itself to adoptive parent authority and control on the other.

In this context the absence, uncovered in the research, of the written post-placement care plans exhorted by the Social Services Inspectorate is, perhaps, unsurprising (Department of Health 1995). Fewer than one in three matching reports included details about such plans and no social worker spoke about having negotiated one which set out the purpose of support and the means by which it would be achieved. However, on the question of where the responsibility might lie for producing and implementing such plans the SSI itself remained uncertain. In the national discussions which formed the backdrop for the development of the Complementary Contract in East Sussex the question was left open as to whether it was the adoptive family support worker or the child's social worker who should take the lead responsibility in this work (Department of Health 1995: 28). The East Sussex social workers themselves held differing views – the case being made for either model. Moreover, they raised the larger issue about the extent to which post-placement care planning and service provision arrangements could be seen as a matter for the professionals. Indeed, it was not at all apparent to these practitioners that any strategic case management function remained once the placement had been successfully made. Practice was firmly based on the assumption that the adoptive parents would soon be fully in the driving seat so far as decisions about post-adoption contact and family support were concerned. This perspective was clearly consistent with the continued legal presumption of the irrevocable transfer of full parental responsibility to new parents on adoption. The research thereby illuminated the extent to which practice is conditioned by the fresh start legacy of British adoption as much as by continued uncertainty about which particular practitioner should take responsibility for taking the lead. Evidence from the decision-making process prior to placement illustrated this fact in two main ways.

At first the matching recommendation itself was justified by practitioners very often by reference to considerations of assimilation. In particular it was suggested that the prospective adopters chosen for a child resembled that child and that they were realistic about his or her prospects. Physical resemblance was important in one-third of the cases reported, sociocultural similarities were central in at least one-half with considerations of class and education particularly salient for practitioners in a largely white English sample group. Class and cultural compatibility was so strongly valued because it seemed to offer some guarantee that new parents would have realistic expectations of the child's capabilities given their difficult backgrounds. Social workers spoke of the need for parents to accept the child for what she was. This search for realism and resemblance in order to discount risks involved in the transplant of a child to a new family was complemented by the approach of the Adoption Panel to post-placement support. Whereas the Contract, with its through-placement and post-adoption care perspective, hoped the panel discussion would focus on the new responsibility of the local authority to offer support to the adoptive family, in fact the scrutiny fell more often, in three cases out of four, on the adoptive parents' responsibility to make themselves available for such support.

Arguably both professional and agency practices in these ways demonstrated a clear recognition of their impending loss of authority and control over the care of the child in question and practitioners adapted their decision-making to the reality of the legally enduring fresh start model of adoption. By contrast exhortations about a new strategic approach to post-adoption care planning based in continued shared responsibility for child care, however well focused in the Complementary Contract, were insufficient in themselves to shift practice.

Changing practice in adoption: the messages from research

The evaluation of the innovative East Sussex/Post-Adoption Centre Complementary Contract provides an insight into a number of policy and practice dynamics that need confronting if the aspiration of establishing comprehensive adoption services in local authorities is to be realized. In its own terms, the new service was delivered as commissioned during the study period (for details of the implementation and development of the contract, see Burnell and Briggs 1997). As the foregoing discussion has shown, the quality of the specialist intervention was never in question. This was a service highly valued by the very large majority of people who made use of it. The research findings strongly endorse the view that skilled, expert and independent advice has an important role to play in adoption services. They also help clarify how best this role might be organized and how, more generally, changing practice in adoption can be achieved.

In respect of the objective of orienting social work decision-making and care planning towards a through-placement and post-adoption perspective the main research message concerns the timing and the focus of any such intervention. The Contract targeted the matching stage and the Adoption Agency decision-making process. On the evidence of the research this was too late to pre-empt the consolidation of the intuitive and incremental patterns of practice reported by the social workers or to dislodge this momentum. If practice is to be influenced it is the local authority care-planning process itself rather than the Adoption Agency that will need to be the prime target for change. The operational lead for the Contract originated in the procedural regime underpinning the Adoption Agency function, not from any fully coherent and clearly articulated permanence policy for all looked-after children. Such policies are essential if the focus of assessment and planning is to be shifted towards the achievement of specified long-term outcomes and away from just the mitigation of past harms and risks.

The research confirmed that expert consultation plays an important, if complex, role in the decision-making process and that social work professionalism rather than procedural injunction provides the impetus for its use. It is clear that practitioners make use, first, of proximal sources of advice and expertise in situations of uncertainty or where justification of proposals is felt necessary. This included consultation with specialist practitioners in the family placement teams. Calls to the Post-Adoption Centre tended to concern particularly disputatious or troubling cases or involve inexperienced practitioners or supervisors. So long as any provision made includes the continued possibility that practitioners can have access to independent advice, which by definition is not readily available in-house, then there must be a case for deploying external expertise to enhance the capacity and capability of the local, internal sources. The need for experimentation with arrangements that use expert agencies to offer training and continuing professional development to practice supervisors and departmental specialists across the continuum of care planning is suggested by the East Sussex experience.

A shift from procedural reform in the Adoption Agency as a means of informing and influencing social work decision-making to the enhancement of policy leadership in the care planning process and the deployment of specialist external support to underpin the strategic case-planning roles of internal supervisors and family placement team consultants is a prerequisite for changed practice. Policy developments must be pursued that reinforce the integration of adoption work within local authority care planning as a whole rather than those which seek to separate the tasks and remove adoption to other agencies. Unfortunately the attempt of government to 'bring adoption back into the mainstream of children's services' through formal guidance (Department of Health 1998: para. 1), while seeming to recognize the central role of local authority adoption agencies, discusses care planning only in relation to political concerns about delays in decision-making and placement and the perceived need to get more children placed in a wider variety of families more quickly. There remains an absence of best practice advice about how to ensure such placements are designed to do more than just mitigate harms (or cut costs).

Even with the reorientation of decision-making towards placement arrangements that seek positively to maximize and support long-term child welfare in adoption, planning and implementation issues will remain vexed. Organizational and practice dynamics are currently institutionalized in accordance with the clean-break philosophy of adoption. There is, as yet, no consensus about the preferred legal status for adoption and hence about the nature of the relationship between adoptive and birth families and between those families and the state. Instead the issues are displaced into an increasingly animated, and at times quite personal, dispute about the benefits of post-adoption contact (see Quinton et al. 1997, 1998b; Ryburn 1998b). Equal uncertainty characterizes the discussion about post-adoption support for the adoptive family. Here, proponents of 'a different model' (Lowe 1997: 371), based on the notion of a contract between the state and the adoptive parents, struggle to reconcile the fact that the 'overall aim [of adoption] should be to continue to provide a legal mechanism by which a new and independent functional family, without the need for public support, can be created' (Lowe 1997: 386), with the recognition that the needs of some children will, however, require just such support. Hence the legally mandated contracts that would secure help for the child would reduce adopters' rights to exercise their independence by declining state intervention as much as they would force the local authority to stop shirking their responsibility in its provision. It is not surprising that social workers report their confusion about the best plans for through-placement support and post-adoption contact or that research shows how difficult it is for a local authority to transform its arrangements in these matters. In lieu of any new philosophical consensus about, and legislative change in, adoption the best that can be expected is that local authorities, first, establish a practice framework for facilitating the support of the adoptive family and the birth family link and, second, clarify the allocation of responsibility for service coordination and provision. This framework must enable the care planning and case management roles associated with the child's 'looked-after' status to be transmuted into the support facilitation role demanded by the child's forthcoming adoption status. The management of the role change is as important as the decision about who will take up the latter task. The allocation of responsibility itself must address the coordination of support, including that required to orchestrate the birth family link whatever the nature and extent of 'contact', as well as the actual provision of that support. The size and complexity of this latter task alone is now becoming understood (see Kedward, Luckock and Lawson 1999). Much work remains to be done before the respective advantages can be assessed of locating coordination (and service provision itself) within the local authority, in generic 'family support' or in specialist placement teams, or in expert, independent agencies.

The East Sussex/Post-Adoption Centre 'Complementary Contract' has demonstrated the importance, in the current emergent policy context, of innovation and exploration. The experiment has not only reinvigorated a permanence approach to care planning in the local authority,[3] but also exposed the kinds of forces at play in the process of changing adoption practice discussed in this chapter.

---

3   In 1997, with local government reorganization, East Sussex gave way to new local
     authorities: the remaining county of East Sussex and a new Brighton and Hove
     Unitary Council. Both have retained the Contract in amended form.

Acknowledgements

With particular thanks to Alan Burnell and Adrian Briggs, architects of the 'Contract', for their bold and hopeful approach at times of caution and conservatism.

References

Beach, L.R. (1997) *The Psychology of Decision-making: People in Organisations.* London: Sage.

Burnell, A. and Briggs, A. (1995) 'The next generation of post-placement and post-adoption services: a complementary contract approach'. *Adoption and Fostering 19*, 3, 6–10.

Burnell, A. and Briggs, A. (1997) 'Partnership in post-adoption services: evaluating the first year of a complementary contract'. *Adoption and Fostering 21*, 3, 50–6.

Department of Health (1992) *The Children Act 1989 Court Orders Study: A Study of Local Authority Decision-making about Public Law Court Applications.* London: Social Services Inspectorate.

Department of Health (1994a) *The Children Act 1989 Planning Long Term Placement Study: A Study of Experiences in Local Authorities of Planning and Achieving Long Term Placements for Children.* London: Social Services Inspectorate.

Department of Health (1994b) *The Children Act 1989 Contact Orders Study: A Study of Local Authority Decision-making around Contact Applications under Section 34.* London: Social Services Inspectorate.

Department of Health (1995) *Post-Placement Services for Children and Families: Defining the Need. Report of the Proceedings of Two Seminars Organised by the SSI.* London: Social Services Inspectorate.

Department of Health (1996) *For Children's Sake: An SSI Inspection of Local Authority Adoption Services.* London: Social Services Inspectorate.

Department of Health (1997) *Children Looked after by Local Authorities: Year Ending 31 March 1996, England.* London: Government Statistical Service.

Department of Health (1998) *Adoption: Achieving the Right Balance.* Local Authority Circular LAC (98)20. London: Social Services Inspectorate.

Department of Health and Welsh Office (1993) (Lord Chancellor's Department) *Adoption: The Future,* Cm 2288. London: HMSO.

Department of Health and Welsh Office (1996) *Adoption: A Service for Children; Adoption Bill – A Consultative Document.* London: HMSO.

Ivaldi, G. (1998) *Children Adopted from Care: An Examination of Agency Adoptions in England, 1996.* London: British Agencies for Adoption and Fostering.

Kedward, C., Luckock, B. and Lawson, H. (1999) 'Mediation and post-adoption contact: the early experience of the Post-Adoption Centre Mediation Service'. *Adoption and Fostering 23*, 3, 16–26.

Lowe, N. (1997) 'The changing face of adoption: the gift/donation versus the contract/services model'. *Child and Family Law Quarterly 9*, 4, 371–86.

Milham, S., Bullock, R., Hosie, K. and Haak, M. (1986) *Lost in Care: The Problems of Maintaining Links between Children in Care and their Families.* London: Gower.

Quinton, D., Rushton, A., Dance, C. and Mayes, D. (1997) 'Contact between children placed away from home and their birth parents: research issues and evidence'. *Clinical Child Psychology and Psychiatry 2*, 3, 393–413.

Quinton, D., Rushton, A., Dance, C. and Mayes, D. (1998a) *New Parents, New Children: Establishing Permanent Placements in Middle Childhood.* Chichester: John Wiley.

Quinton, D., Selwyn, J., Rushton, A. and Dance, C. (1998b) 'Contact with birth parents in adoption: a response to Ryburn'. *Child and Family Law Quarterly 10,* 4, 349–61.

Ryburn, M. (1998a) 'A new model of welfare: re-asserting the value of kinship for children in state care'. *Social Policy and Administration 32,* 1, 28–45.

Ryburn, M. (1998b) 'In whose best interest? Post-adoption contact with the birth family'. *Child and Family Quarterly 10,* 1, 53–70.

Roses in a Pewter Jar

The letter bears an Irish stamp
my own is not so visible
a celtic torque
to be worn around the neck or wrist
the wearing is a kind of bond or tryst

I see it is not written in her hand
I pause on opening
as I might pause before a door
I sense that once I enter here
nothing will be
as it has been before

The card has been carefully chosen
it is entitled
Roses in a Pewter Jar
it is tasteful
the note written
by her niece
is graceful

there is nothing more to say
the card confirms my dream

'We regret to inform you
Kathleen has passed away'

Mindless I form the words
of a polite reply

'It was so good of you to let me know'

Voiceless wordless the sounding
of my birthing
mourning cry

Who does this woman think I am

I breathe as if to catch the scent
of roses that are not really there
I call to mind the Magdalene
and the solace of her hair
I was annointed
yes I too was there
the Nag Hammadi scripture
bears the words
'the scorned one'
'the chosen one'
the story of my birth

13

Clinical Work with Adults who have been Adopted

Rose Golberg

Some things faced by adults who have been adopted transcend time: the implications of Oedipus' adoptive status and his knowledge or lack of it have resonance now. Some of what is faced may also be fixed by our social context: the patients whose experiences will be referred to in this chapter were in a particular situation which will probably be largely not the case in the future for those children who have been adopted since the 1980s. Now the adoptive child is likely to discover over time much about his or her origins: photographs of the birth parents, letters from them to the child, even the medical history of the birth mother and perhaps father will exist for the child, such records looked after by their adoptive parents or contained in an agency file. However, adult patients at present are tantalized by knowledge that can be partial in the extreme: names on a birth certificate and place of registration, perhaps father's occupation. Files when sought may be sparse, maddeningly random in what they contain. One adoptee found after a long quest that her adoptive records had been destroyed in the Blitz of the Second World War. All her and her own children's longing for knowledge about herself had been bombed out of reach. Many adoptions are happy and 'good enough'. But the challenges that adoption makes to all concerned can lead to difficulties, and this chapter is about those adult adoptees who feel themselves to be troubled and who seek help in psychotherapy. Our patients who are adopted are in a peculiarly painful position with regard to that distinctive search that brings many individuals to psychotherapy: for self- knowledge. For adult adoptees, the self and its origins are specifically problematic and complex. Yet, as adoption can be successful and reparative, so psychotherapy for and with these patients is particularly moving and can elucidate in a very acute way phantasies and realities that we all share.

Trauma and beliefs

Caroline Garland (1998) writes of trauma as

> a kind of wound. When we call an event traumatic, we are borrowing the word from the Greek where it refers to a piercing of the skin, a breaking of the bodily envelope … Freud (1920) used the word metaphorically to emphasise how the mind can be pierced and wounded by events, giving graphic force to his description of the way in which the mind can be thought of as being enveloped by a kind of skin, or protective shield. (Garland 1998: 9)

Garland goes on to remind us of how Freud thought that when a piece of traumatic reality is extreme, the mind may defend itself in an extreme way, by the use of delusions: 'A fair number of analyses have taught us that the delusion is found applied like a patch over the place where originally a rent had appeared in the ego's relation to the external world' (Freud 1924: 151). Freud is referring here to the delusions that are found in serious, psychotic illness. But I think that this notion of a patch applied over a rent or trauma can illuminate other situations, such as adoption. Here the trauma may be that of the adoptive parents' infertility, as Lousada (this volume) describes. Or it may be that of the series of moves for the adopted child: their removal, however sensitively thought about and managed, from the birth mother, possibly to a temporary foster placement involving new attachment and loss, before adoption occurs. Rustin (1990) writes of this:

> I think there is a profound ontological question for the child separated from its birth mother – I was born from her body, but she did not hold onto me. This is the issue raised by another of the ways children often speak of the natural mother – the Mummy whose tummy I grew in or came out of. To the shattering caesura of birth is added the disconnection between intra and extra-uterine experience. The mother known from inside – her bodily rhythms and the music of her voice in particular – is lost. (Rustin 1990: 5)

In the rent or trauma of adoption, I would use the idea of beliefs, in the place of delusions, as providing a patch to the ego. Ronald Britton's (1998) work on belief is particularly helpful in understanding how the adoptees (as well as the adopters) may develop precious beliefs about their origins, which it becomes the psychotherapeutic task to identify, explore, and help the patient to relinquish in some cases.

Britton (1998) itemizes the steps in the development and testing of beliefs which include the following:

- Phantasies are generated and persist unconsciously from infancy onward.

- The status of belief is conferred on some pre-existing phantasies, which then have emotional and behavioural consequences which otherwise they do not. Beliefs may be unconscious and yet exert effects.

- When belief is attached to a phantasy or idea, initially it is treated as a fact. The realisation that it is a belief is a secondary process which depends on viewing the belief from outside the system of the belief itself ...

- Once it is conscious and can be recognised to be a belief it can be tested against perception, memory, known facts and other beliefs.

- When a belief fails the test of reality it has to be relinquished ... As a lost object has to be mourned by the repeated discovery of its disappearance, so a lost belief has to be mourned by the repeated discovery of its invalidity. (Britton 1998: 9)

The Oedipus myth, the archetype of family life, includes a story of adoption and it is the misunderstandings and beliefs around this adoption upon which the drama of Oedipus turns.

Adoption and Oedipus

In the story of Oedipus, Laius, the King of Thebes, and his wife Jocasta are warned by Apollo's oracle that their soon-to-be-born son, later named Oedipus, is destined one day to kill his father and to become his mother's husband. The parents attempt to thwart the god's prediction by giving the baby to a shepherd with orders to expose the boy on a mountainside, his feet pierced to prevent him crawling to safety. The shepherd cannot bear to do what amounts to infanticide, and instead gives the baby to a fellow shepherd – of Corinth and a servant of the King and Queen of Corinth – to take him out of Thebes. The baby is brought to King Polybus and his wife, who are childless. They gladly take the child as their own, naming him Oedipus (Swollen-foot), from the injury to his feet. Grown up, Oedipus (now the Prince of Corinth) hears a rumour of his adoption which he ignores, but hears too of the oracle's prediction about him. Believing, or choosing to believe, that this refers to Polybus and the Queen, Oedipus leaves Corinth, hoping thereby to protect his 'parents'. In his wanderings he encounters a surly traveller, who arrogantly strikes Oedipus to push him from the road. Oedipus kills the evidently important traveller, who is, of course, his real father Laius: the fulfilment of the prediction begins. Travelling on, Oedipus reaches Thebes to discover the city in turmoil: its King has been murdered on a lonely road, leaving his widowed Queen, and the city is terrorized by a monster, the Sphinx, who kills all who fail to answer the riddle she sets. The riddle concerns the difference in the generations: who walks on four legs, then two, then three? Oedipus solves the riddle: it is a human being, at first a crawling baby, then upright, then as an old person whose two faltering legs are aided by a stick. The Sphinx's power is destroyed as Thebes joyfully receives Oedipus its saviour. He becomes King of Thebes and marries Jocasta, his mother and Laius' widow. The couple have children. All this emerges only slowly and agonizingly during Sophocles' play, which begins much later, with Thebes again terrorized, this time by plague and a terrible blight on all fertility. The oracle, consulted, reveals that 'there is an unclean thing, Born and nursed on our soil, polluting our soil, Which must be driven away, not kept to destroy us'. It is interpreted that the oracle refers to the unsolved murder of King Laius, and that the killer must be brought to justice in order to purify the city. The subsequent drama is of Oedipus' cooperation with this search, which becomes increasingly faltering and tortured as witnesses, including the shepherd, are produced and tell their stories. Oedipus too tells of what he 'knows' of his early life. It becomes increasingly transparent to Oedipus' hearers and to the reader what the truth is. Part of the drama's agony is in our witnessing of Oedipus' writhing struggle with his inexorable truth and the relinquishment of his beliefs.

Oedipus clings to the contradictory accounts of his origins, which have formed his beliefs about himself, when challenged by the dawning truth as Tiresias, the messenger and the shepherd contribute their cumulative evidence. For Oedipus his beliefs have developed to protect him from the facts which, as Steiner (1993) demonstrates, could have been available to him had he not turned a blind eye. These were the facts not only of Oedipus' actions – the murder of his father and his marriage to his mother– but also of his origins. These latter, which contain the catastrophic ramifications of his subsequent actions, he hides from himself by holding onto the beliefs he has continued to hold, in the teeth of the evidence, that his true parents were the King and Queen of Corinth. Earlier we have learned that Oedipus was long ago told that he is not his father's son. He had been reassured by his adoptive parents but 'the smart (of suspicion) remains' (Sophocles 1947: 47); he had consulted the oracle about his origins but was instead given the warning that he will kill his father and marry his mother. It is because of this warning that he leaves Corinth in order to spare his parents, as he still tries to believe them to be. The action of the play describes Oedipus, in the plague-ridden Thebes which he now rules, interrogating and blustering to discover the murderer of Laius. As the evidence increasingly points to himself as the murderer, and he becomes convinced that he was not indeed the child of the Corinthian King and Queen, he is advised by the chorus that perhaps he is 'the offspring of some primeval sprite', or nymph (Sophocles 1947: 56), fathered by a god: a delusion which is offered, desperately, by the chorus. He ironically thinks that he may be a 'child of Fortune' (Sophocles 1947: 55), and driven by a hunger to know, he cries that 'I must unlock the spirit of my birth ... I ask to be no other man Than that I am, and will know who I am.' The discovery of the truth leads to a moment of overwhelming guilt for Oedipus, but which none the less, as Steiner observes, he is able momentarily to bear. But swiftly guilt turns to hatred towards Jocasta his mother/wife, and then to horror as he finds her hanged body, and he blinds himself. The original rent of his babyhood's trauma had been patched over by his beliefs about his origins. These beliefs are torn from him in a moment of truth. Unable to continue to bear this burden of knowledge, he attacks his eyes, his organs of perception. In Oedipus in Colonus, the patch is now his omnipotent delusion of near divinity.

Oedipus had earlier gained the prize of Thebes, and of Jocasta, because he had braved the Sphinx and solved her riddle: a partial acknowledgement on his part of the immutable differences between the generations. But his actions of patricide and mother-marriage betray his underlying refusal of this reality. Thebes, which seems to represent some internal world struggling with reality, earns only temporary respite. The threat returns, this time in the form of plague. Beliefs must now be examined, and relinquished. This I think happens with some adult adoptees. They have perhaps accommodated and lived with their situation for many years. Then something returns: anxiety, depression, illness, which compels a new confrontation with the Sphinx/Plague's urgent demand for some fundamental confusion to be attended to. These symptoms come from a desperate fear that their origins are random, that their parents had no thought for them, and they have no place in their birth parents' mind. This can lead to a quite dizzying terror of having no place, no identity. Beliefs have shored up such adoptees, enabling them to live and work for a while. It is often at this point that adoptees may decide to see if psychotherapy – a kind of search for the individual's unique truth – may help them.

Why psychotherapy?

Among the different things that may lead someone to seek and then to remain engaged in psychotherapy can be the wish for self-knowledge, and a curiosity about one's origins. This can relate to that person's specific situation, but also to the concerns and confusions we all have about the differences of generation, of gender, of creativity and of death which for psychoanalysis centre on the story of Oedipus. There, the sickness of his city Thebes demanded that the truth be discovered about a great crime, the secrecy about which was corrupting Thebes with plague. Oedipus is quickly turned from a concerned king to a man directly implicated, but how, he does not at first acknowledge. The play traces his agony of whether to follow the need to discover knowledge or rather to recover the knowledge of himself that has always been so near to conscious awareness, as Steiner (1993) interprets the play. Oedipus' longing for and dread of knowledge of his origins is movingly echoed within the psychotherapy setting. Oedipus brings himself to confront his own truth, and, fleetingly, the consequences of his actions. The adult adoptee in therapy is similarly caught between a hunger for knowledge and learning – the epistemophilic impulse – and a dread of it. As seen, fears and cherished beliefs about the birth parents, feelings attached to the adoptive parents and to the adoptive placement of the therapy, these become the stuff of the therapeutic work, in which the patient's internal situation with these 'parents in the mind' can be explored.

The 'parents in the mind'

Lousada (Chapter 4 in this volume) writes movingly of 'the child in the mind' of the infertile couple who hope to adopt. I would like to extend this idea of an imagined child to that of parents in the mind. Adult adoptees come to therapy with, among other concerns and problems specific to the individual, a particular internal configuration which contains two sites, two sets of parents: that of the adoptive parental couple (or parent), and that of the parental couple in phantasy, which in their case is also an objectively real couple: their birth parents. The fears, hopes and other phantasies that other patients have about a phantasied parental couple, which they can explore in psychotherapy, contain a particular edge of reality for the adopted patient. If beginning psychotherapy itself can be characterized as a process experienced by all patients of adoption by and of the therapist, the therapeutic adoption takes on a powerful resonance for both therapist and patient when the latter is already, in reality, an adoptee.

The initial encounter with psychotherapy is usually in the form of an assessment or consultation. Over one or more meetings with a psychotherapist, the therapist tries to gain a picture of the patient, as Jane Milton (1997) puts it,

> of their inner world and the way it functions, and [tries] to understand the nature of the distress that they are presenting with ... The patient will, simultaneously, have the opportunity to assess the nature of the psychoanalytical process, and think about whether or not this is an investigation which they wish to proceed with. (Milton 1997: 47)

As a means to learn about the inner world, the transference of the patient within the assessment is thought about and commented on by the assessing psychotherapist. Transference informs how the patient may speak, behave and interact within the assessment particularly towards the therapist. It includes the patient's particular and unique configuration of feelings towards central figures in the past (such as parents) which are transferred to the present situation and refracted through it. The structure of assessment is likely to reactivate deep, old feelings and responses, which can thus be made evident and so accessible to thought and learning about during the assessment. The patient's phantasies or inner imaginary images and beliefs, usually at a largely unconscious level, operate very powerfully to help form and determine the course of the transference. Such phantasies derive from very early experiences, as well as probably inborn feelings and needs, and continue to be modified and elaborated in subsequent experience.

> Example – A 50-year-old man attends a first assessment meeting. He is too anxious to speak, and looks mutely at the assessor. This contrasts with the fluent, vivid written information that he had provided beforehand. The assessor feels puzzled, and tries to locate where she is with the patient, in his transference to her. It seems that he has split something between his written and his face-to-face contact with her. It emerges that in the former he addresses the phantasied birth mother, eager to hear from him. But the actual meeting with the assessor becomes like his actual encounter with the adopter; the assessor finds herself in the place of his adoptive mother, whom he had feared during his childhood and whom he would, mutely, watch.

Here, the feared parent was the adopter: one might foresee that the patient will experience difficulties in settling into psychotherapy, with a fearful transference towards his therapist and a diminished chance of being sustained by the hope and idealization that may carry many people through their early days in psychotherapy. Here the dominant transference seems to relate to the adoptive rather than to the birth mother. However, the feelings and thoughts about the birth mother came later to emerge in the course of psychotherapy, in the form of a kind of 'articles of faith'.

> Example – A woman reveals to her assessor that she was adopted, information that the referrer and others professionally connected to the patient were unaware of. The adoption had been known about by her as long as she could remember. It had not ostensibly been concealed in the family, with whom this patient's childhood had been happy and where the adoption was apparently successful. It later became clear that the birth parents were a repository for frightening phantasies, and had been quite split off from the day-to-day thinking of the patient. In her friendly and trusting response to the assessor (the benign adoptive mother), and perhaps recognizing that she found a containing 'adoptive placement', the patient was able to intimate the existence of a birth mother.

Here again the adoptive and birth mothers or parental couple provide a vehicle for a split between good enough parents, and a feared parental couple. Splitting is a process whereby the person splits (originally in infancy their mother) into two separate figures: a very good one and a very bad. At the time of infancy and sometimes in adulthood, for example in order to deal with great trauma, splitting can be most important in enabling the individual 'to organise their experiences, bring order into chaos by separating out and keeping relatively safe all those parts of himself and those of mother which promote life from those forces inside and outside him which threaten life and safety' (Salzberger-Wittenberg 1970: 60). However, this does not provide a permanent solution: it is hoped that there will be a movement towards integration. In the absence of integration, the individual is frozen in a world of extremes, where development and growth falter and life is impoverished. In the example just given, the patient came to explore how the adoptive parents' infertility had been rendered a 'non-issue'. The patient's worries about their internal damage of their infertility had therefore been driven underground, and, to protect the adoptive parents, these worries were projected into the phantasied birth parents who became damaged, terrifying figures that could not be entertained in the mind.

The adoptee's protective need to split is particularly evident in these examples: for other adoptees, things are less clear and can be a source of great confusion to those who may be vulnerable mentally.

> Example – A 35-year-old woman had been distressed by symptoms of major mental illness. One source of her distress was her lack of a sense of identity, and fear of being possessed by evil spirits. This seemed to be connected with her feelings around her adoption. She had loved her

adopted mother, also a woman who sounded disturbed. She had known her birth mother, towards whom she also had warm feelings. However, her upbringing had been very difficult and one of her problems seemed to be where to locate her hatred, in her need to maintain both mothers intact. Her phantasy mother was, for her, a real living woman whom she knew and had concern for. In her plight, she split off and projected or pushed outside herself her hate into devil figures, who then threatened to 'possess' her. It would seem that this symptom communicated her feelings about being adopted, which could be seen as a kind of possession.

This woman's solution to the confusion that threatened her mind was to adopt an inadequate paranoid device in order to spare her two mothers from her feelings of hatred and rage. This attempt quickly faltered and she sought help. We might see her as implicitly asking for help to contain and perhaps to integrate her maddening, contradictory feelings. It is this problematic task that is central to analytic psychotherapy. Rustin (1990) talks of how

> In the internal world, the complexity is enormous – there are least two sets of parents to be accorded a place, and often more, though the child's coherent memory of early caregivers may be very sparse. There is a foreclosure on the interplay between internal and external reality in relation to images of the birth parents, and a consequent tendency for these internal representations of the lost parents to remain unmodified and partial, either idealised or monstrous. (Rustin 1990: 6)

We have so far looked at the splits that may operate for the adoptee around their feelings for birth and adoptive parents. More specific issues may emerge, however, determined by the particular circumstances of the adoption. The person adopted because of the infertility of the adoptive parents is likely to bring to their therapy both different issues and in particular a different transference relationship from the person adopted by a single parent for quite other reasons, or by the adopters already with their own child. The patient may feel that they were rescued by their adopters, or in contrast rescued them from the plight of their infertility. The therapist may find himself in the transference powerfully placed as rescuer, or to be rescued from some phantasied profound lack and grief. The issue of creativity and generativity within the therapy may be despaired over or, anxiously, even manically dismissed. The patient may feel tortured by the exclusion from the therapist's 'real family' to a degree that a non-adoptee patient might never quite feel. Tollemache (1998) describes how an adopted child may not feel that she really belongs, that a sense of difference can never be overcome, and the adoptive parents of such a child painfully witness the child's seeking to become part of other families or choosing other parents. Here the child reverses the sense of not belonging by turning from her adoptive parents in quest of a phantasied family. All these possibilities are particularly poignant for adoptee patients in psychotherapy, which offers patients, adopted or not, a phantasied adoption in which vital matters of intimacy and separation, loss and relinquishment are minutely explored. Every adopted person's situation is of course unique, and brings distinctive features to their own parents in the mind which become so central a part of a psychotherapy.

The struggle for knowledge

Bion (1962) developed Melanie Klein's notion of an epistemophilic instinct, which he linked with the baby's way of initially experiencing reality: projective identification with the mother. The mother contains and metabolizes the baby's raw sensations into feelings which he can take back, or introject. In repeating this over and over again, the baby explores and perceives reality, and so comes to learning, in which emotion and cognition are brought together. Taylor (1998) notes that if Klein worked in the area formed by the interrelations between love, hate and reparation, then love, hate and knowledge dominated Bion's (1962) elaboration of Kleinian theory. 'His way of thinking placed knowledge and learning at the centre of the psyche and brought out the importance of knowledge as a modifying ingredient of the mind' (Taylor 1998: 6) Bion came to call learning the 'K' activity, or a 'coming to know'. This learning in which emotion and cognition are brought together describes one, important aspect and aim of psychotherapy. In 'Early stages of the Oedipus Conflict', Klein (1928) writes of the child's situation which describes also what I am trying to convey about the adoptee's situation:

> [The fruits of knowing] are an onrush of problems and questions [resulting in] one of the most bitter grievances we come across in the unconscious [which] is that these many overwhelming questions which are apparently only partly conscious and even when conscious cannot yet be expressed in words, remain unanswered. Another reproach follows hard upon this, namely, that the child could not understand words and speech. Thus his first questions go back beyond the beginnings of his understanding of speech ... In analysis, both these grievances give rise to an enormous amount of hate. (Klein 1928: 188)

The situation of this early hunger for knowledge and its frustrations is revived in the therapeutic setting. In Kleinian theory, knowledge involves that of the mother's body, her possession of the father, and of the babies growing in phantasy or in reality inside her. For the adopted child, at whatever point in childhood he was adopted, the confusions about leaving his birth mother and becoming adopted may both stimulate and muffle curiosity. The adoptee in psychotherapy, like Oedipus, is faced with unconscious material that holds specific difficulties in processing. The complicated early life of the infant, by virtue of leaving the birth mother and then being adopted by other adults, bequeaths to the adoptee a primal scene that is complex and confusing to think about. Risks for the psychotherapist include underestimating its importance to the patient; going along un-thinkingly with a quite possibly successful adoption and neglecting the phantasies connected with the primal scene. Alternatively, the consequences of adoption may be overdetermined, overestimated. There may be an anxious or perverse clinging to its complications, using the adoption as a kind of fetish in which reality is both avowed and disavowed, there can be no development, and the work of mourning cannot take place. A task for the therapist and the patient is to give the adoption its proper psychic space.

Money-Kyrle (1971) writes of the concepts which we all struggle to acknowledge, and of which we will probably achieve only a qualified and inconsistent acceptance. One of these concepts is the supreme creativity of the parental intercourse. Acknowledgement involves a struggle with feelings of envy, exclusion and difference. Many people, because of their own experiences, will have less good images of the parental intercourse, coloured by violence, perversion, loss and so on. The adult adoptee, particularly where the adoption was in the context of infertility of the adopters, may be faced with the absence of a primal scene, an absence of any image which accompanies his or her conception. They are left with an absence of a phantasy of making love. Within such a vacuum, frightening unconscious scenarios may subsist, accessible to therapeutic work only with difficulty. Anxieties about the birth father may emerge, or there may simply be a kind of haunting absence in his place. It is not surprising but it is of interest how little the birth father figures in debates and popular thinking about adoption. He remains invisible, or becomes the receptacle of anxieties about a primal scene of rape and abandonment. The family romance – where children have the passing belief that they are really the child of parents a lot more exciting than those they have actually got – is usually managed and resolved by the eventual acceptance of the less dramatic but solid consolation of the reality. But the adoptee's family romance is in one sense real, and often provides a cold or absent consolation. The happy stories of birth parents reunited with their children who had been adopted are welcome, but they are not the experience of all. Where the birth parents and particularly the father are not or cannot be sought out and 'recovered', the adoptee remains with the absence. This may spawn many thoughts, fears and phantasies, all valuable in psychotherapy.

> Example – I had no concept of being born. I just popped out of the sky. (Words of an adoptee patient)

Here the patient has filled for himself his particular absence or what Lousada calls a gap. His phantasy comes to take on the quality of a belief (Britton 1998) which it will be a task of psychotherapy to examine. For as Lousada continues to explain, the gap is in fact filled with a residue of largely unconscious knowledge of the original mother's care. Rustin writes:

> Even in the most favourable circumstances, there has been an experience of moving from one mode of being mothered to another. This may be felt at quite a primitive level – smells and shape of mother's body are different, the way of being held, fed, put to bed will all be a little different ... Even for a small baby, this transition in primary care is deeply registered, even though it is not understood. (Rustin 1990: 3)

The difficulty of giving thought later to all this, both for adopted children and for their adopters may account for the phantasies and accounts, such as the 'popping out of the sky' story above, which Rustin calls an unconscious reconstruction of the past. One such instance is the image of the changeling. The popular image of the changeling, a persistent and sinister motif of the folklore of earlier ages and domesticated into the notion of the family romance, points to something that the adoptee might have been confronted with. Here, the adopters lack their own, biological baby which in their phantasy has been taken from them. Instead they receive a substitute child, the adopted baby. This phantasy may be shared by their adoptive child. The 'changeling' is in legend attributed with fairy or gypsy or similarly other world or alien blood. I think that this changeling phantasy can sometimes quietly lie within an adoption, including those where there is breakdown of the adoptive placement. Less catastrophically, there is sometimes anxiety about what the adoptee brings with her (mental illness, congenital disease) from her birth parents' histories. The frequent accounts of the adopter and the child somehow recognizing each other at their first encounter is an attempt to establish a choice in a process that is truly random. This is a difficult area and I am aware that using these terms may be upsetting and affront those whose experience has been good or good enough. But I am raising here the phantasies that parents and children often cannot voice, either between the couple or between parent and child. The dread of hurting, saying something that cannot be accepted and tolerated, can be very intense and inhibiting here. Most adoptions do go well, despite the presence sometimes of difficulties that are not expressed at least at the time. But the task of all adoptions is for the child, who has come to the adopters so randomly, even bureaucratically, to become their truly loved child, whom they can lovingly forgive for not being the child they had wanted to create. Similarly, the child to some extent relinquishes, perhaps unconsciously, his or her own birth mother and father, to accept his adopters as parents. This sometimes is finally achieved only when the birth parents can be connected with either in reality, or in therapeutic work.

The story of Oedipus not only is the archetypal story of the family, of gender and generational differences that cannot be overborne by our desire and despair, but also contains a story of adoption, which can help to illuminate some of what comes to be addressed by adult adoptees who have remained troubled by their experiences. I have suggested that this concerns the search for and fear of knowledge, of learning about one's origins. This may demand the contemplation of and relinquishment of apparently precious beliefs. A fear may be for adult adoptees, as for Oedipus, of a horror that can only briefly be endured, ending with the obliteration of contact, sense and perception. Psychotherapy may help adult adoptees through these fears and through a process in which phantasies can be uncovered and explored, beliefs that attach to them can be relinquished, and adult adoptees can mourn their lost hopes and acknowledge the reality and value of what they have.

References

Bion, W. (1962) *Learning from Experience*. London: Heinemann.

Britton, R. (1998) *Belief and Imagination*. London: Routledge.

Freud, S. (1920) 'Beyond the pleasure principle'. In *Standard Edition* vol. 18. London: Hogarth.

Freud, S. (1924) 'Neurosis and psychosis'. In *Standard Edition* vol. 19. London: Hogarth.

Garland, C. (ed) (1998) *Understanding Trauma: A Psychoanalytical Approach*. London: Duckworth.

Klein, M. (1928) 'Early stages of the Oedipus Conflict'. *International Journal of Psycho-Analysis 9*, 167–80. Reprinted in M. Klein (1988) *Love, Guilt and Reparation*. London: Virago.

Milton, J. (1997) 'Why assess? Psychoanalytical assessment in the NHS'. *Psychoanalytic Psychotherapy 11*, 47–58.

Money-Kyrle, R. (1971) 'The aim of psychoanalysis'. *International Journal of Psycho-Analysis 52*, 103–6.

Rustin, M. (1990) 'Aspects of loss in adoption'. Unpublished manuscript.

Salzberger-Wittenberg, I. (1970) *Psychoanalytic Insights and Relationships*. London: Routledge.

Sophocles (1947) 'King Oedipus'. In *The Theban Plays*, trans. E.F.Watling. Harmondsworth: Penguin.

Steiner, J. (1993) *Psychic Retreats*. London: Routledge.

Taylor, D. (1998) 'Learning and some of its problems'. Unpublished manuscript.

Tollemache, L. (1998) 'The perspective of adoptive parents'. *Journal of Social Work Practice 12*, 27–30.

My Mother's Songlines

Storey was my mother's maiden name
telling stories was her way
her words would echo like an old refrain

Her name was Rosemary 'for remembrance'
the telling of her stories
were my mother's prayers for me
her rosaries
the telling of the histories

She was the keeper of the family tree
the keeper of the genealogies
she was the weaver of the golden thread
the holder of the connections
between the living and the dead

My mother's stories were her songlines
and she would tell each story many times
and I could never understand
I could not see that she
was drawing me the map of my familiar land
I did not know that she
was reaching out to me her hand
reaching out to me to say

Look how the pattern weaves this way
this is your pattern can you see
this is how you came to be
the person that you are to-day
these are your threads of being
this is the land where you belong
these are my prayers my rosaries
listen and you too will find your song

Oh there have been times
when I have wondered why
why it is each of these poems rhymes

why these and only these words make the lines
why my words are written with this rhythm
for they have my very breath within them
they are my land's own lines
they are the threads of other times

The flow of water in the rivers
the green of moss upon the stones
the sound of footsteps in the city
the very marrow of my bones
children skipping
chalk peever patterns on the street
the caw of crow rope rhythms
weaving patterns of dancing feet

A child's chant of sticks and stones
these are the names that are my bones

A child's chant of sticks and stones
these are the names that are my bones

A child's chant of sticks and stones
these are the names that are my bones

14

Triangles of Adoption

The Geometry of Complexity

Ilan Katz

The late 1990s was in many ways an unprecedented time for adoption theory and practice in the UK. In this time we had the Bramley and Barrett cases,[1] an adoption summit chaired by the prime minister, government ministers blaming local authorities for an 'anti-adoption culture' and many media articles addressing the adoption debate (e.g. Engel 1999). New performance measures for adoption were produced by the Department of Health (1998) as part of the 'Quality Protects' initiative, which emphasized that adoption should be viewed as a positive resource for children rather than a last resort. Although many of the contemporary debates have been reflected in this book, it is not intended to be a review of policy, practice or research; this job has been comprehensively done by others such as Triseliotis, Shireman and Hundleby (1997) and Parker (1999). Rather it is an attempt to bring together personal experience, research, policy and practice into confront-ation with each other and to understand the dynamics which underpin the complexity of adoption.

There is an underlying theme to the events and statements mentioned above, despite them coming from various different quarters and standpoints; they all challenge the professionalization of adoption. In each case, someone outside of the adoption nexus has questioned the process by which pro-

---

1   The Bramleys are a couple who absconded with their foster children after being turned down as adopters for them. After several weeks they gave themselves up and were allowed to keep the children, who became wards of court. Most of the media supported them rather than the Social Services Department. Barrett is a young man who is suing the local authority with whom he was accommodated, partly on the grounds that they did not place him for adoption.

fessionals select or deal with adopters, adoptees or birth parents. The common thrust has been to challenge the professional hegemony of the adoption process which is portrayed as bureaucratic, unsympathetic and out of touch with the real needs of those involved. Is there a case to answer? Are professionals in a Catch–22 situation, damned if they place children for adoption, and damned if they do not? Or have they really lost their way, requiring a fundamental rethink of adoption policy and practice? This chapter will try to summarize the implications of the contributions in this book to some of the current debates about policy and practice in the field of adoption, and will try to move beyond the polarities which seem to dog the field.

Triangles of adoption: personal, professional and political

Many of the chapters in this book have testified to the pain and difficulty that adoption can bring for all concerned. There is also a growing literature in which the testimony of birth parents, adoptive parents and adoptees is given (e.g. Powell and Warren 1997; Wadia-Ells 1996), mostly demonstrating the problems encountered in the adoption process, but containing many stories of redemption and ultimate resolution. The literature shows that all those in the adoption triangle are likely to feel loss and humiliation. But the process involves much more than a triangle. Although the birth parent, adoptee and adoptive parents may well be the principal stakeholders, there are many others who have an investment in adoption. In particular the professionals involved in the process of assessing, placing and supporting adopters, adoptees and birth parents themselves become part of the dynamic. The adoption triangle also intersects with other 'triangles' – family–child–state; child–mother–father (the Oedipus triangle) – all underpinned by the victim–persecutor–rescuer triangle discussed by Simmonds (Chapter 2). The current 'flavour of the month' in the helping professions is to move towards 'evidence based practice' where interventions in family life are made on the basis of rigorous research which has identified those interventions which will produce positive outcomes for users. This is a linear view of input–process–outcome. But this book demonstrates that far from being 'change agents' who make 'interventions' that result in 'positive outcomes' for children, professionals are people who are inextricably bound up in the multi-triangular dynamics of adoption. They are bound by the same narratives and myths, subject to the same emotional need to rescue and blame, and buffeted by the same powerful media and political forces as the other points in the triangle. One of the frequent surprises of working for CAIS and of editing this book has been the number of people who occupy more than one point in the adoption triangle and therefore how hard it is to box people into the categories of 'professional', 'adopter' or 'adoptee' and this adds yet another twist to the dynamic. Policy-makers, grandparents, siblings and others are also bound up in the adoption dynamic. Many of these stakeholders are represented in this book. Others remain 'silent voices', birth fathers for example.

Why should adoption cause so much trauma for the individuals involved, and controversy for the professionals and public? After all, only a tiny number of children are adopted each year, far fewer than, for example, children who are fostered or in residential care. Adoption, though, is a much more contentious social issue. Fostering and residential care are invariably discussed by the media only in relation to abuse scandals, not as institutions in themselves.

Some of the chapters in this book throw light on this subject. Treacher's introduction (Chapter 1), as well as the contributions of Golberg, Lousada and Simmonds (Chapters 13, 4 and 2); all show how closely adoption is tied in with our understandings and assumptions about family life and the intimate relationships between parents and children. Barn, McCann and Tasker, Richards, and Treseliotis (Chapters 8, 10, 7 and 6) illustrate how the dynamics of adoption have entered into the debates around race and gender, which themselves are emotive and contentious issues in our society. The combination of sex, children and race, as Fanon (1968) wrote, is a powerful cocktail where conflict and dissent are never far from the surface.

It is perhaps because adoption is so bound up with intimate personal experience that the professional, public and policy debates are so convoluted and intense. Many of the contributors to this book have to struggle with how to make sense of their own experiences. Throughout the book there is a constant battle to rise above individual experience in order to place their own situations in a general theoretical, policy and practice context – to create a coherent narrative, if you will.

From a professional perspective, the main imperative for adoption practice is to create a process in which 'the best interests' of the child are served. This involves a process of selection, assessment, representation to the Adoption Panel and placement, post-placement support and counselling to birth parents, adopters and adoptees. On the face of it, adoption should be a win–win situation for all concerned. Parents who are unwilling or unable to look after individual children give them a 'second' chance by giving the children to carefully selected, loving adopters where they are more or less guaranteed a better life than they would otherwise have had. This ideal situation no doubt occurs on occasion, but there are some inherent conflicts in this process, and the ideal is seldom achieved.

First, there is no adequate benchmark about what families are actually the 'best' for children. In the past this was a relatively straightforward issue. Two-parent middle-class families where the adults were healthy, employed and showed a degree of compassion towards and understanding of children were invariably chosen. Adoption itself was seen as a way of giving disadvantaged children a 'second chance'. But gender and racial politics have undermined this cosy view of the family and of adoption. In the 1970s the prevailing ideology of the left was that families were not, after all, a 'good thing',[2] but were the basic building blocks of gender inequalities and abuse of children. This overall suspicion of the family as an institution, begun by 'radical social workers' (Baily and Brake 1975) was compounded by feminist and anti-racist attacks on the liberal consensus. At the same time, the family itself was changing and more and more children were living in single, reconstituted or other non-conventional family configurations. Political attempts to get 'back to basics' or to 'support the family' notwithstanding, the institution has changed to such an extent that the 'normal' family represents a minority of the population in many parts of the UK.

For professionals assessing prospective adopters these social changes have presented enormous problems. It is no longer self-evident what is required of a 'good enough' parent. While these changes were happening to the family, there have also been changes in thinking about what the outcome of 'good parenting' is for children. The aim of parenting is now seen as producing children with a high self-esteem. Self-esteem is increasingly viewed in a superficial and uncritical way as the tendency to feel good about oneself and to conform to other's views about what a mature individual should be. Self-questioning or non-conformity are seen as undermining self-esteem, and as signs of a 'negative' outcome or of poor identity formation.[3]

The problem is that if there is no real consensus about the question of what is 'good enough parenting' or, to be more specific, 'what sorts of people

---

2   Ironically it was the writings of R.D. Laing (1999) during the 1960s which were probably the earliest and most influential roots of the professional anti-family ideology. Laing himself was neither a feminist nor an anti-racist, but he paved the way for others, first, by portraying the family as an oppressive institution which was psychologically damaging for the oppressed members, and second, by politicizing this and relating personal experience of family life to the public issues around oppression. The history of adoption has many examples of people from different and sometimes even opposing political views using each other's arguments to push a particular line.

3   See Katz (1997) for a fuller discussion. This is not to deny the point that Triseliotis makes that a positive sense of identity is crucial to mental health. It is making the point that there are many routes to maturity, and that self-questioning is not necessarily pathological.

will make good enough parents?', then it becomes virtually impossible to make these judgements. Richards (Chapter 7) views this as part of the 'identity crisis' of the social work profession, but cases like that of the Bramleys show that the issues lie way beyond this: society itself is hopelessly divided on these issues. It is arguable, in fact, that the social work profession was one of the first to confront these issues, and that far from lagging behind other professions, it has been in the forefront of addressing race, gender and other issues which the police, for example, have hardly begun to deal with.

Luckock (Chapter 12) shows that social workers (not unlike journalists and probably the rest of the population) show little consistency in the way they make judgements about prospective adopters, relying more on gut feelings and experience than on research or other more objective sources of information. In the end it comes down to the question 'If I had to place my own child with someone else, would I trust these people with my child?' The inadequacies of this approach are well documented by Luckock and others, in particular that gut feelings invariably favour either the cultural norm, situations with which the worker feels personally comfortable, or whatever happens to be in current favour. But the alternative to this – going against one's own instincts and relying on 'objective' research – may not be any better. Researchers are not necessarily more objective than professionals, nor can research provide the answers to some of the more complex situations which professionals have to confront.

Race, gender and adoption

One of the most vexatious areas in this debate about what sorts of people are appropriate adopters is around the question of 'difference'. That is, in what sense should the parents be the same as the adoptee, and in what sense can they be different? Once it has been established that the middle-class nuclear family is no longer the benchmark, what other criteria should be used? Consider the different claims of gays and lesbians, as expressed so vividly by McCann and Tasker, on the one hand, and the arguments around transracial adoption put forward by Barn, Richards and Triseliotis on the other. The gay/lesbian argument is that differences in sexuality should not preclude whole groups of people from being adopters. The 'psychological' opponents of transracial adoption,[4] though, argue that being with a family of a different

---

4   The political (as opposed to the psychological) arguments against transracial adoption point to the one-way traffic of adoptees from the black to the white community as an example of colonialism and exploitation, notwithstanding the psychological effects of adoption on the child.

race places extra burdens on the child, and makes it less likely that the child will achieve a mature identity.

A more subtle look at these arguments shows that this superficial contradiction hides a deeper similarity. First, gays and people from minority ethnic communities are members of minority groups, and it is perhaps this that gives them the understanding and sensitivity to deal with issues which may arise for the adopted child. Both gays and people from ethnic minorities perceive the adoption system not as the 'politically correct' institution so reviled by right-wing (and New Labour) politicians, but as yet another aspect of mainstream society which effectively excludes minorities. In other words, their treatment by the system is part of a political process, rather than a purely technical or professional process of assessment and placement.

As McCann and Tasker point out, it is one thing for an adoption agency to have policies and procedures which assert that gays are as equally appropriate prospective adopters as 'normal' couples. The actual experiences of gays and lesbians belie the official commitment to equality. They are not satisfied with an official line which implies that 'the nuclear heterosexual family is the best, but gays are adequate parents when it is in the child's interests'. Gay people want equality, not acknowledgement. So despite the assertions of Butler-Sloss (Dyer 1999) and the change of policy in the Children's Society, the struggle is not over.

The point about these critiques of the current system is not so much that it is operated by racist or homophobic individuals (although this is part of the problem). The real issue is that the process itself is not geared towards addressing the needs of gay and minority ethnic prospective adopters.[5]

However, the experiences of 'normal' heterosexual middle-class couples are also not easy or conflict free. Engel (1999) certainly felt the brunt of the adoption process despite his impeccably white middle-class background. Richards also expresses bitterness about the selection process and Benton's experiences testify that being assessed as adopters is not an easy or straightforward process (Chapters 7 and 9). Nor was it intended to be. Adopters are

5   These issues were addressed in a BBC2 'Black Britain' television documentary (26 September 1999) on adoption in South Africa, where there are large numbers of black babies needing adoption and few black families coming forward to adopt them. South Africa has a different history of transracial adoption (which became legalized only in 1994). Indeed, it is now illegal to consider race as a factor in placing children or selecting adopters. Nevertheless there are exact parallel arguments which are amplified in the divisive South African society. The argument put forward by the black spokesperson was that the whole adoption process militated against poor black families applying. The white social worker, while sympathetic, saw the solution in terms of 'relaxing' the rules so that more black families would get through the assessment.

deliberately required to go through a tough test which is at least in part designed so that the more faint hearted 'counsel themselves out' of the process. Part of the response of these white middle-class people is perhaps that this is one of the few circumstances in which they are likely to come across social services processes as resource seekers. For minority communities this is often only one of many similar situations in which they are assessed, prioritized and categorized in their quest for services.

Another explanation for this experience of adopters and prospective adopters is the 'script' or 'myth' which portrays adopters as, at some level, 'unnatural' and selfish people whose real motivation is to take children away from less fortunate 'natural' parents. This myth or narrative is sometimes covert and sometimes overt, and like all myths it is bolstered by the occasional verified story of, for example, paedophiles attempting to adopt Romanian children. The myth of the self-seeking adopter is very close to the evil stepmother in earlier days. The Bramley case exemplifies a newer and countervailing myth about adopters – that of the 'ordinary family' who valiantly battle against the faceless bureaucratic forces of the state. The new revelations about this couple have now led media to swing wildly from portraying them as victims to the more familiar modern image of the self-seeking adopter (Gordon 1999).

The myths about the adopter are counterbalanced by myths about the adoptee and the birth parent, of course. As Treacher, Triseliotis and Golberg show in their different ways, adoptees will almost invariably feel abandoned by their birth parents, who are often assumed to be cold and rejecting or else hopelessly inadequate. Adoptees themselves are often viewed as victims or as confused and rootless individuals. These myths not only determine, to some extent, others' perceptions of these different people, but also constrain the responses that different parts of the adoption 'triangle' are able to make towards the process and the institution of adoption. These myths again become apparent in the transracial debate: the common myths here are, on the one hand black children languishing in institutions while politically correct social workers prevent loving white families from adopting them, and on the other hand black children going through identity crises and feeling alienated and rejected by white families and communities. Like all the myths, these have elements of truth, but they also serve to pigeonhole people and to oversimplify complex situations. Fanon in '*The Fact of Blackness*' in '*Race*', *Culture and Difference* (edited by Donald and Rattansi 1992) makes a cri de coeur that as a black man he should be allowed to experience his own pathology and take responsibility for his own life and engage with others without the projections and expectations of both white and black people about what a black identity is supposed to be. For Fanon, true maturity and self-esteem lie not in feeling good about oneself, but in being able to experience one's own pain, rather than allowing others to determine what this pain should be. This plea could be made by all those in the adoption triangle.

It is difficult, if not impossible, for those assessing prospective adopters and working with birth parents and children to be free of these deep-seated myths even though they are mutually contradictory. Assessment is made even more difficult by two other factors mentioned above; the intense emotional resonances of the work for everybody, whether they have been personally affected by adoption or not, and the lack (or rather the impossibility) of an objective standard for prospectively identifying good enough parents. It is also apparent that the relationships which characterize the adoption triangle are inevitably power relationships, and that these power dynamics add to existing power relationships around race and gender.

Narratives of adoption

The history of adoption in the UK is now well documented (Cohen 1994; Parker 1999; Treseliotis *et al.* 1997) as are the narratives associated with adoption itself. For example, it is accepted that adoption started off as a method of 'rescuing' indigent children from starvation, and has to become a process of reparation for children. Treacher (Chapter 1) discusses some of the myths and fantasies that affect all those in the adoption triangle. These are probably fairly constant over time, and as Golberg (Chapter 13) shows, date back at least to ancient Greece. What is interesting is that what is acceptable (rather than what is inevitable) has changed over the years. For example, it is no longer acceptable for adoptive parents to expect gratitude from their children, nor are they permitted by the current narratives to criticize birth parents.

Adoption is now couched as 'a service for children and not for adults'. But there are also contradictions and tensions in this narrative – for example, prospective adopters who take this too literally are likely to be turned down. If their only motivation is to help poor abused children, and adoption does not meet their own needs, then their motivation is likely to be questioned. Similarly if fertile but childless couples choose to adopt, their motivation will be scrutinized closely. Added to this are the much more open and acknowledged debates about gay and transracial adoptions mentioned earlier.

One of the most powerful current myths about adoption is that of reparation for the child. Having gone through traumatic events and separations, the child is placed in a loving family which provides a total environment enabling the child to recover from the trauma. In this sense adoption is the ultimate therapy – twenty-four hours, seven days a week for eighteen years or more. When adoptions fail, then this challenges the effectiveness not only of adoption itself, but also of therapy and ultimately the whole reparative foundation of the helping professions.

These myths or narratives are not unique to adoption; myths such as these pervade the whole of family life and all our relationships. They are part of the fabric of the way people think about themselves and others. There is an ongoing struggle to understand and therefore control the myths, but ultimately this is not possible. There is no one ultimate 'truth' about adoption; it is too complex, conflicted and changeable for that. This is not to say that anything goes, or that every myth is equal. I am not making a postmodernist argument that reduces all human behaviour to 'text' which can be deconstructed. What I am saying is that the truths about adoption are difficult to uncover and are context-bound, so that what may be 'true' at one time for one group of people in the adoption dynamic may well turn out to be problematic or even false in retrospect or for other groups of children.

Life story books

> It's not a story – it all really happened to me. (11-year-old complaining to worker about having to make a life story book)

Life story books have become an integral part of the process of work with children who have been fostered or adopted, especially if the child has been subject to a number of moves and changes. The theoretical rationale for this work is usually provided by attachment theory – that children need to develop a sense of continuity and to internalize the positive experiences and people in their past. Emphasis is placed on allowing children to make their books (tell their story) in their own time and in their own way, using a range of media. It is also emphasized that the book is ongoing and can be added to at different times.

Life story books make sense: it is intuitive that children would and should want to know about their past and the people who have provided care for them. Children, especially those who have had several changes of placement, need to understand where they come from and what has happened to them, and to make sense of their lives. The use of life stories confirms the inherent need for people narrative which is asserted by Ricoeur and which is discussed by Treacher in Chapter 1. They perform exactly the task that all narratives perform – to provide coherence to the child's life. I would like to consider, though, the meta-narratives (myths) involved in life story books, and ask the questions:

- Are there some stories that cannot be told?
- How do the narratives of adoption affect the stories?
- What tensions do the stories mask?
- What should be remembered and what forgotten?
- In what sense are these life stories true?
- What does the literature on life story and identity work tell us about the conflicts and difficulties of workers involved in very painful cases?

Because of the way adoption is now considered, most life story books adhere to the dominant myth of adoption, which has several basic elements:

- Your natural parents loved you, but because of their personal circumstances they were not able to look after you.
- Your adoptive parents chose you because they love and value you.
- You are special.
- (for older children) You have had terrible experiences in your life and our job is to help you overcome those experiences.

Life story books are not just descriptions of events and people; they are representations of reality which are designed to provide children with a sense of themselves. Although all the literature in this area encourages the worker to go at the child's pace, and to let the child lead the process, it is clear that a certain type of narrative is expected to emerge, which is essentially based on the notions of positive identity mentioned above. For example, it is unlikely that the process will allow children to say that their parents were evil bastards who did terrible things to them and that they deserve to be punished. The process also makes it difficult to allow children to claim responsibility for bad things happening, such as the breakdown of a previous foster placement. The book is unlikely to mention administrative or practice failures which may have led to difficulties for the child.

At another level, anything that goes into the life story book (or any biography) cannot be the 'true' story, because language cannot express everything. In time the book itself will become part of the life history and will be subject to interpretation.

There will always be a gap between 'real life' and language. Humans have an innate desire to fill that gap, and are constantly seeking wholeness. It may be that the search for natural parents is part of that search for an imagined family which everybody undertakes; that the desire to rediscover roots is not a specific issue to adoptees and that natural parents provide an object of this universal desire. I am not saying that the situation of adoptees is the same as that of children growing up in 'natural' families. As Golberg and Treacher both show, that would be crass and inaccurate. Our society places enormous significance on 'blood ties', and adopted people are born into a world which does not give adoption the same status as 'natural' family ties. This means that people who have been adopted must struggle with the internal and external perceptions of 'self' in a way that most others do not have to do.

I have said that the notion of identity is constructed by individuals to cope with the fragmentation and lack which is the basis of human existence. It is interesting to read some of the literature on life story work in order to see that there is another lack which is operating – the worker's difficulty in coping with the pain of the child's devastating experiences. Although most of the literature presents life story work in objective, professional terms, there seems to lie, below the surface, a dread that the child's life is not whole, and a need to plug the hole in the child's life, at least symbolically, by doing life story work.

At some level life stories are part of the myth of rescuing and reparation which Simmonds has described. Life story work is a particular exemplar of the difficulty of achieving 'truth' in adoption. Those involved in constructing life story books cannot know how the book will be perceived by the child in the future.

Time and narrative

One of the main difficulties in discussing the dynamics of adoption is that all research, policy and practice in adoption is bound by time, and the time-frames of the different narratives are in tension with each other. Prynn (Chapter 5) illustrates how adoption practice and policy has changed since the 1950s as a response to changes in law, societal values, changing conceptions of the professional task, research, the influence of adopters, practice in other countries and many other influences.

It must be remembered that when a child is placed in an adoptive family she is being given an 'imagined future'. By this I mean that, either explicitly or implicitly, the participants in the adoption triangle are imagining what sort of person this young child will grow into.

The problem is that the people involved in the decisions at the beginning of the process have no idea what the context will be when the child grows up. This means that even if they are successful in their own terms, they may be viewed as failures, acting in bad faith, naïve or ignorant when the decisions are judged retrospectively.

Research on adoption, by contrast, operates retrospectively. The problem for research is that the outcomes of adoption can be legitimately researched only many years after the placement has been made. But by the time the research is done, the situations of people involved in the first stages of adoption are likely to be very different from those being researched (Parker 1999). Thus, for example, it is now axiomatic that most children placed for adoption are not babies (DoH 2000) and many of these will be placed in 'open adoption' situations. Many of them will be placed in 'alternative' family configurations. How can they be compared to babies placed during the 1960s and 1970s?

More importantly, the criteria for judging 'success' also change over time. Barn (Chapter 8) discusses the case of Gill and Jackson's (1983) positive evaluation of transracial adoptions in the British Adoption Project, which is probably the best case in point. Their evaluation was hampered because, rather than seeing racial identity as a core component of the outcomes, they had marginalized its importance. By the 1980s the paradigm had shifted so that a positive racial identity was now seen as a key component of assessing the value of adoptions.

Other examples of this are the apologies by Barnado's and other agencies who were involved in the now notorious transport of large numbers of children from Britain to Australia, Canada and Africa. Again, a policy which was designed (by some accounts anyway) in good faith to give children a better future, has been seen retrospectively as a disreputable scam which involved tearing children away from their roots and placing them in cruel and hostile environments.

It seems to be the case that at least some of the protagonists were acting in bad faith, and that they understood what they were doing. Their desire to see the British Empire populated by 'good white stock' overrode their concern for the children involved. However, there were others who were acting in good faith, and who saw what they were doing as furthering the best interests of those individual children with whom they were working, providing them with a positive alternative to the degradation of lifelong poverty.

It is instructive to contrast the retrospective view of the transport of children to the British colonies (Humphreys 1994) with the Kindertransport discussed by Göpfert (Chapter 3). While the one is viewed as an ignominious and shameful episode in the history of child welfare, the other is seen as part of an heroic struggle in which parents bravely sent their children out of the Nazi sphere of influence into a better future.

These were indeed quite different situations and relationships. In the case of the Kindertransport the parents were making extremely painful personal choices whereas the Barnardo's staff were, on the whole, making bureaucratic decisions. But there is one important similarity. Both the desperate Jewish parents and the Barnardo's officials did not know how history would judge them, nor what the children themselves would, in retrospect, think of the actions they were taking. In both cases they believed that the immediate pain of separation and abandonment that the children inevitably experienced would be outweighed by long-term benefits for them. In this respect their decisions were similar to those being made today by those involved in the adoption process.

There has now been a 'paradigm shift'; children are seen as bearers of rights, rather than being purely objects of concern or beneficiaries of adult welfare. Because it is right to be honest to other adults, we now believe that honesty and openness are right for children. Denying children the right to know of their origins is now a morally unacceptable stance to take. I would like to contend that this stance would hold no matter what research demonstrated. I am arguing here that the primary driver for new ways of thinking about such issues as adoption is not research evidence but new and evolving cultural sensibilities about children and families. Research can be used to test out or back up specific assertions and to deepen our understanding of processes, but the research itself is subject to the same cultural influences as practice and policy, and is therefore only one of the factors influencing them.

Adopting research

Adoption is one of the most researched areas in child welfare. There is a history of research dating back several decades. There have been thousands of research projects into various aspects of adoption, ranging from minute examinations of specific aspects and practices to large-scale evaluations of policy, practice and outcome (Brooks and Barth 1999; Parker 1999). The broad findings in relation to outcomes have been remarkably consistent; we know that adoption is a very successful institution. Most adoptees, no matter what their background, develop into well-adjusted and well-functioning adults. A minority (more than the general population, but less than 'high risk' populations) develop emotional or behaviour difficulties or identity problems. The earlier children are adopted, the better the outcome is likely to be. So in the current parlance 'adoption works!'

Given that these general findings are borne out by so much research, it could be assumed that the evidence base would be solid, and that there would be little argument about the benefits or otherwise of adoption.

But has the issue been resolved? The simple answer must be no: there is still a great deal of debate about adoption, not only about the minutiae of practice, but also about the 'big issues'. Research or evidence cannot, therefore, be the main influence on practice. There are a number of reasons why this is the case. The various contributions to this book demonstrate that although it is important to do research in this area, and research can make a genuine contribution, it cannot, in principle, provide the only evidence base on which practice or policy is founded. One reason for this is the question of timescales discussed earlier; research tells us about adoptions which took place at a time when both the institution of adoption and the 'normal' family were different from now, as were the ideas about parenting and positive outcomes for children. This inevitably limits the reliability and generalizability over time and place of adoption research.

Another problem with the research is that most studies answer questions that are not directly relevant to the actual decisions which practitioners are having to make. This is not because researchers are on the wrong track or are misguided, but because research by its very nature needs to pigeonhole and categorize, and practice must deal with complexity, conflict and phantasy. Practitioners are not faced with choices between different optimum outcomes for children. They are not comparing the likely future of this child with that of 'normal' children. Rather they are faced with trying to find the least damaging choice for a particular child at a particular moment, in a context where there may be a number of people with very strong conflicting feelings about what the choice should be. The research findings cited above would certainly encourage practitioners to think about adoption as an option, but they would not answer the question about whether adoption is better for a particular child.

This must also be seen in the context of more subtle and unconscious processes, both organizational and psychic, which operate all the time. Luckock, Richards and Simmonds all show how organizational dynamics can prevent 'objective' decisions from being made in the 'best interests of the child'. A number of studies (e.g. Gergen, Gloger-Tippelt and Berkowitz 1990; King 1998; Stainton-Rogers and Stainton-Rogers 1992) have contributed to a way of thinking which denies that there is an objective and context-free 'truth' about the best interests of children. Winnicott (1975) famously remarked 'there is no such thing as a baby', by which he meant that babies are inseparable from their mothers, and cannot be seen outside of the context of the mother–infant relationship. We could add 'there is no such thing as a child's best interests' or 'there is no such thing as a positive outcome', by which we would mean that children's best interests are impossible to determine without addressing the ideologies and relationships in which they are embedded.

Nor are the present adoption arrangements inevitable; one of the most intriguing facts about modern adoption is that it is virtually exclusively an Anglo-Saxon institution. In some continental European countries there is virtually no adoption at all, especially where birth parents oppose the adoption (Ellison, Dorthe-Hestbaek and Barker 1998), and yet there is no evidence that the outcomes for looked-after children in these countries are any worse than they are in the UK, the USA or Australia. This means that the cultural and social context are absolutely core to the questions around the effectiveness of adoption.

In a sense this book represents a reaction to 'evidence based practice'. It is the opposite of a practitioner's manual. We are not trying to distil the research, theory and experience of adoption into ten bullet points at the end of each chapter. Rather we have tried to reveal some of the complexities and conflicts inherent in the process and to show how difficult it is for professionals to hold in mind the needs and phantasies of all three points of the adoption triangle – and the other triangles – while at the same time paying heed to their own narratives and fantasies and to institutional dynamics. A new paradigm based on an understanding of complex open systems is creeping up on us from other disciplines such as biology and economics (Byrne 1997; Ormerod 1998). The linearity implicit in the current focus on 'evidence' and 'outcomes' will soon pass into history and become another narrative of adoption. This book should also serve as a warning that we should approach the subject of adoption with humility, and that rigid and self-righteous declarations about the needs or interests of children are unlikely to stand the test of time.

References

Baily, R. and Brake, M. (eds) (1975) *Radical Social Work*. London: Edward Arnold.

Brooks, D. and Barth, R.P. (1999) 'Adjustment outcomes of adult transracial and inracial adoptees: effects of race, gender, adoptive family structure and placement history'. *American Journal of Orthopsychiatry 69*, 87–102.

Byrne, D. (1997) 'Complexity theory and social research'. *Social Research Update 18*. Guildford: University of Surrey.

Cohen, P. (1994) 'Yesterday's worlds, tomorrow's world: from the racialisation of adoption to the politics of difference'. In I. Gaber and J. Aldridge (eds) *In the Best Interests of the Child: Culture, Identity and Transracial Adoption*. London: Free Association.

Department of Health (1998) *Adoption: Achieving the Right Balance*. Local Authority Circular LAC (98)20. London: DoH.

Department of Health (2000) *The Children Act Report 1995–1999*. London: DoH.

Donald, J. and Rattansi, A. (1992) *'Race', Culture and Difference*. London: Open University Press and Sage.

Dyer, C. (1999) 'Judge says gays can raise children'. *Guardian*, October 16, 2.

Ellison, M., Dorthe-Hestbaek, A. and Barker, R. (1998) 'Turning legal principles into practice: the cases of Denmark and the UK'. In BAAF (eds) *Exchanging Visions: Papers in Best Practice in Europe for Children Separated from their Birth Parents*. London: British Agencies for Adoption and Fostering.

Engel, M. (1999) 'My daughter's big brother'. *Guardian*, May 24, 10.

Fanon, F. (1992) 'The fact of Blackness.' In J. Donald and A. Rattansi (eds) *'Race', Culture and Difference*. London: Open University Press and Sage.

Gergen, K.J., Gloger-Tippelt, G. and Berkowitz, P. (1990) 'The cultural construction of the developing child'. In G.R. Semin and K.J. Gergen (eds) *Everyday Understanding: Social and Scientific Implications*. London: Sage.

Gordon, A. (1999) 'Runaway Bramleys faced sex allegations by council'. *Mail on Sunday* 10 October.

Gill, O. and Jackson, B. (1983) *Adoption and Race*. London: Batsford.

Humphreys, M. (1994) *Empty Cradles*. London: Doubleday.

Katz, I. (1997) *Personal Narratives in the Construction of Identity: Implications for Direct Work with Children*. London: CAIS, University of East London.

King, M. (ed) (1998) *Moral Agendas for Children's Welfare*. London: Routledge.

Laing, R.D. (1999) *The Politics of the Family*. London: Routledge.

Ormerod, P. (1998) *Butterfly Economics*. London: Faber and Faber.

Parker, R. (1999) *Adoption Now: Messages from Research*. Chichester: Wiley.

Powell, S. and Warren, J. (1997) *The Easy Way Out? Birth Mothers: The Hidden Side of Adoption*. London: Minerva.

Read, A. (ed) (1996) *The Fact of Blackness: Frantz Fanon and Visual Representation*. London: Institute of Contemporary Arts.

Ricoeur, P. (1992) *Oneself as Another*. London: University of Chicago Press.

Stainton-Rogers, R. and Stainton-Rogers, W. (1992) *Stories of Childhood: Shifting Agendas of Child Concern*. London: Harvester Wheatsheaf.

Treseliotis, J., Shireman, J. and Hundleby, M. (1997) *Adoption Theory, Policy and Practice*. London: Cassell.

Wadia-Ells, S. (ed) (1996) *The Adoption Reader: Birth Mothers, Adoptive Mothers and Adopted Daughters Tell their Stories*. London: Women's Press.

Winnicott, D.W. (1975) *Through Paediatrics to Psychoanalysis*. London: Hogarth and Institute of Psycho-Analysis.

Notes on Contributors

Ravinder Barn is senior lecturer in applied social studies at Royal Holloway College, University of London.

Alison Benton adopted her daughter, and has a son born to her. She is a local co-ordinator for *Adoption UK* and leads a support group for adoptive parents. She qualified and has practiced as a social worker and has published in issues of adoption for *Adoption Today*.

Rose Golberg is a senior clinical lecturer in social work in the Adolescent Department at the Tavistock Clinic, London, and works as a psychoanalytic psychotherapist in private practice. Her social work experience has included a special interest in fostering and adoption.

Rebekka Göpfert works as a literary editor for C.H. Beck Publishing House in Munich. She has a PhD in history from Muenster University on the Kindertransport.

Sallie Greenwood moved to New Zealand in the mid–1980s with three of her daughters. Her first born daughter was given up for adoption over thirty years ago. She is a psychologist and about to embark on a doctoral thesis exploring themes of birth parents and adoption.

Margot Henderson was born to Kathleen and subsequently adopted by Rosemary and David. She works as a poet and a storyteller with schools and other organizations. She has also been a poet in residence for psychiatric units and homeless shelters. She has one daughter – Rowan.

Ilan Katz is head of the Practice Development Unit at the NSPCC. He has had a long-standing interest in issues around race, identity and adoption. He is the author of *The Development of Racial Identity in Children of Mixed Parentage: Mixed Metaphors*. He is a director of CAIS.

Julian Lousada is a senior clinical lecturer in social work and is chairman of the Adult Department, Tavistock Clinic, London. He is a full member of the British Association of Psychotherapists. He is a co-author of *The Politics of Mental Health* and is currently writing, with Andrew Cooper, a book entitled *The Meaning of Welfare*.

Barry Luckock is a lecturer in social policy and social work at the University of Sussex. He is currently working on a study of post-adoption contact in respect of 150 children adopted from care in the mid–1990s.

Damian McCann is a qualified systemic practitioner, supervisor and trainer. He is currently employed as principal family therapist at the Edgware Community Hospital, and is visiting lecturer at City University, Birkbeck College and the Institute of Family Therapy. He specializes in working therapeutically with lesbians, gay men and their families. He is co-editor, with Robert Bor, of *The Practice of Counselling in Primary Care*.

Barbara Prynn has worked in local authority adoption agencies since the late 1970s. At present she is particularly involved with counselling adult adoptees and people who have been in the care of social services. The counselling is in parallel with a research project she is carrying out for CAIS, focusing on the life histories of adults who were adopted or fostered.

Barry Richards is professor and head of the Department of Human Relations at the University of East London. He has written extensively on the psychodynamic dimensions of politics, popular culture and everyday life.

John Simmonds is currently programme coordinator and senior lecturer in social work at Goldsmiths College, University of London. He has a long-standing professional interest in adoption as well as a personal interest as an adoptive father. He has been involved in a number of projects exploring the impact of the adoption experience on individual growth and development of family life.

Fiona Tasker is a lecturer in psychology at Birkbeck College, University of London. She is co-author with Susan Golombok of *Growing Up in a Lesbian Family: Effects on Child Development*. She has published papers on children and divorce and children in lesbian and gay families. She is a member of the Lesbian and Gay Issues in Child Care Strategy Group and a clinical associate at the Institute of Family Therapy.

Amal Treacher works in the psychosocial subject area at the University of East London. Since gaining her PhD on women and identity, she has continued to pursue work on subjectivity (especially children), identity and dual heritage, and issues of adoption. She is a director of CAIS.

John Triseliotis is emeritus professor at the University of Edinburgh and visiting professor and senior research fellow at the University of Strathclyde.

Subject Index

Author Index